AIMING TO EXPLAIN

Theories of Policy Change and Canadian Gun Control

Firearms policy has periodically dominated Canadian politics since the late 1960s. Compared to the United States, however, there is little scholarship on firearms policy to the neighbouring north.

Using Canadian firearms policy, *Aiming to Explain* examines five prominent policy process theories employed during the period from the 1989 Montreal Massacre to the 2012 cancellation of the universal firearms registry. Throughout, B. Timothy Heinmiller and Matthew A. Hennigar present rigorous applications of rational choice institutionalism, social constructivism, the advocacy coalition framework, the multiple streams framework, and punctuated equilibrium. The investigations draw on method-based best practices, while also making use of a wide range of data collection and analysis techniques, including inferential statistics, descriptive statistics, process tracing, congruence analysis, and qualitative content analysis.

The goal of *Aiming to Explain* is not to select a single best theory, but to compare their relative strengths and weaknesses in an effort to direct future research and theoretical development efforts in the study of Canadian public policy.

B. TIMOTHY HEINMILLER is an associate professor and chair in the Department of Political Science at Brock University.

MATTHEW A. HENNIGAR is an associate professor in Department of Political Science at Brock University.

Aiming to Explain

Theories of Policy Change and Canadian Gun Control

B. TIMOTHY HEINMILLER AND
MATTHEW A. HENNIGAR

UNIVERSITY OF TORONTO PRESS
Toronto Buffalo London

ISBN 978-1-4875-4232-0 (cloth)   ISBN 978-1-4875-4235-1 (EPUB)
ISBN 978-1-4875-4233-7 (paper)   ISBN 978-1-4875-4234-4 (PDF)

Library and Archives Canada Cataloguing in Publication

Title: Aiming to explain : theories of policy change and Canadian gun control /
   B. Timothy Heinmiller and Matthew A. Hennigar.
Names: Heinmiller, B. Timothy, 1975– author. | Hennigar, Matthew A.
   (Matthew Aaron), 1971– editor.
Description: Includes bibliographical references and index.
Identifiers: Canadiana (print) 20220203121 | Canadiana (ebook) 20220203164 |
   ISBN 9781487542320 (cloth) | ISBN 9781487542337 (paper) |
   ISBN 9781487542351 (EPUB)
Subjects: LCSH: Gun control – Canada – Decision making. | LCSH: Policy
   sciences – Canada.
Classification: LCC HV7439.C3 H45 2022 | DDC 363.330971 – dc23

We wish to acknowledge the land on which the University of Toronto Press
operates. This land is the traditional territory of the Wendat, the Anishnaabeg,
the Haudenosaunee, the Métis, and the Mississaugas of the Credit First
Nation.

This book has been published with the help of a grant from the Federation
for the Humanities and Social Sciences, through the Awards to Scholarly
Publications Program, using funds provided by the Social Sciences and
Humanities Research Council of Canada.

University of Toronto Press acknowledges the financial support of the
Government of Canada, the Canada Council for the Arts, and the Ontario Arts
Council, an agency of the Government of Ontario, for its publishing activities.

Canada Council   Conseil des Arts
for the Arts   du Canada

ONTARIO ARTS COUNCIL
CONSEIL DES ARTS DE L'ONTARIO
an Ontario government agency
un organisme du gouvernement de l'Ontario

Funded by the   Financé par le
Government   gouvernement
of Canada   du Canada

Canada

Contents

Acknowledgments

This collaboration came about somewhat unexpectedly when two department colleagues – one a specialist in public policy theory, the other in law and politics – got to chatting about the need for a book that tested leading public policy theories using a single Canadian policy area. The result was an engaging and educational few years for both of us, augmented by additional related research projects and graduate supervisions – in short, exactly the sort of rich experience you hope for in an academic department. Along the way we have had the support and encouragement of many individuals. These include the anonymous reviewers, and Dan Quinlan and the production team at University of Toronto Press, whose thoughtful input strengthened the manuscript. Several research assistants did invaluable work collecting and analysing data for the theory-testing chapters: Eleni Nicolaides, Peter Sekyere, Saaka Sulemana, Emmanuel Osei, Samantha Powless, and Jessica Beaupre. Many of these assistants have moved on to become budding scholars in their own right, and that may be the most substantial and gratifying outcome from this project. Dozens of students in Tim's graduate seminar on public policy read and provided welcome feedback on draft chapters, which was especially valuable in achieving one of the project's primary aims: to make public process theory more accessible to Canadian students. We also received helpful input from discussants and participants in conference panels where we previewed some of the book's chapters; they include Kathryn Harrison, Kate Puddister, Dave Snow, Christine Rothmayr Allison, Matt Wilder, Metodi Sotirov, Chris Weible, Michael Howlett, and Byron Sheldrick. As well, Jack Lucas, Anthony Sayers, and Zachary Taylor provided their insights on how to measure the "rurality" of ridings. We greatly appreciate the SSHRC Awards to Scholarly Publication Program's financial support in the book's publication, and Brock University's Council for Research in the

Social Sciences (CRISS) and Match of Minds research grant programs for financial support of the book's research and data collection. Finally, we thank our spouses, who learned more about both policy theory and gun control than they wanted (and thanks for suggesting gun control as our policy area, Kathleen).

Tim Heinmiller
Matthew Hennigar

AIMING TO EXPLAIN

1 Multi-Theoretical Analysis and Theories of Policy Change

This is a book about gun control policy that is not really about gun control. Rather, this is a book about public policy-making and the theories scholars apply to understand and explain how and why public policies are made. This book investigates these theories as they relate to an important case of Canadian policy-making. The objective is not to create a synthetic "super-theory" of the policy process, nor is it to determine, once and for all, which of the theories is superior. The objective is to test competing theories on relatively equal ground, identify where they succeed and fail, and in this way learn important lessons about these theories as ways of understanding Canadian policy-making.

Firearms policy was selected for this study primarily on methodological grounds: it is a high-profile and important policy area in Canada, one that since the late 1960s has at times dominated Canadian politics. Yet it has received relatively little attention from Canadian public policy scholars compared to other major policy areas, and there is almost no scholarship examining Canadian firearms policy using the established theories of the policy process. This makes it rich but unbroken soil for a theoretically based examination of Canadian policy-making. Firearms policy is also distinctive in that none of the established theories "owns" this policy area. Most theories of the policy process have one or two policy areas in which their initial development was grounded and over which they continue to have some ownership. However, none of the mainstream theories was developed based on firearms policy, so it constitutes a relatively neutral policy area in which multiple theories can be fairly tested and compared.

To test the theories of the policy process, we investigate each of them empirically, one by one and on its own terms. This involves identifying each theory's policy change hypothesis or hypotheses and investigating these hypotheses using the most rigorous qualitative and quantitative methods at our disposal. Comparing the results of these investigations is not a simple matter of determining which theories are "right" or "wrong," because in important ways the theories are incommensurate and not mutually exclusive. This makes it impossible to determine a "single best theory," for multiple theories can be supported simultaneously, each explaining a different aspect or dynamic of Canadian policy-making. To accommodate this incommensurability, we will be evaluating the relative success and failure of each theory internally according to its own causal ontology and scope of causal claim. This will allow us to sidestep debates – for now – about the relative merits of theories that make probabilistic versus deterministic causal claims and to focus on the extent to which a theory, regardless of its causal ontology and scope conditions, is empirically supported in an important Canadian policy area.

Our case study approach has limitations. Firearms policy is only a single field of Canadian policy-making, and we must be careful not to overgeneralize from this single field to all of Canadian policy-making. A theory that does well in explaining Canadian firearms policy passes an important test but says nothing about whether that theory has utility beyond this single policy area. Much more research in many more policy areas would be needed to determine whether that theory is more generalizable. Conversely, a theory that does not explain Canadian firearms policy fails an important test, and it is worth investigating these failures further. Unsupported theories should not be rejected automatically, but their assumptions, tenets, and scope conditions should be scrutinized to determine whether they are acceptable and/or correctable.

Studies of public policy-making are characterized by a high (some would say extreme) level of theoretical pluralism, and our objective is to make greater sense of this crowded field by teasing out some of the strengths and limitations of established theories. In this introductory chapter we describe our approach to doing so. The next section outlines three different approaches to multi-theoretical analysis in the study of policy-making and situates our study among these alternatives. After that, we discuss the logic behind our case selection and explain what we can learn by testing policy process theories in our selected case, Canadian firearms policy. We then move on to discuss our approach to theory selection and why we chose to include some policy process theories in our investigation while excluding others. This is followed by a discussion of some of the challenges our study encountered when assessing the theories and the importance of investigating each theory on its own terms. Finally, we lay out this book's structure and tell readers what they can expect in the chapters to come.

Multi-Theoretical Analysis

Any study that utilizes multiple theoretical perspectives faces not only theoretical questions but also epistemological ones. These epistemological questions are about knowledge creation and how different uses of multiple theories can create different types of knowledge. There is no inherently correct (or incorrect) answer to these epistemological questions; that said, it is important to be aware of one's own epistemology in multi-theoretical work and to be clear-eyed about what one's epistemological choices can and cannot accomplish.

Cairney (2013) argues that in policy studies, there are three basic epistemological approaches to multi-theoretical analysis. The first is a synthetic approach that combines insights from multiple theories to develop a single, qualitatively new theory that, ideally, is an improvement on existing ones. The second is a complementary approach that uses several theories to analyse a policy process from multiple perspectives, thereby gaining a more thorough understanding of the process. The third is a contradictory approach in which multiple theories are pitted against one another, evaluated according to social scientific tenets, and assessed on that basis (Cairney 2013, 2–3). Each of these epistemological approaches results in a different type of study and promises a different sort of knowledge generation.

This book follows the third epistemological approach, based on the contradictory use of theories. We are not attempting to create a new, synthetic super-theory of the policy process, largely because we doubt that such a super-theory is possible given the conceptual and ontological diversity among established theories. Nor are we trying to develop the most thorough picture possible of Canadian firearms policy processes, though a more comprehensive understanding of Canadian firearms policy development is one of the by-products of our analysis. Our main objective, rather, is to test theories of the policy process, compare the results of these tests, and draw some conclusions about the efficacy of these theories in an important case of Canadian policy-making. This focus on relative theory efficacy is what makes this study an example of the contradictory approach.

The classic multi-theoretical analysis in policy studies is Allison's (1971) *Essence of Decision*, which mostly follows the complementary approach. Allison studies government decision-making during the Cuban Missile Crisis from three different perspectives: the unitary rational actor model, the organizational process model, and the governmental politics model. Allison's study is an example of the complementary approach in that he emphasizes how each model can be used to fill the analytical voids of other models. He discusses some of the relative strengths and weaknesses of the models, but he does not test the models with data, and he makes few judgments about their relative efficacy. His complementary use of multiple theories does make this valuable and fundamental point: theories "magnify one set of factors rather than another and thus not only lead analysts to produce different explanations of problems that appear, in their summary questions, to be the same, but also influence the character of the analyst's puzzle, the evidence he [*sic*] assumes to be relevant, the concepts he uses in examining the evidence, and what he [*sic*] takes to be an explanation" (251). Thus, using multiple theories in a complementary manner creates a more fulsome picture of decision-making than could be provided by any single model on its own, a point that has been reinforced by Zahariadis (1998), Cairney (2007), and Bandelow and colleagues (2019), among others.

A multi-theoretical analysis that is closer to the contradictory approach is Zahariadis's (2005) study of Greek policy-making between 1990 and 2004 with respect to the Former Yugoslav Republic of Macedonia, now the Republic of North Macedonia. Zahariadis compares the explanations of policy-making offered by three theories: multiple streams, two-level games, and rational choice. His work straddles the complementary and contradictory approaches, analysing the theories from both perspectives, and the complementary dimension of his work largely echoes Allison's findings. The contradictory approach is evident in his explicit evaluation of the theories based on the empirical evidence he collects. For each year in the study period, each theory's consistency with the empirical evidence is rated as strong, moderate, or weak, and the "best" theory is the one that, overall, is most consistent with the evidence (Zahariadis 2005). Zahariadis's work can be criticized on several grounds: the strong/moderate/weak trichotomy is not fully explained, the assessments using this trichotomy involve a considerable amount of subjectivity, and the selection of calendar years as time units for assessing theories' explanatory power is arbitrary and bears little relationship to actual policy outcomes. Nevertheless, this work is representative of the contradictory approach to multi-theoretical analysis, and its findings raise important questions about the efficacy of contending theories of foreign policy development.

In Canadian public policy scholarship, there have been many efforts at multi-theoretical synthesis, but complementary and contradictory analyses have been far less common. One example of a complementary analysis is Anderson and MacLean's (2015) study of New Brunswick forestry policy. They argue that the multiple streams framework (MSF) explains how the idea of increased timber harvests got on the policy agenda and that the advocacy coalition framework (ACF) explains why the idea was adopted by policy-makers; thus, the two theories together provide a thorough understanding of this significant policy change. Another example, this time explaining policy stability, is Morden's (2016) study of the persistence of the federal *Indian Act*. He uses three variants of the new institutionalism – rational choice, historical, and discursive – to explain the policy's persistence despite its apparent dysfunctions, arguing that each perspective helps "fill the gaps that are left" by the others (114). The most recent example of a complementary analysis is Millar, Lesch, and White's (2019) study of Ontario's 2009 *Green Energy and Green Economy Act*, which draws on several theoretical approaches to identify multiple causal pathways explaining the policy's introduction. The only contradictory multi-theoretical analysis in the Canadian public policy literature is Howlett's (1997) study of Canadian agenda-setting. He pits Downs's issue-attention cycle explanation of agenda-setting against Baumgartner and Jones's punctuated equilibrium theory (PET) explanation through an empirical analysis of the acid rain and nuclear energy sectors between 1977 and 1992, ultimately concluding that neither theory is supported by his data.

Given that there is only one contradictory study in the Canadian literature, and that this study focuses on agenda-setting rather than policy change, there is an obvious lacuna when it comes to testing competing theories of policy change in Canadian policy-making. So far, no one has investigated the relative merits of competing policy theories in a single case. Such an investigation could yield important lessons about the strengths and weaknesses of these theories, and that is the task we take up in this study.

Case Selection

Since theory testing is at the heart of our contradictory multi-theoretical approach, it was essential for us to adopt a case study methodology that would facilitate theory testing. As George and Bennett (2005, 80) point out, "single cases serve the purpose of theory testing particularly well if they are 'most-likely,' 'least-likely,' or 'crucial' cases." The strategy employed here was to select a "most likely" case of Canadian policy-making, one that all of the theories selected would likely be able to explain given their tenets and scope conditions. Theories that failed to explain this policy-making, in whole or in part, could then be flagged as problematic, and the reasons for their failure could be further explored. In this way, the analysis would contribute to theoretical development by identifying some of the limitations of mainstream policy process theories as explanations of Canadian policy-making.

The strongest possible strategy for theory testing in a single case is the investigation of a crucial case, but truly crucial cases are exceptional and this strategy was not available for this study. A crucial case "is one in which a theory that passes empirical testing is strongly supported and one that fails is strongly impugned" (George and Bennett 2005, 9). When a case is truly crucial, it is difficult to dismiss a nonconforming case as merely deviant because the finding of deviance is devastating to the theory. Eckstein (1975) first advocated for the use of crucial cases in the social sciences but later admitted that crucial cases are quite rare and that this theory-testing strategy is not always available. In Canadian policy-making, for example, it is difficult to conceive of any single case of policy-making that a theory would have to explain in order to be considered valid. This is especially problematic when some of the most prominent policy process theories are probabilistic in nature and explain policy-making in terms of average causal effects, with non-conforming individual cases regarded as (inevitable) statistical outliers. Thus, it is difficult to sustain the claim that any single case of Canadian policy-making qualifies as crucial, so this theory-testing strategy was not employed here.

When crucial cases are unavailable, the next-best strategy for theory testing in a single case is to utilize a "least likely" or "most likely" case. In a "least likely" strategy, a case is selected that seems unlikely to be explained by a theory, but if the theory explains it, support for the theory is strengthened. The results from a "least likely" study can help to confirm theory but do little to disconfirm theory, making this a confirming strategy. In a "most likely" strategy, a case is selected that should be explained by a theory, and if the theory fails to explain it, the theory is weakened. This means that "most likely" case studies can disconfirm theories but can do little to confirm them, making this a disconfirming strategy (Gerring 2007, 115–22). We opt for the latter strategy, selecting what we consider to be a "most likely" case that all of the theories should be able to explain; if any of the theories have difficulty explaining the case, this result is disconfirming for them. The "most likely" case we selected was Canadian firearms policy between 1989 and 2012.

Canadian firearms policy qualifies as a "most likely" case for the theories we examine because there is no *a priori* reason why any of the theories included in the study should not be able to explain policy-making in this case. All of the theories we have selected make a claim to explain policy-making in a general way within their respective scope conditions, and none of them have limiting scope conditions that would preclude them from explaining firearms policy. All of the theories are, at the outset, expected to explain the case, and those that do not explain the case, in whole or in part, are flagged as problematic in some way. This illustrates the disconfirming approach to theory testing that is inherent in the "most likely" case strategy. One limitation of this approach is that it is only weakly confirming for the theories that do well at explaining the firearms policy case: these theories pass an important test but are not conclusively confirmed because sustaining such a claim would require far more investigation in many additional Canadian policy areas. Another limitation is that the "most likely" strategy meant limiting our investigation to theories with a good chance of explaining Canadian firearms policy, thereby excluding some theories that may be popular but that did not provide likely explanations of this case.

Given that we are testing multiple theories in a contradictory approach, it was also important that the theories be equally likely to explain the selected case, and indeed, that was one of the most important considerations in our case selection. Unlike many other policy areas, firearms policy can arguably be considered a theoretically neutral policy area in which none of the theories are more likely than the others to be successful. The development of most policy process theories has been informed by a specific policy area in which a theory's ideas were developed, tested, and refined. ACF was informed by environmental policy, PET was influenced by budgeting, the social construction framework (SCF) was shaped by social welfare policy, and so on. These policy areas effectively constitute the "home turf" for these respective theories, and testing competing theories in one of these areas would constitute an unfair advantage for one theory over the others; that is, one theory would be clearly "more likely" than the others. Importantly, none of the theories investigated in this study were developed with firearms policy in mind, so no single theory enjoys an advantage in this respect. Admittedly, firearms policy is primarily a regulatory policy area, as opposed to a redistributive or distributive policy area, and this may confer some advantage to theories that were developed with regulatory policies in mind. But any advantage in this respect would be slight, and, given that it is impossible to select a policy area that is *entirely* theoretically neutral, we argue that selecting firearms policy minimizes any such advantage.

In selecting our "most likely" case, we also wanted to investigate a policy area of substantive importance in Canadian policy-making, as opposed to an obscure policy area that might be written off as insubstantial. We contend that since the late 1960s, firearms policy has been a major policy area in Canadian politics. Significant firearms policy reform efforts were undertaken by the Canadian government in 1969, 1975–78, 1990–91, 1994–95, and 2006–12, and are ongoing. Few other policy issues in Canada have received as much attention from policy-makers or generated as much controversy. Gun control is a persistent issue in the Canadian media, it is a significant cleavage in Canadian public opinion, and it is a perennial issue in Canadian elections. It is also representative of the new wave of morality policy issues – along with such things as abortion, same-sex marriage, prostitution, euthanasia, and recreational drug use – that are taking up a greater and greater share of the federal policy agenda and are at the heart of the so-called culture wars in Canada and many Western countries (D.E. Smith 2003; Green-Pederson and Thorup Larsen 2012). For all of these reasons, firearms policy cannot be viewed as insignificant.

Throughout this book, we refer to "firearms policy" rather than "gun control" policy. This is because the former term is more politically neutral, though we recognize that the latter is more common parlance. We restrict our use of the term "gun control" to proposals, efforts, policies, or advocates that specifically try to control guns.

While our results may be wholly or partly disconfirming for some theories, we are under no illusion that our findings will decisively reject or invalidate any of the theories we investigate. These theories are of long standing, with plenty of empirical support in their respective literatures, so failing to explain the Canadian firearms policy case would not be adequate grounds to reject them outright. Prudence requires that the reasons for a theory's failure be investigated before that theory is rejected (Dowding 2020, 54). Moreover, as George and Bennett (2005, 115) point out, theory testing through case study analysis is rarely used "to refute a theory decisively, but rather to identify whether and how the scope conditions of competing theories should be expanded or narrowed." This is painstaking work, but "being able to understand when and how propositions are *not universal*" is an important part of knowledge generation and theory development (Peters 2020, 25).

While disconfirming evidence will prompt us to probe the scope conditions of a theory, we leave it to others to reject disconfirmed theories more decisively based on the totality of empirical evidence, in this study and beyond. This underscores that our purpose is not to reject some theories and accept others, but to explore the theories' limitations based on our findings from this single – albeit important – case. This is also how our study is a building block in the ongoing development of policy process theories in Canada, and it is one of the issues we take up in chapter 9.

In the Canadian public policy literature, no one has yet used firearms policy to investigate contending theories of the policy process as we do here. Some studies of Canadian firearms policy have utilized theories of the policy process, but only to shed new light on firearms policy development, not to test the theories themselves. For instance, Pal (2003) examines how gun control policies impose losses and makes use of institutionalist theory for the purpose of understanding governments' capacity to impose gun control–related losses on gun owners in Canada and the US. Two studies, one by Fleming (2012) and one by Kamal and Burton (2018),[1] compare gun control in Canada and the US and argue that mass shootings put gun control on the policy agendas of both countries; however, differences in institutional design mean that Canada is more readily able to enact gun control measures than is the US. Newman and Head (2017) look at gun control in Canada, the US, and Australia and argue that the problem of gun control can be constructed in various ways, depending on the national context, so that the problem may seem wicked and unsolvable in some contexts but technical and solvable in others.

The rest of the Canadian firearms policy literature is largely atheoretical and descriptive. An inside account of the firearms policy battles of the 1990s is offered by Heidi Rathjen, a founding leader of the Canadian Coalition for Gun Control and a central figure in those battles (Rathjen and Montpetit 1999). A thorough and more objective account is provided by Bottomley (2004), who examines the party and electoral politics of the firearms policy debates and provides several useful insights. The most comprehensive account of Canada's gun control efforts is provided by Brown (2012), a historian, who traces Canada's gun control efforts all the way back to pre-Confederation. Brown's history is a must-read for anyone seeking the historical context of firearms policy debates in Canada today. However, he does not cover the period after the election of the Harper Conservatives in 2006; indeed, this is a significant gap in Canadian firearms policy literature overall. For some reason, very little has been written about firearms policy during the Harper years, even in the scholarly literature on the formation of the Conservative Party and the rise of the right, even though abolishing the long-gun registry was a key plank in the Conservative agenda. Our study benefited greatly from all of the available historical and descriptive literature, providing important contextual and factual grounding for our theory-testing ambitions.

Theory Selection

Given that we were undertaking a contradictory analysis of several competing theories, the issue of theory selection was crucial and, inevitably, controversial. Generally, we chose theories that we viewed as having strong potential to explain Canadian firearms policy-making. This was in keeping with our "most likely" case selection strategy and allowed us to avoid constructing "straw man" explanations that were doomed to fail and would have added little to the analysis.

A preliminary consideration in our theory selection was to ensure that the approaches we included in the study qualified as theories, as opposed to frameworks or models. As Ostrom (2007, 25–6) has argued, there are important differences between frameworks, theories, and models, and all have a role to play in explaining policy processes. Frameworks "provide a foundation for enquiry by specifying classes of variables and general relationships among them. Frameworks organize enquiry, but they cannot in and of themselves provide explanations for, or predictions of, behaviour and outcomes" (Schlager 2007, 293). Explanation is the realm of theories that "place values on some of the variables identified as important in a framework, posit relationships among the variables, and make predictions about likely outcomes" (296). Models are also explanatory but have a narrower range of explanation than theories, applying to more specific situations in which several theorized variables are held constant (294). Implicitly or explicitly, many models are nested within theories and many theories are nested within frameworks, and the interrelations between the three are complex and dynamic (Ostrom 2007). Since our objective was to investigate *theories* of policy-making, we took care to avoid conflating explanatory theories with heuristic frameworks and general theories with narrow models, and to focus our selection on the theory level.

Every theory is at its heart an attempt to explain something. Usually, this means that a theory proposes a hypothesis or group of hypotheses to explain an outcome – in our case, policy-making – that can be empirically investigated (Sabatier 1999). Thus, we looked for approaches that specified policy-making hypotheses or that at least provided a clear explanation of policy-making (if no hypotheses were specified explicitly). While hypotheses are at the core of what makes a theory a theory – and what makes a theory explanatory – there are other important aspects of theories, as well, such as the frameworks within which they are nested. Not all theories are nested within an explicit framework, but when they are, these frameworks identify relevant variables, describe relations between variables, and specify a range of important theoretical assumptions. So understanding these frameworks is necessary for understanding their nested theories, and in our investigations of theories in chapters 4 to 8 we devote considerable space to explaining these frameworks and describing how the theories we investigate are nested within them.

With this conception of theory in mind, four criteria were especially important in our theory selection. First, we endeavoured to select theories of policy change, as opposed to theories of agenda-setting, policy implementation, or some other aspect of the policy process. Second, we limited our selected theories to those that can be considered scientific rather than critical. Third, we selected theories with known applications to, and some success in explaining, Canadian policy-making, avoiding those that have not yet been tested in the Canadian context. Fourth, we chose theories that in our view had a *prima facie* chance of explaining Canadian firearms policy-making and did not have tenets or scope conditions that obviously ruled them out as potential explanations. Below we present our thinking regarding each of these criteria and justify the choices we made as to which theories to include in this study.

Our analysis focuses on theories of policy-making and policy change, but other aspects of the policy process, such as agenda-setting, have also been theorized. An important consideration was to ensure that we investigated like-for-like theories of policy change instead of comparing mismatched theories of policy change and agenda-setting. Some theories of agenda-setting, such as MSF and PET, have also been used as theories of policy change, and following the lead of their respective literatures, we also treated them and investigated them as theories of policy change. Agenda-setting and other features of the policy process are undoubtedly important to investigate and theorize but are beyond scope of this particular study.

The theories in this study are also limited to those that are scientific or aspire to be so. Our understanding of scientific policy process theories is consistent with Weible's definition:

> *Scientific theories ... specify sets of assumptions and conditions under which they apply and posit interactions that come in various relational forms (hypotheses, propositions, principals, or other). Underlying these relationships are causal drivers ... that explain why a relationship could exist. No matter the name, these relational forms serve to enable falsification and learning, to communicate explicitly the relationships under investigation, and to summarize what we know about a given phenomenon.* (Weible 2018, 4)

Scientific theories are empirically based and causally oriented, designed to explain policy-making as it exists rather than advocating what it should be. Scientific theories make few normative assumptions about what policy-making should be, and this distinguishes them from critical theories, such as Marxism, feminism, intersectionality, and others. Critical theories make normative assumptions about ideal states of policy and policy-making and are usually meant to point out inequities and injustices in policy processes and to suggest remedies for them (Orsini and Smith 2007, 1). While these theories have much to offer from a social justice perspective, their primary purpose is to critique policy processes and outcomes, which means they have a different purpose than the scientific theories investigated here.

Given that most policy process theories have been developed in the US with American policy-making in mind, the portability of these theories to Canadian policy-making was an important consideration in our theory selection. To determine the portability of theories, we relied on the existing literature and limited our analysis to those theories that already have a solid Canadian literature featuring several Canadian applications. These applications show that, at the very least, the theories' basic assumptions and central concepts are portable to Canada despite having been developed elsewhere. The applications also show that there is at least some empirical support for the theories in explaining cases of Canadian policy-making, so it is worthwhile to investigate their potential in the case of Canadian firearms policy. Limiting the theories to those with several Canadian applications excluded the narrative policy framework, which has a strong following in the US and is probably applicable to Canadian policy-making but has yet to be demonstrated through Canadian applications.

A final consideration in selecting theories was whether, on their face, the theories stood a chance of explaining the outcomes in Canadian firearms policy. This was based on the assertion that it would be pointless to test theories that have no obvious chance of explaining our case, particularly given our "most likely" case selection strategy. Policy diffusion theory, for example, is explicitly designed to explain how new policy ideas spread between governments but offers no explanation for how originating jurisdictions adopt policy inventions in the first place (Berry and Berry 2018, 253). Since Canada was the first Western country to adopt universal firearms registration in the 1995 *Firearms Act*, making it the originating jurisdiction for this policy idea, policy diffusion theory could offer no explanation for a key policy outcome in our case and was excluded on that basis. Similarly, policy feedback theory (and historical institutionalism, more generally) was excluded because "historical institutionalist analyses centred around a logic of self-reinforcement and path-dependent development have, quite naturally, had far more success explaining stability than in accounting for change" and the Canadian firearms policy case includes at least two major policy changes the theory would have difficulty explaining (Jacobs and Weaver 2015, 441). Weaver (2010), Jacobs and Weaver (2015),

Oberlander and Weaver (2015), Skogstad (2017), Christensen (2020), and others have made strides in their attempts to revise and adapt policy feedback theory to explain both policy stability and change, but a clear and widely accepted version of the theory that would "most likely" explain Canadian firearms policy changes has yet to emerge. For that reason, policy feedback theory was excluded from this study.

A special case was Hall's (1993) policy paradigms theory, which stood a chance of explaining Canadian firearms policy, but awkwardly so. Canada's adoption and subsequent abandonment of universal firearms registration suggests the possibility of a double policy paradigm shift in which a paradigm shifted and then shifted back. This would be an unusual outcome not found in the policy paradigms literature and suggests that firearms policy may be a deviant or extreme case for this theory. This would be interesting to investigate in itself but does not match our focus on theories that, on their face, should stand a good chance of explaining Canadian firearms policy. So despite the theory's potentially general application, its Canadian literature (L.A. White 2012; Skogstad and Whyte 2015; Towns and Henstra 2018; Skogstad 2020), and our personal fondness for it, we excluded policy paradigms theory on the basis that we might be asking it to do something it has never done before. This, admittedly, was a judgment call, and future studies of this sort might do well to include policy paradigms theory in their analyses.

This left us with a group of five theories that are focused on policymaking, that are scientific, that are demonstrated as portable to Canada, and that have a *prima facie* chance of explaining the Canadian firearms policy case: the advocacy coalition framework (ACF), the multiple streams framework (MSF), punctuated equilibrium theory (PET), the social construction framework (SCF), and rational choice institutionalism (RCI). Detailed descriptions of the theories are provided in the theory investigation chapters (chapters 4–8), but it is worth discussing here the considerable diversity among these theories, since that diversity has implications for what we can expect from our contradictory multi-theoretical analysis.

The most obvious source of diversity among the theories is the array of factors they identify as causal in policy change. Some of these causal factors include: the number of veto players along with their coherence and congruence (RCI); the power of advocacy coalitions and the opening of policy change pathways (ACF); the onset of positive feedback through shifting policy images and venue shopping (PET); the power and social construction of target populations (SCF); and the actions of policy entrepreneurs during fortuitous and brief policy windows (MSF). These various causal factors are not only diverse but also unique to each theory. The theories also provide similarly unique explanations of policy stability, some explicitly and others implicitly. In other words, the theories provide five distinctive causal stories with respect to policy outcomes, and our purpose is to probe the plausibility of these accounts by determining how well these causal stories match with empirical experience. But because these causal stories are not – for the most part – mutually exclusive, finding support for one theory does not automatically result in a rejection of the others.

Although all of the theories explain government policy-making, each of them focuses on slightly different phenomena due, in part, to their varying conceptions of public policy. Depending on the theory, public policies are conceived as sets of rules (RCI), as translations of beliefs into policy attributes (ACF), as bundles of benefits and burdens aimed at target populations (SCF), or as levels of government spending (PET). Because the theories conceive of public policies in these various ways, they are each explaining slightly different things, even when analysing the same policy outcome. This can create some confusion and raise some challenges when we try to assess the competing explanations using a contradictory approach. Also, it means that multiple theories might be empirically supported in explaining a single policy outcome.

The theories also differ in their working assumptions, particularly as regards their units of analysis and their causal ontologies. A theory's unit of analysis refers to the portion of the political world that is assumed to be most relevant in explaining policy outcomes. Some theories assume that the entire political system is the necessary unit of analysis (RCI and MSF), others assume that policy subsystems of limited geographical and topical scope are most relevant (ACF), and still others have a role for both policy subsystems and macropolitical institutions in their accounts (PET). The theories also vary in their ontological understandings of causality. Some theories take an explicitly probabilistic approach to causality (MSF), outlining factors that are likely to produce policy stability or change, on average, across cases. Other theories take a deterministic approach to causality (ACF), specifying factors that are necessary, sufficient, or contributing to policy stability or change in all cases. And some theories are unclear or ambivalent as to whether they are probabilistic or deterministic (PET, SCF, and RCI). These different assumptions are a further potential source of confusion in applying and comparing the theories.

Because the theories identify unique causal factors, explain slightly different policy outcomes, and have divergent working assumptions, they are incommensurate. Our task here is not to arbitrate which of these explanations is "truest" or "best" but to probe the limits of these explanations on their own terms. This is less satisfying than pronouncing a single best theory, but it is more in keeping with where we are at in the ongoing project of understanding and theorizing Canadian public policy-making.

Assessing the Merits of Contending Theories

Inherent in the contradictory approach to multi-theoretical analysis is the notion that contending theoretical explanations will be investigated and evaluated according to scientific standards – that is, their ability to explain empirical outcomes. Zahariadis (2005), for example, evaluated the theories in his study of Greek foreign policy by assessing their ability to explain policy outcomes in each year of his study period. The shortcomings of this approach were noted earlier. Notwithstanding those, his was an attempt to investigate and evaluate theories according to their consistency with empirical evidence. We endeavour to do the same in this study of Canadian firearms policy, though our empirical evaluation aims to be more sensitive to the scope and causal ontology of each theory.

We will be evaluating each theory on its own terms. Each contains an explanation of policy-making, usually in the form of a testable hypothesis that is subject to empirical investigation. As just explained, these hypotheses differ not only in how they explain policy-making but also in their scope and causal ontology. Given these differences, we investigate each theory on its own terms; no theory will be (unfairly) tested on another theory's terms.

Because we are investigating and assessing each theory on its own terms, we will be tapping a considerable diversity of research methods and data. Given that investigating probabilistic theories requires different methods and data than investigating deterministic theories, a "one size fits all" approach to data collection and analysis was not viable for this study. Instead, each theory is investigated using research methods and empirical data that are appropriate to it; in this way, we endeavour to meet (or exceed) existing best practices in each theory's literature. Some of the methods utilized include: process tracing, congruence analysis, qualitative content analysis, and large "n" statistical methods. The various methods used to investigate each theory are briefly explained in the theory chapters (chapters 4–8), with more detailed explanations sometimes provided in chapter appendices. Also, because of scope differences, the policy outcomes investigated vary from theory to theory: some chapters investigate all of the firearms policy changes in the

1989–2012 period, while others investigate only the two major policy changes during this period. In short, the methods used and the policies analysed in this study vary by theory and are derived from the nature and scope of the theories' respective causal claims. This is all part of our effort to ensure that each theory is tested on its own terms.

The common metric between the parallel theoretical investigations is the extent to which each theory's explanation of policy-making is consistent with the empirical evidence, setting aside that the relevant empirical evidence varies from theory to theory. This allows for some comparisons between the theories insofar as some are completely supported by the empirical evidence, some are partly supported, and some are not supported at all. However, given the theories' incommensurateness, this is the extent of the comparisons that can be drawn in terms of the theories' relative merits. We focus predominantly on probing the limits of each individual theory.

This book has three sections. The first provides important background information on Canadian firearms policy; the second examines the various policy process theories included in the study; the third collects and summarizes the results of our theoretical investigations and explores their implications for the future of public policy theory. Readers of this book may want to skip to one of the sections based on what they hope to get out of it.

Chapter 2 provides important background on the technical aspects of firearms policy and Canada's history with firearms policy; chapter 3 lays out the structural dimensions of Canadian firearms policy and the basic politics of contemporary Canadian firearms policy issues. Readers who are new to firearms policy should read chapter 2, and those who are new to Canadian policy-making should read chapter 3, as these chapters provide basic knowledge that is assumed in the theoretical investigations that follow. Those already familiar with both firearms policy and Canadian policy-making can safely skip to the second section of this book.

The second section contains the five theoretical investigations that are the core of the book's analysis. Chapter 4 begins the investigations with one of the long-standing and most popular policy process theories in Canada, RCI. From there, chapter 5 investigates SCF, chapter 6 tests ACF, chapter 7 explores the old and new versions of MSF, and chapter 8 looks at PET. This order is not meant to suggest our priorities or preferences; we are simply showcasing the diversity of assumptions and causal stories at hand. Some of the chapters include methodological appendices outlining the data collection and analysis methods used within them, for those who are methodologically inclined.

In the final chapter, we collect and explore our findings from the five theoretical investigations and the implications of those findings for the future of policy theory, with particular emphasis on any potential scope conditions revealed by our analysis. For readers who want to skip the investigations and get straight to the results, chapter 9 is the place to go. However, to fully understand the empirical bases of our findings and their theoretical significance, reading the theoretical investigations is strongly recommended.

2 The Evolution of Canadian Firearms Policy

A key goal of this book is to explain the various major developments in Canadian firearms policy from shortly after the Montreal Massacre in 1989 to the cancelling of the long-gun registry in 2012. In scientific parlance, our study's dependent variables are the three most significant policy episodes regarding gun control in this period. This chapter describes these episodes while providing some historical context of gun regulation in Canada prior to 1989. As we will see, and as expertly detailed by Brown (2012), gun control in Canada did not begin after 1989; indeed, it has a long and volatile history that predates Confederation. Notably, our goal regarding the post-1989 period is simply to describe the policy developments. As the rest of the book is dedicated to exploring the various possible explanations, this chapter does not go into much detail about the massacre and its political fallout.

The Parameters of Firearms Policy

Before detailing the specifics of Canadian firearms policy, it is important to understand what "gun control" can mean, in general terms. There are essentially three dimensions of gun control (Bottomley 2004; Pal 2003; Brown 2012): rules on *who* can use guns, on *how* guns can be used, and on *what* can be used. All three are present in Canada. The "who" can include age restrictions, licensing or safety training requirements, and background checks that forbid certain groups of people from owning or using firearms. The last of these might include people with a record of committing violent crime, who have certain mental illnesses, or who are on a terrorist watch list. Specific ethnic, religious, and ideological groups have also been targeted at various points in Canadian history, both pre- and post-Confederation. The "how" dimension of gun control can also take several forms, often of the "time, manner, and place" variety. Seasonal limits on hunting, minimum distances that firearms can be discharged from roads, and bans on carrying firearms within town limits (as in Quebec City in 1865) are all examples, as are rules governing the storage and transportation of firearms (Pal 2003). Another is specific penalties for certain types of gun use, such as additional penalties for committing crimes with a firearm. Finally, under "what," the state may regulate firearms and related equipment directly, by restricting or banning particular kinds of guns, ammunition, or parts. A recent example is the issue of regulating "bump stocks" that help a semi-automatic weapon shoot like a fully automatic machine gun, after they were used by the shooter in the October 2017 Las Vegas massacre that took a then-record 58 lives and injured more than 500. This third dimension of gun control can also regulate the manufacture, sale, and trade of firearms and related equipment.

The sections that follow use some legal terms that are important to understand. First, firearms policies can come in the form of either *legislation* or *regulations*. Legislation refers to laws passed by the legislative branch, that is, Parliament or provincial legislatures with Royal Assent. Regulations are rules adopted by the executive branch (ministries and the bureaucracy) to implement legislation; they may "flesh out" broad legislative goals or provide direction to those members of the bureaucracy who are responsible for enforcing the law or delivering a government program. Another distinction it is important to recognize is the one between *offences* and *crimes*. An "offence" is "a law or regulation that, if broken, is punishable by fine or imprisonment" (Hausegger, Hennigar, and Riddell 2015, 34). While both the provincial and federal legislatures can create offences, only the latter can create "crimes," which are those offences contained (primarily) in the *Criminal Code*. As such, "all crimes are offences, but not all offences are crimes" (34). We explore the jurisdictional divisions over criminal law and offences that shape Canadian firearms policies in chapter 3.

Limiting Only the "Disloyal": Gun Control from Pre-Confederation to the First World War

During much of Canada's early history, the state actively promoted the use of firearms. Guns were largely seen as "normal," particularly in rural areas for pest control, subsistence hunting, and self-defence, but gun ownership and gun crime were relatively uncommon before Confederation (Brown 2012, 44–5). In the mid-nineteenth century, however, there began a trend toward greater regulation. This was for a variety of reasons, including rising rates of gun-related crimes, suicides, and

accidents; the use of firearms during the 1837–38 rebellions; and growing concern about disruptive immigrants – specifically, impoverished
Irish Catholics who had arrived in large numbers as refugees from the
Great Famine and to work on the many canal construction projects
during this period (30–1). The pre-Confederation Canadas disarmed labourers in 1838 and passed legislation in 1845 limiting gun possession
on public works. Similarly, several municipalities regulated firearm
use within their boundaries in the 1850s. These measures represented
the first significant, albeit limited, efforts at gun control in Canada and
were intended to discourage gun possession by those deemed a threat
to public order – First Nations, Irish Catholics, labourers, the unprop-
ertied, and new non-British immigrants. At the same time, firearms
possession was encouraged for law-abiding, British, middle- and up-
per-class men, especially after 1860, when it was feared that the US
Civil War would spill over into British North America. There was also
increasing conflict between European settlers and Indigenous peoples
in the Prairies and British Columbia.

After the US Civil War, a massive surplus of cheap, high-quality
American guns flooded the world market, especially British North
America. Interest in hunting and sharpshooting among both men and
women surged with pro-imperial sentiment from 1890 until 1914, fos-
tered by the Boer War (1899–1902) and rising international tensions. In
that climate, Canada did little to restrict long guns (i.e., rifles and shotguns) for citizens deemed loyal, and Canada became heavily armed
compared to other developed democracies (9).

For those deemed disloyal or a threat to the state, it was a different
story. In the years immediately after Confederation, anxiety among British Canadians about Indigenous peoples in the West and Irish Catholics
in the East led to firearms restrictions targeting those groups. The temporary measures adopted after the 1837 rebellion were revived and made
permanent after the 1866 Fenian raids. With respect to First Nations, the
Macdonald government established new restrictions on the sale of ammunition to Indigenous peoples in the West (60; Gwyn 2012). In subsequent decades, discriminatory attitudes toward new immigrants from
Asia and southern and eastern Europe led authorities to target such individuals disproportionally for possession offences (Brown 2012, 125) or to
impose higher licensing fees. For the most part, however, Canadian governments did not introduce new gun laws targeting ethnic minorities.

An important trend emerged in the decades between Confederation and the First World War: the Liberals attempted to introduce gun
control, particularly for handguns, and the Conservatives (particularly under Macdonald) resisted this (see Table 2.1 for a summary of

Table 2.1. Chronology of major firearms policy changes

Year	Change
1838	(Pre-Confederation Canada's) ban on gun possession by labourers
1845	(Pre-Confederation Canada's) ban on gun possession on public works
1877	Ban on carrying handguns (with exceptions)
1878	Temporary restrictions on carrying guns in public
1892	Ban on concealed handguns, further increased penalties for gun crimes, gun sellers must record names of buyers
1913	Greater penalties for gun crime, repeal of exemptions for carrying handgun in public
1914	Ban on firearm possession by "enemy aliens" during First World War
1919	"Aliens" require firearm possession permit
1920	Firearm possession permit extended to all Canadians (except for shotguns)
1921	Firearm possession permit requirement lifted for long guns, retained for "aliens"
1933	Increased sentences for illegal possession of handguns and crimes committed with a firearm, ban on concealed firearms in public, permit system for gun sellers
1934	National (RCMP) registry for handguns
1940	National registry of all firearms, ban on firearm possession by "enemy aliens" during Second World War
1946	End of national firearms registry (except handguns)
1951	Automatic weapons added to registry
1969	New codification system for firearms: unrestricted, restricted, prohibited; almost nothing prohibited
1977	Firearms acquisition certificate (FAC) required to purchase any firearm, criminal record check for FAC applicants, ban on fully automatic firearms (grandfathered)
1991	Prohibited category includes many military weapons and automatics converted to semi-automatics; FAC application requires more background information, character references, mandatory training, and four-week waiting period; increased sentences for firearms offences and bans on gun possession for those convicted
1995	Universal firearms registry, new Possession and Acquisition Licence (PAL) needed for all firearms and ammunition purchases, further increased penalties for serious gun crimes
2012	Registration of unrestricted long guns ends, records destroyed

firearms policy changes). The next chapter will explore this issue in greater detail, but we note here that Macdonald was a leading proponent of the view that the 1689 English *Bill of Rights* gave law-abiding British (male) citizens the right to own guns (Brown 2017). Macdonald opposed greater restrictions even after the high-profile murders of two Fathers of Confederation with pistols: Thomas D'Arcy McGee in 1868 and George Brown in 1880. In 1877 the first Liberal government, under Prime Minister Alexander Mackenzie, increased punishments for crimes committed with a handgun and banned the carrying of handguns, albeit with a generous exception for those with "reasonable cause to fear an assault or injury to himself, to his family, or to his property" (Brown 2012, 72). Further temporary restrictions on carrying weapons in public were introduced in 1878, accompanied by expanded police search-and-seizure powers. When the *Criminal Code* was introduced in 1892 – under the Conservatives, but notably a year after Macdonald's death – it required gun sellers to keep detailed records of their sales, banned concealed handguns, further increased penalties for gun crimes, and restricted handgun purchases to those who could prove their "good character" to a justice of the peace (Friedland 1975–76). A Conservative government in 1913 increased penalties for gun crimes and repealed the generous 1877 exemption concerning public possession of firearms, but it also created new exemptions for those who carried handguns in their own homes or businesses – an implicit form of discrimination against those without property, usually labourers, the poor, and recent immigrants.

An Emboldened State: Gun Restrictions from the First to Second World War

The First World War saw the federal government introduce new firearms restrictions in the name of national security. Those restrictions targeted "enemy aliens" in Canada, including the roughly 100,000 immigrants who had been born in Germany or Austria-Hungary and were still citizens of either. Ottawa required 80,000 enemy aliens to register and issued an Order in Council to disarm them all, including by police search and seizure without a warrant; in addition, 8,500 were placed in internment camps (Kordan 2002). The Bolshevik Revolution in Russia in October 1917 led to fears that leftist radicals in Canada would threaten the war effort, the government, and the economy, and those fears only intensified after the war on the heels of widespread labour unrest, including the Winnipeg General Strike in 1919. The government's initial postwar response has rightfully been called "hysterical," for it scapegoated enemy aliens, who were falsely accused of owning virtually all of the concealed weapons in Canada (Brown 2012, 136–7). Parliament passed legislation in 1919 requiring aliens to have a permit to possess any firearm; in 1920, this law was extended to all Canadians, even for guns already in their possession. The only exception was shotguns, as a concession to farmers, thus marking an end to the long-standing preferential treatment of rifles (137–8). The government's crackdown was surprisingly short-lived, however: in 1921, the permit requirement was lifted for long guns (though retained for "aliens"). No significant new firearms restrictions were introduced for the next twelve years.

The Great Depression and the growth of organized crime associated with Prohibition spurred new firearms restrictions in the 1930s. In 1933, Parliament enacted tougher sentences for unlawful possession of handguns and for crimes committed with a firearm, banned concealed firearms in public, and introduced a permit system for gun sellers. A year later, Parliament created the first permanent, national gun registry in Canada by requiring the registration of all handguns with the RCMP. By 1940, almost 200,000 handguns had been registered, with little public resistance or criticism (152). Additional restrictions throughout the 1930s banned short rifles and again increased penalties for crimes committed with a firearm. The Second World War saw further state regulation of firearms, the most important development being the creation in 1940 of the first national gun registry for *all* weapons, with registration records copied to the RCMP. Notably, the registry generated little public outcry. Enemy aliens (Germans, Italians, and Japanese) – including those who had become naturalized British citizens after 1929[1] – were again prohibited from owning firearms or ammunition. A shortage of pistols for the military prompted a ban on sales to the public of several popular handgun calibres, and there was a spike in the enforcement of permit requirements and seizures of illegal firearms by police (153). Immediately after the war, Parliament banned enemy weapons brought back to Canada (i.e., as war trophies). As Brown (2012) observes, gun regulation in the 1930s and 1940s reflected not only the growth of state power but also the state's growing confidence in its capacity to administer coercive programs at a national level, assisted by new computing and sorting machines (e.g., the 1940 registry employed equipment from IBM). Federal enthusiasm for firearms regulation quickly subsided, however, and the long-gun portion of the registry was destroyed shortly after the war. However, Ottawa did retain mandatory registration of handguns – which has survived into the present day – and added fully automatic firearms to the registry in 1951, the same year that record-keeping was centralized in the office of the Commissioner of the RCMP (Friedland 1975–76, 45).[2] Many provinces introduced licensing and mandatory safety training programs for hunters in the decades after the Second World War, but otherwise gun control "largely disappeared from public debate for more than twenty years" (Brown 2012, 159).

A New Policy Status Quo: 1969 to 1989

Gun control largely fell off the political agenda for two decades; however, several social and political developments throughout the 1960s were working to change that. The assassinations of President John F. Kennedy, his brother Robert, and civil rights leader Martin Luther King shocked the world and led to new (albeit weak) gun controls in the US. There was growing social unrest in 1960s associated with counterculture movements, including the civil rights, anti–Vietnam War, and women's movements, and rates of both crime and gun ownership were rising. Prime Minister Pierre Trudeau introduced new gun laws in 1968–69 as part of the sweeping omnibus reform of the *Criminal Code* (*Criminal Law Amendment Act, 1968–69*, SC 1968–69, c 38), after extensive consultations with well-established interest groups representing hunters and sport shooters (Brown 2012, 166). The result reflected the considerable influence of these groups, and introduced few new limits besides bans on sales of firearms to those of "unsound mind." Also, judges could prohibit those convicted of a firearms offence from carrying or possessing a firearm or ammunition for up to five years.

The main change was a new codification system for firearms, still in place, that created three classes of weapons: unrestricted, restricted, and prohibited. Unrestricted weapons were those considered "safe" and in 1969 included hunting rifles and shotguns; these required no new permits. Restricted weapons were those considered more dangerous, such as handguns, fully automatic and some semi-automatic firearms, and short-barrelled rifles and shotguns, and each restricted weapon required a permit ("registration certificate") for possession (RCMP 2016). Especially dangerous weapons could be classified as prohibited and thus banned, with exceptions for the military and possibly police. However, nothing was prohibited in 1969, not even firearms that *had* been banned in the 1930s, such as short-barrelled (and thus easily concealable) rifles and sawed-off shotguns; all were reclassified as "restricted" in 1969. Even by 1975 no firearm was prohibited in Canada (Friedland 1975–76, 37), despite alarm caused by the terrorist activities of the separatist Front de libération du Québec (FLQ) in the early 1970s. As such, the 1969 amendments arguably *weakened* firearms regulation overall, in line with the demands of gun enthusiasts and lobbyists.

Rising per capita crime rates throughout the 1970s – particularly with guns, and in Canada's cities, where the overwhelming majority of Canadians lived – prompted calls for tougher gun laws. There was also growing concern over gangland shootings with automatic weapons and the mix of drug use and gun crime, as well as public shock at a string of school shootings in 1975 and 1976 by youths using unregulated hunting rifles and shotguns. An independent study for the federal Solicitor General in the mid-1970s, by leading criminal law scholar Martin Friedland, called for tougher sentences for gun-related crimes, the prohibition of sawed-off shotguns and automatic weapons, and universal licensing for all gun users or new owners, but rejected the idea of a universal gun registry (Friedland 1975–76). Other studies by Statistics Canada and the RCMP around the same time estimated that Canadians (at the time numbering around 23 million [Statistics Canada 1977]) owned between 5 and 10 million firearms, with 1.5 million Canadians reporting that they had used a gun within the twelve months preceding the survey (Brown 2012, 173–4). After the appointment of a more pro–gun control Minister of Justice in 1975, Ottawa proposed another omnibus bill aimed at criminal law. Bill C-83 would have yet again increased sentences for gun-related crimes; it would also have required all gun owners, whether active users or not, to obtain a licence; moreover, officials could refuse to license individuals judged mentally unstable or "potentially dangerous." However, C-83 would not have altered the existing classification scheme and thus would have left most rifles and shotguns unrestricted, and automatic weapons and sawed-off shotguns would still be available with a simple permit. Despite these weak measures, and the Liberals' holding a majority government, Bill C-83 was left to die on the order paper in 1976. Brown attributes the bill's failure to divisions within the Liberal caucus that had been inflamed by the gun lobby's "sustained and emotional resistance" (188). Critics of gun control repeatedly invoked conspiracy theories that the government was planning to ban and seize all firearms, and called instead for even tougher sentences for gun-related crimes (even though decades of stiffening penalties had proven ineffective) (186–7). Bill C-83 thus marked the first time that a government committed to gun control backed down in the face of organized public resistance.

The Trudeau government responded in 1977 with a watered-down gun control bill, C-51, which Parliament passed thanks in large part to the (assiduously courted) support of the pro-gun lobby. C-51's main policy change was the introduction of a requirement that all new gun owners obtain a Firearms Acquisition Certificate (FAC), including for unrestricted (hereafter "regulated") firearms; existing owners were exempted. FACs would be valid for five years and permitted a holder to purchase an unlimited number of rifles and shotguns; also, purchasers would not have to provide a reason for their purchases or find guarantors (i.e., character references) (Friedland 1984, 118). Implementation of the FAC regime was delayed until 1979, by which year provinces were empowered to require FAC applicants to take a safety training course (RCMP 2016). As with previous gun control bills, C-51 increased punishments for gun-related crimes (including reintroducing mandatory minimum sentences[3]) and expanded police search-and-seizure powers. The bill also reclassified fully automatic weapons as "prohibited" (albeit while grandfathering automatics already registered as "restricted") and banned private citizens from carrying a restricted weapon to protect property. Despite unsuccessful bills by private members and backbench MPs to amend Canada's firearms laws, and a mass shooting at Quebec's National Assembly in 1984, C-51 was the policy status quo at the time of the Montreal Massacre.

The Montreal Massacre and Post-1989 Firearms Laws

When twenty-eight people were shot and fourteen women killed at École Polytechnique on 6 December 1989, it was by far the worst mass shooting in Canadian history, and the shooter's explicitly misogynistic motive shocked Canadians. Moreover, the gun he used – a Ruger Mini-14 semi-automatic – was entirely legal, and legally obtained. The galvanizing effect of the shooting on pro–gun control forces will be discussed in the chapters that follow; suffice it to say there were immediate calls for tougher gun controls from Montreal Massacre survivors, the public, the media, and politicians. In particular, Liberal opposition MP Warren Allmand, who as Solicitor General had championed Bills C-83 and 51 in the 1970s, suggested new restrictions on FACs only two days after the murders: a two-week waiting period on applications, FAC expiration after two years instead of five, a requirement that applicants provide two guarantors, and a further requirement of a FAC for all ammunition purchases (*Debates, House of Commons* [8 December 1989], 6658). Shortly thereafter, he proposed these measures in an unsuccessful private member's bill, C-283 (*Debate, House of Commons* [2 February 1990], 7778).

Despite widespread calls for action, Brian Mulroney's Progressive Conservative government did little in response. Even before the shooting, it had proposed to ban the importation of automatic weapon models that had been converted to semi-automatics but could easily be reconverted. After the Montreal Massacre, Minister of Justice Doug Lewis simply promised to follow through on this measure, even though it would have had no effect on the shooter's weapon, which had been manufactured as a semi-automatic. To those demanding a ban on semi-automatics, Lewis replied: "You can't legislate against insanity ... There are many thousands of gun owners who act responsibly. Semi-automatics are used for sporting purposes" (Bottomley 2004, 30).

Kim Campbell replaced Lewis as justice minister in late February 1990 and a few weeks later announced her intention to introduce new firearms legislation (Fleming 2012, 115). On 26 June 1990 she tabled Bill C-80, which mostly followed through on Lewis's pre-massacre commitment to ban automatics that had been converted to semi-automatics (Bottomley 2004, 32). Campbell also proposed banning certain military and paramilitary weapons and high-capacity magazines, but not semi-automatics. Instead, some semi-automatic models of assault weapons, such as the Uzi and AK-47 – notably, however, not the one used in the massacre – were to be added to the "restricted" list (Rathjen and Montpetit 1999, 57). Campbell also proposed a four-week waiting period for FAC applications. Gun control advocates criticized the bill as inadequate; even so, it encountered significant resistance from gun rights advocates, including many within the Progressive Conservative caucus. In an unusual move, Campbell sent C-80 to a Special Committee before second reading for re-evaluation, which critics interpreted as a stalling tactic (63). Such fears proved accurate: although the Special Committee report ultimately recommended thirty-two amendments, Bill C-80 died on the order paper when Parliament prorogued (for not even twenty-four hours!) on 12 May 1991.

Only two weeks later, Campbell introduced revamped gun control legislation in Bill C-17[4] with the promise that the new bill would "take the wrong guns out of all hands, and all guns out of the wrong hands" (*Debates, House of Commons* [6 June 1991], 1250). C-17 included the main provisions of C-80 but also some of the demands made by gun control lobbyists. Despite attempts by pro-gun Tory MPs to weaken the bill at the committee stage, it actually emerged even stronger (Rathjen and Montpetit 1999, 113–19). Bill C-17 was adopted by the House 189–14 on 7 November, 1991, although the Tory MPs were under party discipline by order of Prime Minister Mulroney. Many MPs did not show up for the vote to avoid having to support the bill (Brown 2012, 209–11).

According to Pal (2003), the changes in C-17 "were largely technical, and although they represented some important departures, for the most part, they built on the existing regime and simply broadened and deepened it" (249). That said, the new law addressed several dimensions of gun control. First, the FAC screening process was made more rigorous. It now required applicants to provide more background information, a photograph, and two character references; it also introduced a twenty-eight-day waiting period. Firearms officers were empowered to interview the applicant's neighbours, social workers, spouses, and family before issuing a FAC. The law made safety training mandatory for applicants and raised the minimum age for applicants from sixteen to eighteen, although those aged sixteen or seventeen could apply for a FAC with parental consent. FACs continued to remain valid for five years.

Second, the law increased the penalties for firearms-related offences. For example, it doubled the sentence for the illegal importation of prohibited weapons from five to ten years' imprisonment. It also ordered judges to consider imposing firearm prohibitions as a bail condition for individuals charged with a violent offence or as a peace bond condition in domestic disputes. Existing firearm prohibitions for those convicted of violent offences were extended from five to ten years and made permanent for repeat offenders. As well, firearm prohibition orders as bail conditions or upon conviction were extended for the first time to drug trafficking offences. Some new firearms offences were also created, as well as new regulations for the storage, handling, and transportation of firearms. In particular, gun owners would now have to store firearms and ammunition separately, store firearms in an inoperable condition, and hide and lock guns during transport.

Third, the law expanded the models of firearms that were restricted or prohibited, moving about two hundred models into these categories (Brown 2012, 211). As promised even before the Montreal Massacre, fully automatic firearms converted to semi-automatics were banned, although registered collectors could keep any that they already possessed. As well, military, paramilitary, and other particularly high-powered guns were prohibited, as were large-capacity cartridge magazines for automatics and semi-automatics (RCMP 2016). In a telling comment aimed at the gun lobby, Campbell justified these measures by arguing that "the most dangerous firearms … are not weapons for personal or civil defence. These roles are very capably performed by the police and the armed forces of Canada, and should not serve as a justification for the private ownership of firearms" (*Debates, House of Commons* [6 June 1991], 1254). Yet many semi-automatic models – including, surprisingly, the one used in the massacre – remained unrestricted or only restricted, with the emphasis placed instead on limiting magazine size (ten rounds for semi-automatic pistols and five for rifles above .22-calibre). However, the law empowered MPs or senators[5] to demand that firearm regulations (i.e., those made by Order in Council) be reviewed at the draft stage by a parliamentary committee. This limited the power of the justice minister to make unilateral regulatory changes – for example, regarding which gun models and ammunition would be prohibited or restricted. That power had generated intense criticism and anxiety among pro-gun lobbyists (Brown 2012).

Although the vast majority of Opposition MPs voted in favour of Bill C-17, some strongly criticized the bill. Ian Waddell, a NDP MP from

British Columbia, and Benoit Tremblay, a former Tory MP from Quebec now sitting as an independent (and part of the group that would shortly become the Bloc Québécois), called for a national registry of all restricted weapons (*Debates, House of Commons* [6 June 1991], 1268–9). Tremblay was especially critical of the bill's failure to prohibit the "paramilitary weapon" used in the Montreal Massacre, which was "already prohibited elsewhere, even in the United States, for instance in New Jersey" (*Debates, House of Commons* [6 June 1991], 1270). For her part, Minister of Justice Campbell explicitly rejected a national registry as too expensive and ineffective.

Following the passage of C-17, the federal government's political agenda was dominated by the national unity crisis sparked by the failure to pass the Meech Lake Accord in 1990 and by the subsequent attempts to negotiate constitutional reform that led to the failed Charlottetown Accord and 1992 referendums in Quebec and the rest of Canada. The Mulroney government was also busy negotiating what would become the North American Free Trade Agreement (NAFTA) with the US and Mexico, as well as dealing with the sluggish economic recovery from the 1990–91 recession. Gun control did not entirely disappear from the political agenda, however, due to the efforts of advocacy groups and the high-profile shooting by disgruntled Concordia professor Valery Fabrikant of four colleagues with a legally acquired handgun in August 1992.

The 1993 Federal Election and the *Firearms Act* (Bill C-68)

Brian Mulroney stepped down as prime minister in February 1993 and was replaced by Kim Campbell, who called an election for 25 October 1993 – the first to be contested by the separatist Bloc Québécois and by Liberal leader Jean Chrétien, as well as by an invigorated Reform Party in the West. Gun control was not a major issue during the election campaign, arising only once during the English-language leaders' debate, during which Chrétien and BQ leader Lucien Bouchard offered brief and vaguely worded support for stricter gun laws (Bottomley 2004, 33). The Liberal's widely circulated "Red Book," detailing the party's campaign platform, promised little on gun control except to crack down on illegally imported firearms and prohibit gun possession by anyone convicted of an indictable drug-related, stalking, or violent offence (Liberal Party of Canada 1993). No other party leader raised gun control during either the debates or the campaign (Bottomley 2004, 33). The Liberals won a majority government, and the PCs were nearly obliterated, reduced to just two seats; the BQ formed the Official Opposition, just ahead of the Reform Party. As Bottomley observes, "the Red Book and the campaign of 1993 gave no indication that, within months of being elected to a majority government, the Liberals would announce and then pass into law by far the toughest, most comprehensive, and most controversial gun control legislation in Canadian history" (34). Surprisingly, the new government would soon claim that it had an electoral mandate to pursue such changes, a "revisionist assessment … [that] went largely unchallenged" and "became an important rhetorical pillar for the government" (34).

Toronto MP Allan Rock was appointed justice minister in March 1994 and soon after announced his support for extremely strict gun control, including possibly a total ban on private handgun ownership (Wills 1994a). A month later, he publicly admitted that he personally believed no one should possess firearms except "police officers and soldiers" (Vienneau 1994, A1), although he reassured gun owners that he had no intention of proposing such a ban or of confiscating firearms (Bottomley 2004, 36). The Liberals' policy conference in May 1994 overwhelmingly approved Rock's proposals, sponsored by the National Women's Liberal convention, to strengthen restrictions on handguns and assault weapons and "to examine the possible creation of a national registry of all guns held in private hands" (38). Prime Minister Chrétien promised a new gun control bill in the House's fall session.

As it happened, the new *Firearms Act*, Bill C-68, was not tabled until mid-February 1995. After vigorous debate and the Liberals' aggressive use of legislative fast-tracking and enforcement of party discipline to deal with caucus dissent (Docherty 1997; Pal 2003; Bottomley 2004), the bill received Royal Assent on the sixth anniversary of the Montreal Massacre. Pal (2003) writes that unlike the Tories' C-17, C-68 "was not cosmetic or incremental; it introduced a whole new regime" (250). The centrepiece of the new regime was a universal national firearms registry, the first since the Second World War as well as the first during peacetime for long guns (Stenning 2003). The bill made owning an unregistered firearm a criminal offence, with a criminal record upon conviction. Registration and the registry were administered by a new office, the Canadian Firearms Centre headed by the Firearms Registrar, which was separate from the Chief Firearms Officer – now one for each province – who was responsible for issuing, renewing, and revoking firearms licences. Besides establishing a registry, C-68 replaced the FAC system with a new and significantly more comprehensive licensing system. FACs had been required only for those purchasing a firearm, whereas the new Possession and Acquisition Licence (PAL) would be required for those who already possessed a firearm, as well as to purchase ammunition (as

Warren Allmand had proposed in 1989). Like FACs, PALs would have to be renewed every five years. The new law also banned many models of handguns and assault rifles and required handgun owners to justify possession every five years (Brown 2012, 216). Finally, as with previous rounds of amending firearms laws, sentences for serious gun crimes were increased. In deference to the *Firearms Act*'s sweeping changes, and to the political firestorm it set off among gun enthusiasts and some Indigenous peoples, the Liberals delayed implementation of the law until 1 December 1998 and created the User Group on Firearms to help advise the government on the development of related regulations. The User Group included "representatives from hunters, gunsmiths, gun clubs, firearms retailers, competitive shooters, aboriginals, outfitters, firearms safety trainers, and collectors." The government took almost two years to develop new gun regulations (Pal 2003, 252).

Registry Implementation Problems and Cancellation

From the start, policy-makers struggled to estimate the financial cost of creating and maintaining the registry, primarily because the government had no clear idea how many firearms were in Canada – a problem the auditor general of Canada had flagged as early as 1993. As Brown (2012, 216–17) notes, estimates of gun numbers ranged from 6 to 20 million, and the registry would require investment in new information technologies such as computers and the Internet to function. Justice Minister Rock pegged the cost of the registry at $85 million, claiming that most of this would be recouped through user fees (230). This would prove to be spectacularly inaccurate. In June 1998, Rock's replacement as justice minister, Alberta MP Anne McLellan, admitted that the administration costs for the Firearms Program would be much higher than $85 million, but she did not specify by how much (Pal 2003, 253). In August 2001 the Canadian Firearms Program reported that the registry had cost $527 million to date, blaming the massive cost overruns on a poor computer system for tracking licence fee collection; moreover, it would require "massive change" and "significant investment" to fix (CBC News 2015). An audit of the registry in April 2002 found the cost now at $629 million, including $227 million for computers alone, and a further $60 million for public relations programs (CBC News 2015), $18 million of which went to the advertising agency GroupeAction, a firm tied to the federal Liberals that would soon be implicated in the sponsorship scandal (CBC News Online 2006).

On 3 December 2002, Auditor General Sheila Fraser released her damning report on the gun registry. She found that costs had ballooned to \$688 million, with only \$59 million recouped from user fees, and criticized the Department of Justice for providing "insufficient financial information and explanations for the dramatic increase in the cost of the Program" (Auditor General 2002). The report included the Justice Department's estimate that by 2004–5 the registry would cost "at least \$1 billion" while collecting only \$140 million in fees, and that this did not include all financial impacts on the government (Auditor General 2002). These forecasts proved to be inflated, and besides that, most of the money had been spent on screening and licensing gun owners rather than on registration (Cukier and Thomlinson 2004); even so, it was clear that the registry had cost much more than initially promised. The auditor general identified several factors that had contributed to the cost overruns, including poor planning; lack of leadership; program restructuring; underestimation of the cost and complexity of the IT systems needed; the unexpected refusal of some provincial governments to help implement the registry, which forced Ottawa to pay for implementation in those provinces and for a more expensive centralized system; and user fee reductions and waivers to encourage licensing and registration (Auditor General 2002). As well, she found that 85 per cent of the applications submitted by gun owners were incomplete, which meant they had to be processed manually at much greater cost (Auditor General 2002), which in turn required Ottawa to spend millions on revising the forms and on advertising to encourage registration (Brown 2012, 233). Fraser further noted that the government had undermined the program's accountability by withholding these implementation problems and cost overruns from Parliament, in violation of its own regulatory policies (Auditor General 2002).

Even before the auditor general's report, questions had been raised about the quality of the registry. In June 1999 the Canadian Firearms Centre claimed that 411,000 people had been licensed and that 1.3 million firearms had been registered in the first six months of the program, yet an access-to-information request by the Reform Party revealed that only 5,500 people had been licensed and 66,000 firearms registered (Bottomley 2004, 59). The situation had apparently improved by the beginning of 2003, when it was reported that "seventy-five per cent of all gun owners [met] the Jan. 1, 2003 deadline for registering their non-restricted firearms, signing up 5.8 million firearms" (CBC News 2015). However, in June 2003, the Solicitor General announced that many of the gun registrations before the January 1 deadline had been lost due to IT problems and that anyone seeking to obtain a licence or register a weapon after the deadline will not be prosecuted (Bottomley 2004, 70). Nonetheless, the following month the Canadian Firearms Centre reported that over

90 per cent of Canada's gun owners had acquired a licence and that 6.3 million of an estimated 7.9 million long guns had been registered, and that roughly a million firearms had been surrendered by owners who did not wish to obtain a licence (Brown 2012, 225).

Meanwhile, provincial governments and Indigenous peoples had launched constitutional challenges against the registry. The Alberta government referred the *Firearms Act* to its Court of Appeal in 1997, where it argued that the registry violated the province's jurisdiction over "property and civil rights" in s.92(13) of the *Constitution Act, 1867*. After a close decision (3–2) in favour of Ottawa, Alberta appealed to the Supreme Court of Canada, with the support of the governments of Manitoba, New Brunswick, the Northwest Territories, Nova Scotia, Ontario, Saskatchewan, and Yukon, as well as several pro-gun groups. The Supreme Court unanimously rejected the provinces' challenge, finding that while the *Firearms Act* had regulatory aspects that touched on property and civil rights, it fell well within the federal government's criminal law power (*Reference re Firearms Act (Can.)*, 2000 SCC 31). Indigenous groups argued that the *Firearms Act* infringed on their constitutionally protected treaty rights and traditional hunting practices and objected to paying new licensing fees (Brown 2012, 221). The Federation of Saskatchewan Indian Nations had also intervened in the *Firearms Reference* to argue that the law violated their treaty rights, but as the case was only about the federal division of powers, the Court did not pursue this issue except to invite a new challenge specifically on such grounds (*Reference re Firearms Act* 2000, para. 56). In fact, the government had heard and responded to Indigenous complaints early in the implementation process, consulting with Indigenous groups and adopting the *Aboriginal Peoples of Canada Adaptations Regulations* in March 1998. These regulations permitted elders in Indigenous communities to participate in screening firearm licence applicants, allowed Indigenous children under twelve to take part in traditional hunts, and exempted Indigenous people from the mandatory safety course if they could show informally "that they possessed an understanding of firearms laws and safety guidelines" (Brown 2012, 221). Nonetheless, in July 2003, while a court challenge was pending, a judge granted a temporary injunction that exempted Inuit hunters in Nunavut from the registry or licensing fees due to unique promises made to that community (CBC News 2015). It appears that the case was never heard, and the injunction stayed in place until the long-gun registry was cancelled in 2012.

The Liberals left power in 2006 after thirteen years as the governing party. They were replaced by the Conservative Party – the result of a 2003 merger between the Canadian Alliance (previously, the Reform

Party) and remnants of the Progressive Conservatives – as a minority government under Prime Minister Stephen Harper. As detailed in the next chapter, the Conservatives and their predecessor parties had long been vocal opponents of the *Firearms Act* and the gun registry, and soon after taking power they launched the first of several attempts to eliminate the registry and weaken gun control laws. In May 2006, the government cut $10 million from the program's budget, issued a one-year amnesty (repeatedly renewed) for those who had not yet registered their firearms, eliminated and refunded registration fees for long-gun owners, and transferred administration of the *Firearms Act* and the Canadian Firearms Centre to the RCMP (CBC News 2006). Repeated attempts to cancel the long-gun registry were unsuccessful, however, as bills died on the order table when Parliament was prorogued in 2007 (Bill C-21) and dissolved in 2008 for an election (Bill C-24). That election returned another Conservative minority government, which introduced three separate bills to abolish the long-gun registry. The first of these was a private member's bill tabled by outspoken gun advocate and Conservative backbench MP Garry Breitkreuz (Bill C-301 on 2 February 2009); the second was a Senate bill by Deputy Government Leader Gerald Comeau (Bill S-5 on 1 April 2009); the third was another private member's bill tabled by Conservative MP Candice Hoeppner (Bill C-391 on 15 May 2009). Breitkreuz's and Comeau's bills did not proceed past first reading, despite two attempts for C-301, which failed when Breitkreuz did not show up (*Debates, House of Commons* [15 June 2009], 1100). C-391, however, passed second reading and was sent to committee in November 2009. It was later reinstated after Parliament was controversially prorogued at the end of the year (CBC News 2009). In June 2010, the opposition party members on the House Standing Committee on Public Safety and National Security – who, in a minority government, formed the majority of the committee – banded together to ensure that the committee's report on Bill C-391 would recommend against proceeding. On 22 September 2010, the House narrowly accepted the committee's report, and C-391 officially died.

In March 2011, the government was brought down by a vote of non-confidence. An election was called for May, with the Conservatives once again promising to end the long-gun registry. This time, the Conservatives were elected with a fairly comfortable majority, and on 25 October 2011, the government tabled Bill C-19, the *Ending of the Long-Gun Registry Act* (S.C. 2012, c. 6) – its final, and ultimately successful, attempt to undo the Liberals' extension of gun registration from handguns and automatic firearms to all guns. That bill received Royal Assent on 5 April 2012. The same law removed the obligation on gun sellers to keep detailed sales records. This said, it is important to appreciate the limited scope of C-19: despite its expansively titled name, the bill did not eliminate registration for all "long guns," only those in the "non-restricted" category. Registration continued for restricted and prohibited weapons (the latter only held by collectors who had made them inoperable or those with special permission, such as security guards). As well, the significant changes brought by the new PAL regime in 1995 were left untouched, meaning that possession and acquisition of all firearms and ammunition required a licence. This said, Bill C-19 was certainly a blow to gun control advocates, as many models of powerful rifles and shotguns were now unregistered, and the expensive registry was destroyed.

While the gun control issue faded in prominence between 2012 and 2020, despite the replacement of the Conservatives by Justin Trudeau's Liberals in the fall of 2015, there are three important codas to the story. The first is that the government of Quebec made a last-ditch attempt through the courts to retain gun registration records from that province, in the hope of maintaining its own registry, but its initial success at the trial court was overturned on appeal (*Quebec (Attorney General) v. Canada (Attorney General)*, 2015 SCC 14).[6] In 2016, however, Quebec passed legislation (Bill 64, *Firearms Registration Act*, 2016, chapter 15) to create a provincial registry for the very guns that had been removed from the federal registry. The second is that the Harper government passed Bill C-42, the *Common Sense Firearms Licensing Act* (S.C. 2015, c. 27), which drew criticism from both gun control and pro-gun lobbyists. That law loosened restrictions on the transportation of firearms within the province of possession but retained strict controls on inter-provincial transportation. It also required a classroom-based firearms safety course for first-time licensees, which the gun lobby argued would cause undue hardship on rural and northern residents (National Firearms Association 2014). In addition, C-42 empowered the minister of justice to reverse RCMP (Firearms Officer) decisions to reclassify weapons and ammunition, thus opening what was an administrative process to partisan interference and potentially hampering the RCMP's ability to respond quickly to gun manufacturers' attempts to circumvent restrictions through design changes (Coalition for Gun Control 2014, 6–7). The law also removed the restriction on the minister of justice's authority, introduced in 1995, to change the classification of particular models of firearms and ammunition, but only in this telling direction: the minister could now move models to *less* restrictive categories (from prohibited/restricted to restricted/non-restricted) unilaterally, but not to *more* restrictive categories. The minister's discretion to make a firearm model more restrictive is subject to Cabinet approval and cannot proceed if the weapon "is reasonable for use in Canada for hunting or sporting purposes" (*Criminal Code*, s. 117.15(2)). Finally, C-42 strengthened the *Criminal Code* provisions "relating to orders prohibiting the possession of firearms where a person is convicted of an offence involving domestic violence" (RCMP 2016). The third is the April 2020 mass shooting spree in Nova Scotia that killed twenty-two and injured three. Prime Minister Trudeau's government almost immediately banned 1,500 models of "assault-style" firearms, including the ones used in the Nova Scotia shootings and Montreal Massacre (Tasker 2020).

Conclusion

Firearms policy in Canada has a long and conflicted history and has been tied closely to political and social developments domestically and internationally. While many rightly see the gun registry adopted in the wake of the Montreal Massacre as the high point of the state's attempt to control firearms, large-scale registration was not unprecedented, and for many types of firearms, including all handguns, it continues to this day. Arguably as important as the 1995 registry was the significant expansion that year of mandatory licensing for all holders and buyers of firearms and ammunition, a policy change that largely remains in place. For the analytical purposes of the chapters that follow, we can summarize the three main post-1989 policy episodes as follows. The initial policy response by the Progressive Conservatives to the Montreal Massacre was slow, muted, and ultimately unsuccessful; their second attempt, with Bill C-17, was somewhat more ambitious and adopted successfully, but was essentially an incremental extension of the existing gun control regime established in 1977. The same cannot be said of the second episode, which culminated in the Liberal government's *Firearms Act* (Bill C-68) in 1995, which introduced a national, universal firearms registry and possession-and-acquisition licensing regime. In the third episode, Conservative governments under Stephen Harper demonstrated a persistent commitment to end the registration of non-restricted long guns, and succeeded at this with Bill C-19 in 2012 after repeated failed attempts.

The next chapter examines the broader context of Canadian politics in which firearms policy-makers operate, including key institutional structures, social forces, ideology, public opinion, party systems, and external events. Armed with the policy history and an appreciation of these contextual factors, we will then be able to test how well the various policy theories explain developments in firearms policy between 1989 and 2012.

3 The Canadian Policy Environment

Cairney (2012, 130) observes that "we know that policy-makers make choices, but recognize that policy-making does not begin with a blank slate or operate in a vacuum." This chapter introduces the policy-making environment in which firearms policy-making occurs, identifying possible explanatory factors that will be elaborated upon and tested in the theory-focused chapters that follow. There is no assumption at this stage that all of these factors influence firearms policy. The factors identified here, however, are drawn from previous studies of gun control in Canada and abroad, and of Canadian policy-making more generally.

"Policy environment" is an umbrella term that captures a variety of contextual factors that may influence actors and decision-makers. That is, they are factors that are external to policy-makers, as distinguished from "agent-level" factors such as personal preferences (9–11). The first theory we apply, Rational Choice Institutionalism (RCI; chapter 4), emphasizes the agency of policy-makers while recognizing the influence exercised by their environment. The policy environment includes various "structural" factors, such as the formal and informal institutions of Canadian politics: the federal division of powers; Indigenous, Charter, and common law rights; the judiciary and judicial review; the Westminster parliamentary system and the concentration of power in the political executive, particularly the prime minister; the role of the bureaucracy, including parliamentary officers like the auditor general; and the party and electoral systems. More broadly, structures can include the "socio-economic background of states" (such as capitalism and thick welfare states) and the effects of globalization (trade pacts, dependence on foreign investment or aid, and so forth) (11). Relevant contextual factors can also include demographic structures (regionalism, urbanization, age, sex/gender, ethnic diversity, etc.), social attitudes and political ideology, and the presence or absence of organized advocacy groups and social movements. In the specific case of firearms policy, we can further imagine that crime rates, gun ownership levels, gun culture, and a recent history of high-profile gun crime can all exercise some influence. Finally, there is the broader international context, especially the US experience with gun crime and firearms regulation, as well as Canada's shared and highly permeable border with the US.

Constitutional Law

Constitutionalism is the principle of limited government – that is, that there are limits on what the government can do even when it has been democratically elected by a majority of the people. In Canada, constitutional limits are both formal (written in constitutional law), and informal (unwritten conventions, such as responsible government) (Heard 2014). The former are the "supreme law of Canada" according to s.52(1) of the *Constitution Act, 1982*. Canada's written constitution consists of many documents, but chiefly the *Constitution Acts* of 1867, which created Canada via Confederation, and of 1982, which adopted domestic constitutional amending formulas,[1] the *Charter of Rights and Freedoms*, Aboriginal and treaty rights (Section 35), and various provisions related to the federal division of powers.

The Federal Division of Powers

The most important and pervasive constitutional constraint in Canada is federalism: the formal division of sovereignty between the national ("federal") government and the ten regional ("provincial") governments.[2] The 1867 constitution and subsequent amendments outline federal and provincial responsibilities, mainly in Sections 91 and 92 respectively. For our purposes here, the most pertinent provisions are those related to criminal justice and the regulation of property. Under s.91(27), the federal Parliament has jurisdiction over "The Criminal Law, […] including the Procedure in Criminal Matters." This has been interpreted over the years to mean that Parliament can create crimes by prohibiting conduct and assigning penalties for non-compliance, including incarceration, and can also specify the rules governing criminal trials, the use of evidence, and so forth. The most obvious expression of this power is the *Criminal Code of Canada*. The criminal law power's scope is not unlimited, however; Parliament cannot simply criminalize anything it wishes. The precise boundaries are contested, but criminal law must promote a "public purpose" such as "public peace, order, security, health, [or] morality" (*Reference re Validity of Section 5(a) of the Dairy Industry Act*, [1949] S.C.R. 1). Despite that generous definition, some parliamentary attempts to exercise criminal law jurisdiction have been rejected by the courts as being really ("in pith and substance") attempts to regulate (rather than prohibit) behaviour in areas of provincial authority. Recall from chapter 2 that the gun registry was subject to such a challenge by the Alberta government but was upheld unanimously by the Supreme Court of Canada (SCC) as a valid exercise of Parliament's criminal law power (*Reference re Firearms Act (Can.)*, 2000 SCC 31).

Although many aspects of the criminal justice system as a whole fall under provincial jurisdiction – mostly notably, administering the courts that hear virtually all criminal law cases (Hausegger, Hennigar, and Riddell 2015), and most of the prosecutions and policing – criminal justice *policy-making* rests with Ottawa. Newman and Head (2017, 47) are therefore correct to conclude that Ottawa can enact "gun restrictions through amendments to criminal justice legislation ... without the cooperation of the provincial governments." This fact is underscored by the 1995 *Firearms Act* and long-gun registry: despite announcements from Alberta, Manitoba, Ontario, and Saskatchewan that they would not enforce the registry (Lindgren and Naumetz 2003), Parliament was able to enact the law. Although this not the focus of our study, it should be noted that provinces do have some regulatory authority over firearms outside of criminal law, for example in making rules about firearm use related to hunting (limiting the types of weapons and ammunition allowed, establishing hunting seasons and locations, requiring licensing and firearm training for hunters, and so forth). That authority comes from provincial jurisdiction over "Property and Civil Rights in the Province" in s.92(13), and "Generally all Matters of a merely local or private Nature in the Province" in s.92(16) of the *Constitution Act, 1867*. If such regulations directly conflict with federal criminal law, however, the latter is "paramount" (*The Attorney General for Ontario v The Attorney General for the Dominion of Canada, and the Distillers and Brewers' Association of Ontario* [1896] UKPC 20, [1896] AC 348 (9 May 1896), P.C. (on appeal from Canada) [*Local Prohibition Case*]).

The Charter of Rights and Freedoms

Significant civil, legal, and human rights were added to the constitution in 1982 with the *Charter of Rights and Freedoms*. These include classic liberal freedoms, such as of expression and religion, as well as equality and voting rights and some distinctly Canadian rights such as to minority-language education in English or French. The most pertinent provisions related to gun control are the legal rights in Sections 7 to 14, which are triggered when an individual is subject to the criminal justice process.[3] Of particular note are Section 7's right to life, liberty, and security of the person – the right to liberty being "engaged" any time an individual faces state incarceration or compulsion – and the Section 8 right against unreasonable search and seizure. These provisions constrain government action both procedurally, limiting *how* the state adopts and enforces laws, and substantively, limiting *what* the state can seek to do. Perhaps more importantly, Section 24(1) of the Charter explicitly empowers judges to enforce the document's rights by issuing any remedy for infringed rights "as the court considers appropriate and just in the circumstances."

The courts have embraced this role (Kelly 2005), but the Charter's potential policy impact is limited in two key ways. First, many rights are internally limited, including Sections 7 and 8. Section 7's rights can be infringed "in accordance with the principles of fundamental justice," a novel phrase in 1982 that the courts have elaborated over the years to preclude a wide range of actions (including those that are arbitrary, overly broad, or grossly disproportional) (Stewart 2012, 2015). Searches and seizures must be "unreasonable" to be unconstitutional under Section 8. In addition, Section 1 specifies that all of the Charter's rights are subject to "reasonable limits," and the courts have been somewhat deferential to governments on this point, albeit the SCC decreasingly so since its first Charter case in 1984 (Choudhry 2006; Muttart 2007, 161–2). All of this suggests that the Charter *can* constrain government policy-making, but only if it is interpreted and enforced vigorously. However, like all constitutional law, the Charter is not self-enforcing; it relies on either judicial enforcement (see below) or on political actors anticipating constitutional limits, for example, through internal Charter-vetting mechanisms during the policy-making process (Hiebert 2002; Kelly 1999).

Finally, in the context of gun control, arguably the most important aspect of the Charter is what it does *not* contain: a right to bear arms. There is simply no analogue in the Charter to the US's controversial Second Amendment. Similarly, an individual right to own property was intentionally excluded from the Charter in 1982 for fear that it would unduly limit the state's ability to legislate for the common good, as the Fifth Amendment has at times in American history (Augustine 1986; Johansen 1991). Conceivably, such a right might have frustrated government regulation and seizure of property like firearms and ammunition. These absences deprive opponents of gun control of a potentially powerful legal tool, although it has not prevented them from claiming that they have a right to own firearms (Brown 2017) – a right categorically rejected by the SCC in *R. v. Hasselwander* ([1993] 2 S.C.R. 398) and *R. v. Wiles* (2005 SCC 84).

Aboriginal and Treaty Rights

Another major addition to the constitution in 1982 was the recognition and affirmation in Section 35 of "the existing aboriginal and treaty rights of the aboriginal peoples of Canada," identified in s.35(2) as "Indian, Inuit and Métis peoples." These rights are rooted in the prior occupancy of Canadian territory by Indigenous peoples, as previously recognized in the Royal Proclamation of 1763 (Russell 2017), or in the terms of treaties signed between Indigenous peoples and British and subsequent Canadian governments. Many of these rights concern hunting and fishing, which can employ post-European-contact technologies, including firearms. There is thus the potential for conflict between Indigenous rights and government attempts to limit firearm ownership or use, as seen when Indigenous groups challenged the 1995 *Firearms Act* (see chapter 2). These rights may also be invoked as part of the larger effort by Indigenous communities to assert their cultural identity and demands for self-government, even though many Indigenous people live in urban settings and have little connection to traditional uses of firearms (Sheptycki 2009, 312).

Common Law Rights

In addition to the rights entrenched in the constitution, there are other, older, rights contained in the common law, the body of laws and legal traditions inherited from Britain. The most notable of these is the rule of law, which, while having no single agreed-upon definition, is widely understood as including at least the following: no one, including the government, is above the law; governments must act through the legislature and not arbitrarily; and disputes under law should be resolved by independent courts (Dicey 1959). The rule of law was famously enforced by the SCC against the autocratic premier of Quebec, Maurice Duplessis, in *Roncarelli v. Duplessis* ([1959] S.C.R. 121) and was subsequently recognized in the preamble to the *Charter of Rights and Freedoms* and incorporated into several of its rights.

Brown (2017), following on the work of Malcolm (1994) and Schwoerer (2000), examines another English common law right that was cited during debates about gun control, both in the time of Sir John A. Macdonald and more recently. That is the right to bear arms for self-defence, which appears in Article 7 of the English *Bill of Rights, 1689* (1 Will & Mary, sess. 2, c. 2): "That the subjects which are Protestants may have arms for their defence suitable to their conditions and as allowed by law." As Schwoerer (2000) observes, this right was clearly limited to Protestants of the upper classes and subject to regulation by Parliament (216–19). Nevertheless, Prime Minister Macdonald invoked it to justify his refusal to introduce tighter controls on pistols in 1872, and other MPs of that era cited the *Bill of Rights, 1689* when opposing firearms restrictions (Brown 2017, 99). After the creation of the long-gun registry, this argument re-emerged when it was claimed by the pro-gun lobby and those charged with violating the 1995 *Firearms Act*. Court decisions in *R. v. Hasselwander*, *R. v. Wiles*, *Hudson v. Canada (Attorney General)* (2009 SKCA 108), and *R. v. Montague* (2010 ONCA 141), however, emphatically rejected the notion of an unrestricted common law right to possess and use firearms for self-defence. As such, while this right appears to have had some constraining influence on policy-makers in the nineteenth century, it is safe to say that it did not represent a serious legal impediment during the period of our study.

The Judiciary

As noted earlier, the judiciary can serve as an institutional constraint on policy-makers, as judges are tasked with both interpreting and enforcing constitutional law, which may include striking down statutes and regulations that are unconstitutional. Similarly, courts routinely interpret and enforce statutes and regulations in the process of resolving legal disputes and may thereby alter the meaning of those laws or find that governments are not respecting their own rules. Collectively this function is known as judicial review (Hausegger, Hennigar, and Riddell 2015), and it is an essential part of ensuring the rule of law, especially when conducted by strongly independent courts such as Canada's. While it is well-known that the Supreme Court of Canada – the highest court of appeal in the country for all legal disputes – performs judicial review, this power is also held by most lower courts to at least some degree (36).

Courts can also provide opportunities to policy-makers by legitimizing policies that survive judicial review and thus weakening the political position of opponents. Although judicial review is usually initiated by individuals or groups who are subject to but oppose a law, Canadian governments not infrequently seek out judicial legitimization by "referring" proposed or existing laws for judicial review (Puddister 2019). The federal government (specifically, the executive) can refer directly to the

SCC, and a provincial government can refer to the province's highest court of appeal (the Ontario Court of Appeal in Ontario, for example) with a right of appeal to the SCC. Conversely, one unit of government (a province, the federal government) can use references to challenge the legislation of another unit, as we saw with the *Firearms Act Reference*. As the preceding sections suggest, while the prospect or exercise of judicial review may constrain policy-makers, it ultimately did not do so overtly in the case of firearms policy during our period of study.

Parliament

In light of the federal responsibility for criminal law, arguably the most important institution in the firearms policy environment is Parliament, Canada's primary law-making institution at the national level. Canada's parliament broadly follows the Westminster model. It is bicameral, that is, composed of two chambers that must both agree to approve proposed legislation, via majority vote in each body. The lower chamber is the elected House of Commons, and the upper chamber is the Senate, whose members have been appointed by past and present prime ministers (in practice; technically by the Crown). The two chambers possess the same legislative powers, except that "money bills" and the budget must originate in the House; however, senators have generally deferred to the House when they disagree, given the latter's stronger democratic mandate. Parliament also includes the Crown, as represented by the governor general, whose Royal Assent is required before bills become law but is given as a formality.

The House of Commons and Responsible Government

The House's Members of Parliament (MPs) are elected at least every five years, though on average about every three years.[4] The currently 338 MPs (295 between 1988 and 1997, 301 between 1998 and 2003, 308 between 2004 and 2014) are distributed roughly according to representation by population and are organized around political parties (see Electoral and Party Systems, below). The defining feature of Westminster parliaments is that the government – the political executive, or Cabinet – is "embedded" in the House and drawn primarily from MPs of the party with the most seats (i.e., the plurality of seats) (Franks 1987). This means that voters do not directly elect the government (let alone the prime minister), but only the MPs in their individual ridings, with government determined by the aggregate outcome; the prime minister is simply the leader of the party that forms government

(Heard 2014, 113). Although governments usually have a majority of the House's MPs, "minority governments" are not uncommon at the federal level; there have been fourteen since 1867, including three during the period of our study (2004, 2006, and 2008) (Russell 2008).

The democratic cornerstone on which the government rests in a Westminster system is the principle of responsible government, which in turn relies on the "confidence convention": the government "must always have the confidence of a majority of elected MPs in the House of Commons" (Aucoin, Smith, and Dinsdale 2004, 11). In other words, the Cabinet is responsible to the House, which represents the electorate. If the government loses the House's support, it typically resigns, and either an election is called or the governor general offers another party the opportunity to form a new government. However, not all votes are automatically confidence measures. Throne Speeches, budgets, and most other money bills are, while opposition parties can formally call for a vote of non-confidence; also, the government can make any vote a confidence measure. In light of the confidence convention, it is surprising that parties in Canada have usually preferred governing alone when in the minority, or in an informal alliance with a smaller third party, rather than forging formal power-sharing coalitions or multi-party Cabinets.

Responsible government goes a long way to explaining the extremely strong emphasis on party discipline in Canada, as the future of the government quite literally depends on it, especially during minority parliaments. As with other Westminster-style parliaments, "the principal consideration determining the way in which Parliament works is the party system" (Griffith and Ryle 1989, 7). As thoroughly documented elsewhere (Franks 1987; Savoie 1999; Docherty 2005; Russell 2008; Aucoin, Jarvis, and Turnbull 2011; Samara Centre for Democracy 2011; Loat and MacMillan 2014), party discipline erodes an MP's ability to represent their riding's voters, particularly when party leaders have the power to eject MPs from caucus, to block them from representing the party in the next election, or to remove them from (or reward them with) plum appointments to Cabinet, legislative committees, or (after leaving the House) various commissions, agencies, boards, Crown corporations, diplomatic posts, or even judgeships. During periods of majority government, the only threat to Cabinet is a backbench rebellion, and all of these tools help keep MPs in line. As Hiebert and Kelly (2015, 11) write, "the voting behaviour of MPs in Westminster-based systems has become so cohesive that their deviations from the party line are both infrequent and often inconsequential." Backbench rebellions are even less common in relatively small parliaments such as Canada's (338, compared to the UK's 650), as there are more MPs in the latter who have little or no hope of appointment to Cabinet or another coveted post (Franks 1987).

From a policy-making perspective, all of this means that the House is essentially subservient to the government and its leaders. Franks identifies a corollary of this fact – that "strong party discipline has the often unrecognized advantage of protecting the individual MP" from intense interest group lobbying – and notes that the lack of party discipline in the US Congress makes its members "very vulnerable to this sort of pressure from single-interest groups such as the moral majority or those opposed to gun control" (96).

The Senate

Senators are appointed and serve until age seventy-five; as such, they routinely outlast the prime minister who appointed them. There are 105 senators, who are distributed according to "regional" parity, with the regions defined as Atlantic Canada, Ontario, Quebec, and the West.[5] The Senate was originally conceived of as a chamber of "sober second thought," a body in which regional and propertied interests[6] would temper the power of democratic majorities. This "anti-democratic" character contributed to the Senate's perceived illegitimacy, which was augmented by the institution's (often deserved) reputation for being stuffed with dubiously qualified patronage appointments; this in itself discouraged the Senate from blocking the will of the House. Moreover, until very recently,[7] the Senate was organized around parties that paralleled those in the House, even sharing caucuses. As such, by the period of our study (1988–2012), the Senate was not seen as a major impediment to the Cabinet's ability to make policy, and as we will see in the following chapter, it was not in the case of firearms policy despite some expectations to the contrary.

The Legislative Process and Parliamentary Committees

A bill that proposes a legislative amendment, repeal, or new law can be introduced by any MP or senator, but bills are usually introduced by the government of the day. To be successfully adopted as a law, a bill must go through three "readings" in each chamber and examination by one or more parliamentary committees. Once a bill passes third reading, it moves to the other chamber, where all of these stages are repeated. Any amendments adopted in the second chamber go back to the original chamber for approval, with rejections sent back to the second chamber; this back-and-forth can be repeated as many times as parliamentarians are willing to allow it. As noted earlier, the Senate has tended to defer to the House when conflicts arise. The process ends when the bill receives Royal Assent and formally become a law.[8] As we will see in chapter 4, a number of firearms-related bills stalled part way through the legislative process.

When people think of Parliament they may picture the noisy ex-changes and heckling of Question Period, but the real work of both the House and the Senate is done in committees (Franks 1987; Docherty 2005; Samara Centre for Democracy 2011) after a bill has proceeded to second reading. This is particularly true of Senate committees, whose members – by virtue of being appointed until age seventy-five – serve for much longer than their elected counterparts in the House and so ac-quire deep policy area expertise. There are three types of committees – standing, special, and legislative – and they can exist in the House or the Senate[9] or as joint committees with members from both chambers. Standing committees have permanent mandates for a given policy area, such as the House's Standing Committee on Justice and Human Rights or the Standing Senate Committee on Legal and Constitutional Affairs – both of which would consider firearms-related bills – and it is by such committees that bills are usually reviewed. Special committees, such as the Special Joint Committee on Physician-Assisted Dying, conduct specific inquiries or studies on something the chamber considers im-portant, even before bills are drafted. Legislative committees are *ad hoc* and created to study a particular bill referred to it by the chamber, or to help prepare a bill; once the bill reaches the report stage, the legislative committee is dissolved (Parliament of Canada – House of Commons, n.d., *Compendium of Procedure – Legislative Process*). Parliamentary com-mittees in Canada are still subject to party discipline; nevertheless, they can play an important role in policy-making. In particular, they provide an opportunity for stakeholders to appear as witnesses and to try to influence the outcome, either by persuading parliamentarians directly or by drawing the attention of the media and the public to per-ceived flaws in the bill. Policy-making theories that emphasize the role of advocacy groups, policy entrepreneurs, and issue framing – such as SCF (chapter 5), ACF (chapter 6), MSF (chapter 7), and PET (chapter 8) – often analyse what occurs during parliamentary committees.

Officers of Parliament

Finally, Parliament has created officers and bureaucracies that are in-tended to help it hold Cabinet to account. Chief among these are the auditor general of Canada, the parliamentary budget officer (who provides independent analysis of the government's budget and other spending proposals), the commissioner of official languages (to help enforce official bilingualism), and the Canadian Human Rights Commission (to enforce the *Canadian Human Rights Act*). The auditor general has a broad mandate to review government spending to ensure that it complies with the law and is reported accurately by Cabinet (McGlashen 2014). These financial audits are reported annually by the auditor general, and "it always commands media attention, highlighting, as it does, administrative breakdowns, program overspending, the construction of a road to nowhere, or irregularities in the expense accounts of senior officials" (Savoie 1999, 289). For example, as we saw in the previous chapter, the auditor general issued high-profile, scathing reports detailing implementation problems and massive cost overruns related to the Liberals' gun registry. The auditor general is also empowered to conduct "performance audits" on areas of its own choosing, which ask two questions: "Are programs being run with due regard for economy, efficiency, and environmental impact?" and "Does the government have the means in place to measure the effectiveness of its programs?" (McGlashen 2014, 5). The auditor general is well-supported in these tasks: in 2012–13, the Office of the Auditor General had around six hundred employees, including more than four hundred audit staff (4). Summing up, critical review (or the threat thereof) by officers of Parliament, specifically the auditor general, and the negative media and public attention such reviews can generate may influence or constrain policy-makers.

The Executive: The Prime Minister, Cabinet, and Central Agencies

Franks (1987, 21) astutely observes that "the structure of power in Canada is executive-centred. It became moulded in this form shortly after Confederation, and has retained the form to this day." Franks here is referring to the dominance of the *political* executive: the politicians who become the Cabinet and the prime minister, and the people they appoint to central agencies – chiefly, the Prime Minister's Office (PMO) and Privy Council Office (PCO) – to advise them and to help carry out their policy goals. Ironically, this system is rooted in the principle of holding the executive responsible to the House. Cabinet ministers are (technically) responsible for policy development and implementation in broad topic areas, such justice, finance, and public safety, and they are accountable to Parliament for these areas. Ministers oversee large staffs of permanent, merit-based bureaucrats, but they also have more political advisers, whom they or the prime minister appoint personally.

Throughout its history, Canada has had some very powerful and independent ministers, and there is still evidence of influential regional ministers (Bakvis 2001; G. White 2010; Brodie 2018) and Cabinet personalities "who can take charge of a government department and give it direction" (Savoie 1999, 273). However, there is little question that prime ministers have for some time generally dominated Cabinet, and thus the government and Parliament, even to the point that Cabinet is seen as "a focus group for the Prime Minister" (260). Based on his extensive interviews with former ministers and senior bureaucrats, Savoie concludes:

> Only the prime minister and, to a lesser degree, the minister of Finance, through the budget, can decide when and how to land on a policy issue or even on a new spending commitment. Other ministers must know either not to land or, if they strongly want to do so, they have to look to the prime minister, not Cabinet, for permission to land and guidance on when and how to go about it. (273)

Surveys of federal ministers confirm that throughout the period of our study, cabinet members continued to feel that centralization was still a prominent feature of government (Lewis 2013).

The remarkable concentration of power in the prime minister is rooted in constitutional convention rather than law. Many Royal prerogatives left to the governor general in the *Constitution Act, 1867* are in practice exercised by the prime minister, given the convention that the governor general follows the prime minister's "advice." These prerogatives include the power to prorogue (suspend) Parliament, call elections ("dissolve" Parliament), and fill a staggering number of positions, such as judgeships, ambassadorships, and Senate seats. It is the prime minister who appoints the Governor of the Bank of Canada as well as members of government agencies, commissions, and the boards of Crown corporations. Most importantly for our purposes here, it is the prime minister who appoints Cabinet ministers, heads of central agencies, and senior bureaucrats. Cabinet ministers thus owe their positions to the prime minister, and they can be removed or "demoted" at the latter's discretion; moreover, resignation from Cabinet is typically the only way for ministers to signal their strong disagreement with their leader's policies – a high cost that few are willing to pay (Savoie 1999, 273). When we add to this the aforementioned powers the prime minister wields as party leader, the result is a concentration of power in one person that is unparalleled in the democratic world (O'Malley 2007) and that some have even termed a dictatorship (Wallace 1998; Simpson 2001). This is not an entirely new phenomenon – early Prime Ministers John A. Macdonald and Wilfrid Laurier managed their governments and the extensive patronage networks needed to keep them running virtually single-handedly (Bakvis 2001, 65; Gwyn 2012) – but it is generally agreed that the concentration of prime ministerial power accelerated under Pierre Trudeau and was particularly acute during our period of study, under Chrétien and Harper (Savoie 1999; G. White 2010).

Key to the concentration of prime ministerial power was the development of central agencies, the institutions that help the prime minister oversee and coordinate ministers and departments. The most important agencies facilitating centralized policy development are the Prime Minister's Office (PMO) and the Privy Council Office (PCO). The PMO is the "unabashedly partisan powerhouse of government" (G. White 2010, 52), personally appointed by and accountable to the prime minister, whose staff advise him or her on policy and media strategy and convey his wishes to ministers.[10] The PCO is the elite of the permanent civil service, who advise the prime minister and Cabinet on policy matters and the machinery of government and help coordinate and direct government activity. The PCO is non-partisan; however, the head of the PCO (Clerk of the Privy Council) is selected personally by the prime minister, and the unit's mandate is to implement the prime minister's policy goals. Savoie (2008) has found that the senior non-partisan civil service has been made highly "responsive" to the centre's political agenda. The resources of central agencies enable the prime minister to announce major policy decisions and appointments without the input of Cabinet, bypassing even the minister responsible for the policy area, a phenomenon Savoie (1999, ch. 10) characterizes as "governing by bolts of electricity." Central agencies can also help prime ministers address – though not entirely overcome – an important limitation on their power, that of overload (G. White 2010, 55). Even the sharpest critics of prime ministerial power recognize that the centre cannot focus on more than a few key issues at a time, nor can the centre "repeatedly run roughshod" over ministers without provoking resistance (Savoie 1999; G. White 2010, 55; Brodie 2018). As well, it is important to note that PMs can be weakened or even forced out by the party if they become very unpopular with the public or within the party, particularly if there is a strong challenger waiting in the wings, as was the case with Jean Chrétien's finance minister and long-time rival Paul Martin Jr. All of this has led some to conclude that prime ministers must deliberate carefully before imposing their authority (G. White 2010, 55–6). Nonetheless, it is clear that prime ministers can usually be a dominant force in policy-making when they want to be, and chapter 4 provides examples of this with respect to firearms policy. The centralization of power around the prime minister will be an important theme in the chapters on ACF and MSF as well.

The Electoral and Party Systems

The electoral and party systems may exert an influence on policy-making by shaping the partisan incentive structure for political parties and their leaders. Put another way, firearms policy may reflect the broader dynamics of party competition, which in turn are shaped by the electoral system. The House of Commons is elected using the single member plurality (SMP) system, often (misleadingly) referred to as "first past the post."[11] Each constituency, or riding, is represented by one representative, who is the candidate who received the most ballots cast (i.e., the plurality). Canada's electoral system is ostensibly based on "representation by population"; however, that would require ridings to be of roughly equal population, and the law and those with the power to set electoral boundaries have long sought to prevent rural and northern interests from being weakened by the urban majority (J. Smith 2002; Courtney 2004; Pal and Choudhry 2007). The result is that urban areas are significantly underrepresented relative to rural ones.[12]

SMP has been widely criticized for its distorting effects on representation (Cairns 1968; Clarke et al. 1996; Milner 1999; Pilon 2007). In this regard, two related effects on the party system are of particular note. The first is that when elections are contested by more than two parties, governments can win a majority of the seats with less than 50 per cent of the popular vote – often significantly less, as seen in the federal elections of 1988 (Progressive Conservatives 43%), 1993 (Liberals 41%), 1997 (Liberals 38.5%), 2000 (Liberals 40.9%), 2011 (Conservatives 39.6%), and 2015 (Liberals 39.5%).[13] Given that federal voter turnout is historically around 70 per cent, and has been trending downward since 1988 (Elections Canada 2017), virtually no MP represents a majority of the eligible voters.[14] The second effect of SMP is that it "favours minor parties with concentrated sectional support, and discourages those with diffuse national support" (Cairns 1968, 62). Moreover, since each riding has only one representative, SMP undervalues the partisan diversity of both individual ridings and regions in aggregate, thus rendering the parliamentary composition of each party (i.e., caucuses) less diverse, regionally speaking, than its voters (Cairns 1968, 62).[15]

Taken together, SMP, rural overrepresentation, and low voter turnout have discouraged political parties from appealing to the Downsian median voter (Downs 1957) and encouraged them to act opportunistically, targeting appeals to particular regions or communities. This is most obviously so for "sectional" parties like the Bloc Québécois, which only runs candidates in Quebec, but it is also true historically for national "brokerage" or "catch-all" parties (Carty 2013) with strong regional bases: for example, the West is "home turf" for the Progressive Conservatives, the Reform Party, the Canadian Alliance, and (after 2003) the Conservatives; and Quebec and Ontario for the Liberals. A brief review of the party system during our period of study reveals that it was highly competitive and underwent a remarkable amount of disruption and instability, even for a country characterized by weak voter ties to political parties and high potential for electoral volatility (Clarke et al. 1996; LeDuc 2011).

The 1993 federal election saw the end of what was widely termed the third party system (Carty, Cross, and Young 2000), which was characterized by three parties – the Liberals, the Progressive Conservatives, and the social democratic New Democratic Party (NDP) – running national campaigns. Under that system, the Liberals dominated, being the most successful brokerage party. By the 1980s, this system was breaking down – the Liberals were almost shut out of the West by 1980,[16] and in 1984 the PCs under Brian Mulroney finally shattered the Liberals' historic hold on Quebec and won a majority of the seats in all ten provinces (it was also the last federal government to win a majority of the popular vote). The PCs won again in 1988, but heated disputes over constitutional reform – specifically, the failed Meech Lake (1987–90) and Charlottetown (1990–92) Accords – aggravated already deep regional divisions over the fundamental nature of Canada and fractured Mulroney's electoral coalition (Russell 2004). The 1993 election ushered in the fourth party system, which has been characterized as "balkanized" along regional lines (Bickerton, Gagnon, and Smith 1999; Carty, Cross, and Young 2000, 34). In a stark illustration of Cairns's (1968) argument, two national parties with diffuse support – the PCs and NDP – were almost annihilated (two and nine seats respectively), both losing official party status despite receiving 16 and 7 per cent of the popular vote respectively. In contrast, the three regionally based parties thrived. The Liberals almost swept Atlantic Canada, Manitoba, and Ontario, won heavily in Montreal, and took a smattering of urban seats in the West and were able to form a majority government (177 of 295 seats, or 60%) with only 41 per cent of the popular vote The new pro-separatist and social democratic Bloc Québécois (BQ), running only in Quebec, formed the Official Opposition with 54 seats (18.3%) but only 13.5 per cent of the national popular vote. And the right-wing populist Reform Party, which did not run candidates in Quebec and had as its founding motto

"The West Wants In," came third with 18.7 per cent of the popular vote and 52 seats (17.6%), almost all of them in Alberta and BC, despite also winning over 20 per cent of the popular vote in Manitoba and Ontario.[17] Notably, Reform won 22 of 26 Alberta seats with only 52 per cent of the province's popular vote. This pattern was largely reproduced in the 1997 federal election, with Reform displacing the BQ as the Official Opposition and the PCs and NDP rebounding somewhat with seats mostly in Atlantic Canada (Elections Canada 1997).

By 2000 the system had begun to shift again. The Reform Party re-branded itself as the Canadian Alliance in an attempt to "unite the right," a move initially rebuffed by the PCs. The 2000 election produced no major changes in the party system (although the Liberals pulled ahead of the BQ in the popular vote in Quebec), but a prolonged pe-riod of electoral instability was on the horizon. In 2003 the PCs and the Canadian Alliance merged to become the Conservative Party of Canada under Stephen Harper's leadership, and by the end of that year Prime Minister Jean Chrétien had been pushed out as Liberal leader and replaced by Paul Martin Jr. The 2004 election produced the first of three consecutive minority governments, the first led by Martin, in which the Conservatives (and, to a much lesser extent, the NDP) loos-ened the Liberals' hold on Ontario, while the BQ made a comeback in Quebec. The 2006 election brought Harper's Conservatives to power, with re-election in 2008, and finally a majority government in 2011 as Liberal support in central Canada collapsed.

A few features of this last, arguably "fifth party system" (Walchuk 2012; Patten 2016) warrant brief mention. The first is that the party sys-tem effectively split into two after 2000 (Pruysers 2014): a "renational-ized" system in English Canada much like the third party system, with three parties competing across the country outside Quebec but with the Conservatives dominant in the West and steadily eroding Liberal support in Ontario; and a regional system in Quebec dominated by the BQ and the sovereignty question (Gidengil et al. 2012), in which the other parties ran different campaigns than their national ones. Second, the Quebec system underwent a massive shift in 2011 with the sudden collapse of the BQ and the movement of many of its voters (as well as former Liberals) to the ideologically similar NDP, which formed the Official Opposition for the first time.[18] Third, the gains made by the Conservatives were skewed toward rural areas and vote-rich suburbs (such as the "905" around Toronto), and they remained largely shut out of the three largest cities of Toronto, Montreal, and Vancouver, as well as Halifax (Elections Canada 2011).[19] Fourth, spurred no doubt by the extended period of minority government, all parties were in essentially "permanent campaign" mode after 2000 (Flanagan 2013). This led Harper's Conservatives in particular to adopt "almost military-style hierarchy in the organizational structure and operations of parties" (Patten 2016, 19), with message discipline and secrecy strictly enforced (Flanagan 2013, 91; Lewis 2017). Thus, during the later period of our study that led up to and included the end of the long-gun registry, the party system was unstable and competitive, still fairly regionalized, and somewhat skewed along rural/suburban–inner-city lines outside of Alberta and Saskatchewan.

The electoral and party systems are explored in the next chapter, on rational choice institutionalism, where we test explanations for firearms policy between 1989 and 2012 that are based on partisan competition.

Advocacy Groups

An advocacy group (or "interest group") is "any organization that seeks to influence government policy, but not to govern" (Young and Everitt 2004, 5). Such groups are the vehicles whereby many people in Canada seek to effect policy change. They do so through a wide range of activities: lobbying politicians, testifying before parliamentary committees, using public demonstrations and mass media to raise awareness or to pressure political actors, and engaging in litigation and legal education (M. Smith 2018). As such, they can be a source of policy ideas, civil society allies or opponents of government, or agents of agenda-setting. Groups come in many different forms, from well-resourced, institutionalized groups with paid staffs and permanent offices, such as those representing elite professions like medicine and law, to *ad hoc*, grassroots groups of volunteers that form to address a single issue, such as a particular law or local real estate development. Think tanks like the Fraser Institute and the Canadian Centre for Policy Alternatives also function as advocacy groups (Savoie 2010). Networks of groups and individuals seeking "to fundamentally transform social practices" are often termed social movements; examples include the temperance, women's, civil rights, peace, environmental, LGBTQ, and anti-globalization movements (M. Smith 2018, 45). It bears noting that a distinctive feature of the post-1989 Canadian gun control movement has been its close alignment with the women's movement, due to the inherently misogynistic nature of the Montreal Massacre. As chapter 6 on the advocacy coalition framework explores the role of advocacy groups in gun control, we restrict our comments here to the broader context in which such groups operate in Canada.

That context has two key features. The first is that groups are free to form and to express their collective interests and demands; indeed, these freedoms are protected in the constitution via the Charter's freedoms of "thought, belief, opinion and expression," of peaceful assembly, and of association (ss.2(b), (c), and (d)), although they may be limited when "reasonable" under Section 1 (see above). The second is that despite these freedoms, Canadian political institutions offer advocacy groups somewhat limited access to decision-makers, especially by comparison to the US with its separation of powers. The highly centralized nature of power in Canada is the main reason for this; lobbying an individual MP, for example, is unlikely to influence policy-makers in the PMO and the Cabinet. But even venues that are more open, such as legislative committees, may give preference to more powerful groups or raise financial barriers to entry (e.g., travel costs to Ottawa) that disproportionately affect non-institutionalized groups (Young and Everitt 2004, 97–8). Also, governments often initiate consultations outside of parliamentary channels, overtly privileging some groups and types of interests over others, even to the point of completely excluding some voices (Young and Everitt 2004, 98–9). Young and Everitt conclude that "some government consultation processes are designed only to legitimize decisions already made, rather than consulting interested groups" (103). Nonetheless, advocacy groups have the potential to shape government policy-making in a variety of ways.

Quebec

It is well-known that Quebec has a distinctive place in Canada by virtue of its unique linguistic, cultural, and legal features and that the successful brokerage of Quebec – with its large number of House seats (75 from 1989 to 2011, 78 since) – was traditionally a crucial part of any majority government (Johnston 2017). The key point for our purposes is that policy-making during the first and especially second episodes of our study was taking place in the context of heightened sensitivity to Quebec. In view of this, any distinctive political attitudes in Quebec are potentially salient.

By the beginning of our study period, in 1989, there was a constitutional crisis about Quebec's place in Canada. Under Prime Minister Mulroney, the crisis was about how to reform the constitution to accommodate Quebec's unmet demands from 1982. With the failure of that exercise by 1992 there was a serious threat of secession as Quebec's most nationalist voters mobilized around a rejection of the status quo (86). This found expression in the federal party system with the formation of the BQ and its election to Official Opposition with fifty-four of seventy-five Quebec seats in 1993, but also at the provincial level with the 1994 election of a separatist Parti Québécois (PQ) government that promised to hold a referendum on Quebec "sovereignty"[20] the following year. (That attempt was very nearly successful, the "No" side winning with only 50.6%.) For pro-unity federal parties – particularly the Liberals and their Québécois leader Jean Chrétien – the very future of Canada depended on winning over "soft nationalist" Quebec voters, and this became a central concern in the early 1990s. Moreover, with the Reform Party and its successors' insurmountable hold on the West, the Liberals needed to maintain their dominance in eastern Canada and try to grow in Quebec; gun control was an obvious issue that would both appeal to Quebecers and distinguish the Liberals from their rivals outside Quebec (Bottomley 2004, 64).

It is also notable that early in the fifth party system, Quebec voters became alienated from the federal Liberals over the sponsorship scandal: the revelations, unearthed by the auditor general and the high-profile Gomery Commission (2004–6), that the Liberal Party was implicated in fraudulent spending during its advertising campaign in the 1990s to promote national unity and the profile of the federal government in Quebec (Nadeau and Bélanger 2012, 147). The scandal created an opening for the Conservatives and the BQ; both these parties eroded the Liberal popular vote in Quebec. The Conservatives' successful expansion into Ontario and Quebec at the Liberals' expense resulted in it forming three governments, two minority (2006, 2008) and one majority (2011) (Pruysers, Sayers, and Czarnecki 2020). By 2011, the existential threat of Quebec secession had receded with the electoral collapse of the BQ and with the PQ out of power provincially. The distinctive place of Quebec in Canada and the party system after 1989 are examined in the chapter on rational choice institutionalism.

Gun Ownership Levels, Urbanization, and Rurality

The prevalence of guns in society and patterns of ownership might reasonably structure firearms policy by raising questions about potential political resistance and institutional capacity. If firearms are seen as a regular part of people's lives, any government attempt to restrict them will be a challenge, because it will involve taking away something from people, adding burdens to them, or suggesting that they are part of a group that needs to be regulated. More simply, new restrictions suggest that the way things are, and perhaps have been for a long time, are no longer acceptable, and this may provoke backlash.

With respect to institutional capacity, an example is instructive. After the Port Arthur massacre in 1996, Australia – a country of 18 million people at the time – undertook a buy-back program for firearms, which succeeded in removing about half a million of an estimated 1.5 million prohibited guns from circulation, at a cost of $500 million (Australian National Audit Office 1997; Parliament of Australia 2017). While widely seen as a success, Australia's approach would be difficult to replicate for financial and technical reasons in the US (even setting aside the well-known ideological and political reasons), where there is roughly one gun per person for 325 million people (Krouse 2012, 9). Canada is somewhere between these two examples: at the time the universal registry was introduced, about 26 per cent of Canadian households owned at least one firearm (Block 1998), and by the early 2000s there were roughly three guns owned by civilians for every ten people, or about 10 million firearms (Karp 2007, 47). In 2011, the year before it was abolished, the universal registry included 7.86 million civilian weapons: 7.13 million unrestricted (mostly shotguns and hunting rifles), 531,735 restricted, and 197,024 prohibited (RCMP 2012, 20). In short, guns are actually quite prevalent in Canada, especially long guns, but they are distributed unevenly.

One of the strongest predictors of gun ownership is the size of one's community. In the mid-1990s, residents of Canada's two largest cities of Toronto and Montreal were very unlikely to own a gun – less than 2 per cent of households by some estimates (Block 1998, 22) – compared to more than one-third of households in smaller towns (fewer than 10,000 residents) and rural areas, and between 15 and 20 per cent for intermediate-sized communities (8). The firearms were overwhelmingly long guns used for hunting, with sport shooting and collecting a distant second and third (13). Rural residents may also use firearms for vermin control, wildlife and crop protection, euthanization of livestock, and personal safety in remote areas. By the 1990s, however, only about 20 per cent of Canadians lived in rural areas and another 13 per cent in small population centres,[21] with the highest rates in Atlantic Canada, Manitoba, and Saskatchewan (Statistics Canada 2011b). The vast majority of Canadians nationally and within every province except those in Atlantic Canada thus live in cities (Statistics Canada 2016); almost 60 per cent of Canadians live in large cities with more than 100,000 residents, where gun ownership is much less common. The upshot is that public reaction to stricter gun control is likely to be skewed along rural–suburban–urban lines, although this is likely to be mediated through other institutions (such as rural overrepresentation in Parliament). Patterns of gun ownership are incorporated into several of the explanatory approaches in the following chapters, including RCI (where we test for the effect of rural representation in the party system), ACF (where we examine the role of pro-firearms advocacy groups), and SCF and PET (which focus on the framing of gun use and users).

Ideology

Rural residents are more likely to own guns, but that does not automatically entail greater opposition to gun control; they might, for example, see themselves as law-abiding and responsible users and thus not threatened by greater regulation. This is not the case in Canada, however, where opposition to gun control is greatest in rural and suburban areas and appears to be rooted in the greater conservativism of those populations, even after controlling for socio-economic factors like education, ethnic diversity, income, and age (Thomas 2001; Blais et al. 2002; Cutler and Jenkins 2002; Wasko and O'Neill 2007; Segaert 2008; Roy, Perrella, and Borden 2015).[22] As we noted earlier, value differences along geospatial lines are most likely to be conveyed through things like the party and electoral systems.

Ideology can also be a broad structuring factor in policy-making, by establishing the outer boundaries of legitimate political action or facilitating policies that are more congruent with dominant values. A simple example helps makes the point: severe physical punishment for minor offences is simply incompatible with contemporary Canadians' basic values about justice; as such, it is virtually inconceivable that a government would amend the *Criminal Code* to order convicted litterers to be whipped. As Nevitte and Cochrane (2011) and Patten (2016) observe, neoliberalism was the dominant ideological paradigm during the period of our study, marked by a strong (but not uncritical) belief in free markets and growing hostility to or scepticism about the Keynesian welfare state, as well as decreasing traditionalism regarding morality and family values (albeit skewed along urban–suburban–rural lines).[23] While ideological values do find expression in the party system, especially with the rise of the Reform/Alliance/Conservatives and BQ, the different value dimensions – economics, morals, family – do not "run together" for Canadians, and this complicates partisan campaign strategizing and policy-making (Nevitte and Cochrane 2011, 267). Gun control occupies a particularly complex space in this regard, as it taps into free market/libertarian values as well as traditionalism regarding a "way of life" and masculinity (Brown 2012; Cukier and Sheptycki 2012). Ideology thus permits a wide range of policy-making approaches to gun control in Canada, although it probably precludes some extremes: for example, governments' forcibly seizing all firearms, as this would offend mainstream values regarding due process and state respect for private property and likely raise doubts about state capacity to disarm the public and especially criminals. At the same time, Canada's culture is not "weaponized" or "pistolized," in that most individuals do not carry personal firearms in the context of daily life or believe they need a gun for protection, and the state has retained its monopoly on legitimate lethal force (8).

Public Opinion

Ideology refers to broad and fairly persistent value orientations; public opinion is more ephemeral and can change quickly in light of current events (although some events or experiences are so profound as to shape ideology). There is a wealth of public opinion data on gun control in Canada going back to 1989 (Page 2006, ch. 8). Our goal here is not to try to summarize it but simply to emphasize that polls usually matter to partisan policy-makers. This is especially true in the "permanent campaign" era of "marketing-oriented politics" (Marland, Giasson, and Lees-Marshment 2012; Flanagan 2013; Patten 2016), where "parties developed the capacity to employ polling and big data analytics to develop the sort of fine-grained understanding of the electorate that allows researchers to identify the characteristics, interests, and political attitudes of clusters of like-minded voters" (Patten 2016, 19). Polling helps policy-makers assess support levels for proposed or existing policies, which may be obscured by the "active" expressions of opinion by advocacy groups (Page 2006, 15). Gun control provides a classic example: polls told the Liberals there was strong majority support – even in Alberta – for a universal gun registry, despite the fact that opponents outnumbered supporters at public meetings (Bottomley 2004; Page 2006). As Heidi Rathjen, co-founder of the Coalition for Gun Control, observes, "an impartial observer could have been excused for believing that the country was 95 per cent against restrictions on guns" (Rathjen and Montpetit 1999, 155).

Crime Rates, Firearms, and High-Profile Shootings

Closely tied to the influence of public opinion, gun crime rates and high-profile shootings are part of the broader environment that may shape policy-making regarding firearms by raising demands for stricter regulation (or depressing them, if rates are low and such shootings are absent) (Fleming 2012). The Montreal Massacre is an obvious example, and its effects, along with gun crime rates, are explored more fully in chapters 7 (multiple streams framework) and 8 (punctuated equilibrium theory). What we can say here is that there was evidence of increasing crime, including violent crime with a firearm, that peaked around 1990, but that crime rates have generally been declining ever since (Leesti 1997; Perreault 2013). As well, very few violent crimes involve a firearm – only 2 per cent in 1995, the year the universal registry was established (Leesti 1997). Homicide rates have followed a slightly different pattern regardless of firearm use, trending downward since the mid-1970s but increasing around 1990 and again in the early 2000s (Cotter 2014). During the period of our study, handguns were used in two thirds of firearms-related homicides (Dauvergne 2005; Boyce and Cotter 2013).

While gun crime in Canada is far less common than in the US, is it high compared to peer countries in the developed world (Karp 2007; Grinshteyn and Hemenway 2016). Moreover, crime statistics often ignore gun suicides, as suicide is not a crime in Canada. Between 2003 and 2012 at least 5,616 people shot and killed themselves, a rate more than twelve times that of England and Wales (Overton 2016). A study in the mid-1990s found that about 80 per cent of firearm-related deaths in Canada were suicides (Dandurand 1998, 18). As well, between 2008 and 2012, 3,688 Canadians died from firearm injuries, including from accidents, suicides, and homicides (Statistics Canada 2013).

Perhaps more important than actual crime rates, however, is the *public perception* of crime, which for many years has significantly overestimated its prevalence, particularly with respect to violent crime and youth crime. Put simply, the public tends to believe that rates are increasing or stable even when they were in fact declining (Stein 2001; Perreault 2017). Yet in the same surveys, respondents overwhelmingly indicated that they felt safe in their own communities. On a related note, Sheptycki (2009, 311) points to the disconnect between popular images of rural dwellers using firearms as tools, versus urban gangs committing gun crimes, and the reality that the "risk of death or injury from firearms [is], on a per capita basis, actually higher in rural Canada than in the urban centres." A series of high-profile shootings can also keep gun crime in the public's mind. For example, during our study period, Canadians were shocked by school shootings at Concordia University (1992), Taber (1999), and Dawson College (2006), the shooting deaths of innocent bystanders Georgina Leimonis (1994) and Jane Creba (2005) in Toronto, the murder by a BC man of his estranged wife and nine family members with a legally obtained firearm in 1999, and the 2012 gang-related shootings at the Eaton Centre and at a Danzig Street block party (the last of these the worst mass shooting in Toronto's history). During the writing of this book, Canadians were further shaken by the horrific killing spree in rural Nova Scotia that claimed twenty-two lives, the worst mass shooting in Canadian history.

International Context

Finally, Canadians do not live in a vacuum and are especially aware of events and politics in the US, which is an outlier in terms of gun manufacturing, possession, crime, and violence, as well the power of the gun lobby in politics. The high-profile horrific mass shootings that have become so common in the US,[24] but also events like 1996's Port Arthur massacre in Tasmania and school shooting in Dunblane, Scotland, and the 2019 attacks on mosques in Christchurch, New Zealand, helped keep gun crime in Canadians' minds.[25] The Canada–US border is highly permeable, both for materials – high levels of gun exports and illegal smuggling from the US have been remarked upon since at least the American Civil War (Brown 2012), if possibly overstated (CBC Radio 2018) – and for ideas (particularly from the NRA, but also gun control initiatives during the 1930s [Friedland 1984, 126–7]) and gun culture (Cukier and Sheptycki 2012). There is also a pragmatic element at work here, in that high numbers of illegal firearms smuggled into the country can feed the perception that Canada cannot prevent guns getting to the "wrong people." Although our study does not explicitly test for international influence on Canadian firearms policy, it is likely that it helps shape advocacy strategies, policy ideas, and perceptions of gun ownership (particularly the association with the US), which are the subject of the ACF, MSF, and PET and SCF chapters respectively.

   This chapter has illustrated that a remarkable number of structural and other contextual factors are at play in the firearms policy-making environment. To reiterate, these are factors that may influence policy-makers, such as how the electoral and party systems create incentives for political leaders to emphasize issues that strengthen their regional appeal, especially in Quebec. Or how Canada's parliamentary system and convention of responsible government concentrate power around the prime minister and empower majority governments to make sweeping policy changes. Those structural influences related to the formal institutions of Parliament are the focus of the next chapter, on rational choice institutionalism. Public opinion and ideology – and, as we'll see, the party system – play key roles in the social construction of firearms users, which is the focus of chapter 5. The activities of advocacy groups and the institutional features that facilitate them, such as parliamentary committees, are the primary concern of the advocacy coalition framework in chapter 6. This is also true, if to a lesser extent, of chapter 7 and the multiple streams framework, which along with punctuated equilibrium theory in chapter 8 draws heavily on the institutional centralization of power around Cabinet and the prime minister, the role of external events such as mass shootings, and the nature of firearms ownership in Canada. While the policy environment is complex and suggests that many factors influence firearms policy, our goal in the chapters that follow is to test for such influences in a rigorous manner by applying leading public policy theories and frameworks, and in the process assess the applicability of such theories to policy-making in a novel and Canadian context.

4 Policy as Strategic Decision-Making: Rational Choice Institutionalism

For many, the starting point for explaining public policy is the assumption that policies are the product of intentional, logical choices by political actors who are pursuing a particular goal or set of goals. Inspired by theories of human behaviour from the field of economics that see individuals as "utility maximizers," rational choice theory rapidly became one of the leading approaches in political science by the 1960s. However, the approach has been refined over the years: it is now acknowledged that many factors limit or shape the ability of individuals to choose their preferred course of action. Of particular importance are institutions, such as the formal structures and processes of the state, that reward or punish certain actions and frustrate or facilitate knowledge and cooperation. In this chapter we employ a form of rational choice institutionalism (RCI) to assess the impact of federalism, the Westminster parliamentary system, and the electoral and party systems on gun control policy from 1989 to 2012. While some have applied the logic of RCI to earlier episodes of gun control (Mauser and Margolis 1992; Pal 2003; Bottomley 2004; Fleming 2012; Kamal and Burton 2018), they have not done so systematically and their analyses end before the era of Conservative Party governments under Stephen Harper.

Rational Choice Institutionalism

Unlike the approaches in later chapters, which employ distinct assumptions and methodologies, RCI represents a diverse family of approaches (Hall and Taylor 1996; Shepsle 2008). These include actor-centred institutionalism (Scharpf 1997), veto player theory (Tsebelis 2002; König, Debus, and Tsebelis 2011), nested games (Tsebelis 1990), and institutional analysis and development (IAD) (Ostrom, Gardner, and Walker 1994), among others. What unites them is the observation that existing institutions often frustrate rational actors as they pursue their sincere preferences, leading them to instead accept the best outcome possible under the circumstances. A real-world example that illustrates this well is the majority decision-making rule on the nine-member Supreme Court of Canada: each judge has an equal vote on how to resolve the case, but a majority of the judges is required to create a binding precedent. That may mean some judges have to compromise on their *sincere* preference in order to get others on board – that is, they agree to a *strategic* position as close to their sincere preference as possible to get four other judges to agree. But this dynamic is entirely a product of the majority decision-making rule, that is, the institutional rule for how the court operates. Imagine how different their decisions might be if instead all of the judges had to agree, as is the rule in some countries!

RCI has been applied in a wide variety of policy studies – far too many to attempt to capture in a comprehensive literature review – but relatively rarely in the Canadian context, and even then often without self-identifying as RCI. Examples include analyses of how veto points in federalism and the parliamentary system shaped public health insurance (Maioni 1997) and economic stimulus programs after the 2008 recession (Constantelos 2014), and Cooper and Marier's (2017) study of how "executive style" (merit- versus patronage-based bureaucracy) affected home care policies in New Brunswick and Nova Scotia. Explicit applications of RCI include explanations for the "staying power of the legislative status quo" regarding abortion after the Supreme Court's ruling in *Morgentaler* (Flanagan 1997), devolution negotiation outcomes in Canada's northern territories (Alcantara 2013), and the persistence of the *Indian Act* (Morden 2016). Hennigar (2010) uses Tsebelis's concept of nested games to explain the federal government's policy strategy concerning same-sex marriage. The study of foreign policy elsewhere was long dominated by RCI-driven theories such as realism or Allison's (1971) classic approaches based on bureaucratic and organizational politics, yet few Canadian academics have ever embraced the "realist" label; nevertheless, "structural-realist" assumptions are widely employed in the literature analysing Canadian foreign policy (Haglund 2017). Finally, RCI approaches have been used to study policies concerning common-pool resources, an example being Elinor Ostrom's (1990) famous case study of the Nova Scotia inshore fishery. Ostrom's later IAD framework has been applied to water regulation (Sproule-Jones, Johns, and Heinmiller 2008).

The central unit of analysis in RCI is those political actors who have the power to make policy decisions, or "methodological individualism." Actors are assumed to have preferences and to act rationally to maximize the realization of those preferences in public policy, albeit within the incentive structures created by institutions. Although individual actors are typically the focus in RCI, many studies treat collective actors (such as political parties) as if they are individuals, because decision-making power within the group is highly centralized (Tsebelis 2011). As discussed in chapter 3, Canada's Westminster parliamentary system of government is distinguished by the extraordinary centralization of power in the prime minister and their inner circle, especially during periods of majority government. Similarly, Canadian political parties are highly centralized in terms of their governance and campaign strategy.

A signature feature of RCI, and of rational choice theory generally, is the use of *simplified* assumptions about actor preferences. No one seriously disputes that people have complex and sometimes conflicting goals, and that there are practical and cognitive limits on their ability to examine their goals and all possible strategies – in other words, that actors are "boundedly rational" (Simon 1956, 1957). But simplification allows for what is the greatest strength of rational choice theory: the deductive testing of hypotheses based on those assumed preferences. A common critique of inductive research – which starts by observing empirical evidence and pulling out (inferring) a theoretical explanation – is that it is vulnerable to selective reading by the researcher in order to find their preferred conclusion (more colloquially known as "cherry picking"). The inductive approach may also lead to circularity, or tautological conclusions, since there may be no independent evidence to confirm the hypothesis other than the very evidence used to generate it. The assumed preferences used to create hypotheses in RCI are based on previous research or logical reasoning and then tested against new evidence to determine whether at least part of the explanation is correct (Flanagan 1998). That is, the hypotheses are falsifiable and may lead researchers to reject or refine their assumptions, hypotheses, or explanatory variables (Scharpf 2000).

A critical assumption in RCI regarding elected politicians is that policy preferences are secondary to the desire to obtain and retain power (Downs 1957), since the ability to make policy requires first winning the election. This may be less true for parties that have little hope of winning, or in highly fragmented party systems with coalition-style government where there's an advantage to strong party branding. But it is more likely to apply to competitive parties where single-party government is the norm, as in Canada, which also helps explain the leading parties' historically weak attachment to ideology and rapid swings in policy positions (including often promising one thing during the campaign and doing another once in power). In this account, office-oriented politicians make policy in order to win elections (Shepsle 2008); contrast this with other theories (such as ACF) that assign primacy to policy goals. Put simply, the competitive landscape of the party system, and the incentive structures contained in the electoral system, condition the policy choices of politicians.

The definition of "institutions" and how they matter vary greatly within RCI. First, we can distinguish between structured and unstructured institutions. The former are durable over time and usually formalized – things like the constitution (including the federal division of powers and the *Charter of Rights and Freedoms*), the electoral system, and the structure of the legislative branch (Shepsle 2008). Unstructured institutions are more fluid and informal and include certain norms or cooperative arrangements, such as executive federalism (First Ministers' Conferences). Constitutional conventions, such as responsible government in Canada, fall somewhere between these poles as they are highly durable but technically informal. As we are focusing on firearms policy made by Parliament, the institutions relevant to our analysis will include both structured and unstructured institutions. Second, institutions may be "exogenous" – taken as givens by political actors – or "endogenous" – created by the current actors themselves (e.g., when the dealer in poker declares that deuces are wild). For our purposes, the institutions will be treated as mainly exogenous, and our focus will be on the constitution, the structure of Parliament, and the electoral system. Finally, to use Hall and Taylor's (1996) terminology, institutions can be thought of as "constitutive" of actor preferences or as affecting the "calculus" of actors seeking to maximize their pre-existing preferences. The constitutive account holds that institutions help form actor preferences by encouraging certain values, norms, or role perceptions that "go with the job," such as judicial impartiality. In contrast, the calculus approach sees actors as already having preferences, and institutions are (usually exogenous) incentive structures that influence how much actors can pursue them. The calculus approach is the dominant one in RCI (Shepsle 2008) and is the one used here. This view also contains an important caveat about institutions: they may shape behaviour, but they are not automatic or deterministic (Scharpf 1997, 42); thus, actors can choose to ignore them if they are willing to pay the price. To return to our Supreme Court example earlier, a judge may prefer to be in the minority rather than compromise on a key principle.

A key concept associated with RCI is that of "veto points" or "veto players" (Immergut 1990; Tsebelis 1995; Maioni 1997; Tsebelis 2002; Zohlnhöfer 2009).[1] A veto point is an institution – or more accurately, those actors who occupy an institution – that can block policy change. In general, the more veto points or players that exist, the less likely policy change will occur and the less likely that any change will be dramatic. It has often been observed that the American "separation of powers," with its robust bicameralism and the presidential veto over legislation, creates more veto points than the Canadian Westminster parliamentary system, where during periods of majority government the Cabinet executive is able to dominate the legislative branch and the unelected upper chamber almost always defers to the elected House. Similarly, in many democracies formal coalition government – with a multiparty Cabinet – is the norm, in which case some or all of the parties in the coalition are veto players. Coalition government is very rare in Canada, however; even when the party with the most seats does not have a majority, it almost always chooses to govern alone as a minority government rather than formally share power.[2]

Constitutional rights and the federal division of powers, enforced via judicial review, can make courts and other levels of government potential veto points as well. In the US, the Second Amendment's right to bear arms and the Fifth Amendment's property rights create significant barriers to gun control laws. As discussed in chapter 3, there are no analogous rights in the Canadian constitution (Augustine 1986; Johansen 1991).[3] As Constantelos (2014) concludes in his study of economic stimulus policies in Ontario and Michigan after the 2008 recession, we should not expect robust policy changes from a single level of government unless it has unfettered jurisdiction. In Canada, gun control falls under the federal Parliament's expansive criminal law power (s.91(27) of the *Constitution Act, 1867*), which is paramount in cases of conflict with provincial jurisdiction over such areas as "property and civil rights" (s.92(13)) and "the administration of justice" (s.92(14)). That means Ottawa can enact gun control laws without the cooperation of the provinces (Pal 2003; Newman and Head 2017), as was definitively confirmed by the SCC in *Reference re Firearms Act (Can.)* (2000 SCC 31). This means that in Canada, there are very few veto players in the policy area of gun control. The two primary ones are the opposition parties in the House of Commons during periods of minority government and (potentially) the government caucus itself.

While veto points can be individuals (such the US president), they usually involve a collective veto player (Tsebelis 2002), that is, an institution that can block policy change but is composed of people who individually cannot; legislative chambers are a good example. Collective actors come in many varieties (Scharpf 1997, 51–96) and may inject much greater complexity into one's analysis. A key factor is the degree of *internal cohesion* (Tsebelis 2002) or hierarchical control within the collective veto player: the more rigidly centralized it is, the more we can treat it like an individual actor. Chapter 3 emphasized that governing parties in Canada are distinguished by the exceptional degree to which they are centralized and dominated by their leaders, as the institutional convention of responsible government and relatively small government caucuses produce extremely strong party discipline in the caucus (Franks 1987). Moreover, Cabinets – another potential veto point – are usually subservient to the prime minister, at whose pleasure the members of Cabinet serve. Based on these factors, we can make the simplified assumption that governing parties in Canada can be treated as individual actors, with policy direction coming from the leader or a minister with the leader's support; the evidence will indicate to what extent that assumption proves accurate in the context of gun control.

The number of veto points and the internal cohesion of collective veto players are important, but insufficient on their own to explain policy change. Equally important are the respective policy positions within and among the veto points (i.e., the extent of policy *congruence*) (Weaver and Rockman 1993; Tsebelis 2002). If, for example, a minority government wanted stronger gun control and all major parties agreed, then the mere fact of minority government should not be a significant obstacle to policy change. This is precisely what occurred in New Zealand in 2019, when a strict new gun law banning "military-style" semi-automatics was passed only twenty-six days after the horrific mosque shootings in Christchurch left fifty people dead. Policy positions are very difficult to map in an abstract or predictive manner (Tsebelis 2002; Ganghof 2003),[4] but fortunately our goal is to explain policy change after the fact, not to predict it (Scharpf 1997, 25). It is therefore relatively easy to determine which parties opposed or supported policy change at the time, or what we can think of as the veto players that are *external* to the governing party. Measuring policy positions within the governing party – that is, the *internal* veto point of the caucus – is considerably trickier, however, given the strong tradition of party discipline and that disagreements within caucus are only infrequently made public.

A final concept worth mentioning is game theory, which is the branch of rational choice theory concerned with situations when decision-making choices and outcomes are interdependent. Decision-makers rarely act in isolation. The classic example is the prisoners' dilemma, where the outcome (the sentence received) for each of the two partners in crime depends on what the other person does – admit nothing or implicate their partner – but they each decide in isolation. In that example, although it would be best for both of them if neither confessed, the individual payoff structure – which harshly punishes the person who admits nothing if the other confesses – encourages both of them to confess. Game theory typically involves complex quantitative modelling, and while it would be possible to use it here, we employ a more qualitative approach that simply acknowledges game theory's insight that political parties react to one another's positions. In a public policy context, we know that parties take positions either to distinguish themselves from other parties or to "steal the thunder" of another party that is promoting a popular policy. "Wedge politics" (Wilson and Turnbull 2001) is a particularly aggressive version of the former: a party highlights an issue that is very important to at least some of its voters (but of low importance nationally) and produces dissention within opposing parties (Giasson and Dumouchel 2012). Giasson and Dumouchel (2012) conclude that gun control became a wedge issue for the Conservatives under Prime Minister Stephen Harper. This was arguably not the case for the Chrétien Liberals in the 1990s, though as discussed below, gun control allowed the party to distinguish itself from the Reform Party while appealing to Quebec voters.

Hypotheses

In light of the foregoing, we can offer some hypotheses about the likelihood of gun control policy change based on the number of veto points, the relative policy positions of the veto players, and the internal cohesion of the government. Majority governments from 1989 to 2012 faced virtually no veto points, given that neither federalism nor bicameralism[5] represented any significant limit on the government's ability to enact its preferred policies. The government's own caucus was its most significant potential barrier, and in normal periods party discipline should weaken this threat considerably. However, during minority governments the opposition parties in the House of Commons become a collective veto player, and the government caucus potentially more so since the Cabinet is vulnerable to non-confidence votes. As such, we follow Constantelos (2014) in hypothesizing that policy change is more robust – that is, there is lower policy stability – in Canada's Westminster parliamentary system when there is a single-party majority government, so that when the government lacks a majority, we can expect to see a delayed, blocked, or less ambitious policy response. As noted earlier, the effect of veto points is tempered by the internal cohesion of the primary collective decision-maker (the governing party) and the policy positions of the key external veto players (the opposition parties) relative to the government's.

Combining these factors produces two general hypotheses about the capacity of governments to change gun control laws:

H_1: There will be lower policy stability (robust change more likely) in periods of majority government, but only if party cohesion is high.
H_2: There will be higher policy stability (robust change less likely) in periods of minority government, but only if there is low congruence between government and opposition parties.

Both hypotheses speak to the capacity for governments to act; they also reflect what are in effect the most and least likely institutional conditions under which policy change will occur. They also predict the anticipated *magnitude* of policy change, understood as the degree of change from the status quo: majority governments that can act decisively are more likely to undertake significant changes than minority governments that face opposition.

But what about the anticipated direction of policy change? The most obvious starting point in building hypotheses for direction is to consider what factors are likely to influence the government party's position on gun control. Two immediately stand out: (1) the degree of rural representation in the government caucus, and (2) how much the government party relies on seats in Quebec. These require some elaboration, along with an explanation of how – consistent with RCI – various institutions amplify the importance of rural and Quebec voters.

For decades, it has been commonplace for media and political commentators to suggest that rural voters are less likely to support gun control and that rural MPs fear that supporting such measures will endanger their prospects for re-election (Bottomley 2004; Page 2006; Ibbitson 2010; Mitchell 2010; EKOS Politics 2017; Rana 2017). The rationale is captured nicely by a recent quote from Global News: "A standard response to why government doesn't go further to crack down on guns is politics and the perception that urban Canadians view the issue far differently than rural dwellers, who use guns to hunt for food or protect themselves in remote regions beyond the every-day reach of law enforcement" (Levitz 2017). More generally, there is much evidence that rural residents tend to vote differently from urban and suburban residents (Cutler and Jenkins 2002; Roy, Perrella, and Borden 2015), with Bittner (2007) calling it "one of the main cleavages of Canadian politics" (939). It is also the case that since 1989 rural MPs have been more likely to oppose tighter restrictions on firearms (Page 2006). It is therefore reasonable to assume that parties that have more rural MPs will be less likely to support gun control, or at least less likely to support robust new restrictions. Moreover, as explained in chapter 3, Canada's electoral system numerically overrepresents rural areas, meaning both that rural MPs carry disproportionate weight in the House and that parties have an incentive to appeal to rural voters.

H_3: The greater the level of rural representation in the governing caucus, the less likely the government will adopt new restrictions on firearms and the more likely it will weaken gun control.

This hypothesis is not uncontroversial. Notwithstanding the conventional wisdom about greater rural opposition to gun control (which is accurate regarding the US; Igielnik 2017), there is little evidence that this is actually true in Canada. Repeated polling over the past thirty years, by both advocates and opponents of gun control, finds that a majority of rural voters favour stronger gun control; indeed, they even favoured the federal long-run registry when it was first introduced (Mauser and Margolis 1992; Rathjen and Montpetit 1999; Bottomley 2004; Page 2006; Angus Reid Institute 2019). The main finding to the contrary was a 2002 Ipsos-Reid poll that found rural residents were about 10 per cent more likely than urbanites to favour cancelling the long-gun registry (Fleming 2012, 101), but that may reflect greater frustration with the soaring cost of the registry rather than more hostility in principle to gun control. Nonetheless, it is clear that rural MPs are historically less supportive of gun control; indeed, Page (2006) concludes that gun control is a policy area where many rural MPs ignored public opinion polls and thus did not accurately reflect their constituents' views.

Since the Montreal Massacre in 1989, support for gun control has consistently been strong in Quebec, as well as higher there than in other regions (Page 2006). No doubt some of this is because the massacre happened in Quebec, only five years after a gunman shot sixteen government employees – three fatally – at the National Assembly (add to this two later high-profile shootings in Montreal, at Concordia University in 1992 and Dawson College in 2006). Voters in Quebec are not significantly different from those elsewhere in Canada (Nadeau and Bélanger 2012; McGrane and Berdahl 2013), but with two key exceptions. One relates to the centrality of the sovereignty issue, at least until 2011. The other, more relevant here, is that Quebecers are less morally and religiously conservative. For example, they are more supportive of feminism and a "softer" (less punitive) approach to crime, as well as – most importantly for our purposes – restricting access to firearms and requiring their registration (Nadeau and Bélanger 2012, 146). Moreover, for the reasons explained in chapter 3, we would expect such differences to be salient to political parties eager to appeal to Quebec voters. So it is reasonable to assume that MPs from Quebec are more likely to support strengthening gun control and to oppose attempts to weaken it, which produces the following hypothesis:

H_4: The larger the proportion of Quebec seats in the governing caucus, the less likely the government will be able to weaken gun control, and the more likely to adopt new restrictions on firearms.

Before proceeding to our operationalization of these factors, let us pause to underscore the nature of the causal claim in our application of RCI. The hypotheses we have developed are stated in probabilistic terms rather than the strict deterministic language of "necessary" or "sufficient" causes. More specifically, we identify the most and least likely institutional conditions under which robust policy change will occur, and the factors we have hypothesized will shape the direction of policy change. This approach to causality is in keeping with Tsebelis's veto player theory and best suited to our particular scenario and research interests. It must be stressed that in general RCI is highly flexible about the causal claim being hypothesized and tested and that other variants of RCI may be formulated in deterministic terms. This points to the adaptability of RCI as an approach, which is one of its major strengths.

Operationalization

While our hypotheses are admittedly simple, and the conditions arguably self-evident, they allow us to operationalize several testable variables:

Independent Variables

x_1 = Is there a majority government? (yes/no)
x_2 = Was there unwhipped dissent in government caucus? (yes/no)
x_3 = Did opposition parties opposed to the government's policy preference represent a majority of the House? (yes/no)
x_4 = Percentage of government caucus from rural ridings
x_5 = Percentage of government caucus from Quebec

Dependent Variables

y_1 = Did policy change occur? (yes/no)
y_2 = Direction and magnitude of proposed policy changes (see below)

To test Hypotheses 1 and 2, we employ three independent variables: whether there was a majority government (number of veto players); whether there was open dissent in the government caucus on the change to gun control legislation that the prime minister did not whip to overcome (internal cohesion); and whether the opposition parties *who opposed the government's proposed change* represented a majority of the House (congruence). Given party discipline and the power of the prime minister, open caucus dissent by government party MPs is rare in Canada and as such usually receives media attention when it does arise. We therefore use media and secondary sources (such as Bottomley 2004; Page 2006; Brown 2012) to identify when the PM whipped caucus. To clarify, higher internal cohesion is signified both by a *lack* of open caucus dissent (i.e., whipping was not necessary) and by the prime minister's exercise of the whip. The policy positions of the opposition on legislation regarding firearms were obtained from media sources and the parties' statements in the House; assessing whether opposition parties constituted a majority involved simple arithmetic based on the composition of the House. It should be acknowledged that x_1 and x_3 are not truly independent of each other, for if x_3 is true then x_1 is "no" by definition: opposition parties cannot represent a majority in a majority government situation. This would be more of a problem if we were combining these variables in a quantitative formula such as multiple regression, but we are not. (Although RCI studies often use quantitative analysis, the approach does not require it, and our more qualitative method is in keeping with several applications of RCI to Canadian policy-making [Flanagan 1997; Maioni 1997; Alcantara 2013; Morden 2016].) X_3 should simply be understood as a refinement that allows us to test both for the effect of minority government by itself (x_1) and for the effect of the external veto players' policy positions.

Turning to the directional variables, surprisingly there is no uniform definition of a "rural riding." To date, Sayers (2013) has taken the most sophisticated approach to measurement, using a multi-factor index to determine the "urban-ness" of Cabinets and federal government parties. His data on individual ridings are not publicly available, however, and the analysis ends in 2008. Several authors examine rural/suburban/urban distinctions in voting behaviour and public opinion (Walks 2005; Wasko and O'Neill 2007; Roy, Perella, and Borden 2015; McGrane, Berdahl, and Bell 2017), but such studies only measure the respondents' immediate community, not their riding. We follow the OECD (2011) and a *Maclean's* (Taylor-Vaisey 2015) study in using a population density of less than 150 people per square kilometre as the threshold for a "rural" constituency. While population density is an admittedly crude indicator (and can be misled by gerrymandering that combines cities with vast rural areas, as in Saskatoon's three ridings), "density does increase as one moves from country to suburban and finally city ridings" and is "a widely used measure with the advantages of being both linear and simple to apply" (Sayers 2013, 98).[6] Statistics Canada's census provides population density for federal electoral districts (FEDs) after 2001; for earlier elections it was calculated using census population counts for FEDs and area data from digital mapping software.[7] Ridings were then cross-referenced to the party of the winning MP, using information from Elections Canada and PARLINFO at the Parliament of Canada website,[8] and the rural proportion of caucus calculated; the same was done for Quebec ridings at the point in time when the bill was introduced.[9]

Our first dependent variable is simply whether policy change occurred via legislation; the restriction to legislation follows logically from our focus on the veto points in the parliamentary system, which do not apply to regulations, which can be issued solely by the executive. To capture the direction and magnitude of policy change, we constructed a composite measure to reflect the fact that gun control can regulate *who* can use guns, *how* guns can be used, and *what* guns can be used (Bottomley 2004; Pal 2003; Brown 2012). In recognition of the fact that policy is not made in a vacuum, the policy status quo at the time of the attempted change is used as the point of reference, and we measure whether the government's policy strengthened or weakened gun control along several dimensions (see Table 4.1). While this approach does not allow us to assess how much change occurred with mathematical or categorical precision,[10] the qualitative analysis will tell us in general terms whether changes on each dimension were marginal or significant, and also whether there was change along multiple dimensions. It is expected that a policy reform that affects multiple dimensions is more robust, though we acknowledge that a dramatic movement on a single dimension may also represent major policy change.

A decision to grandfather new restrictions is evidence of less robust change, as is replacing legal requirements with voluntary guidelines. While the dimensions above are phrased in dichotomous terms, we

Table 4.1. Dimensions of firearms policy

General categories of firearms regulation	Sub-categories/definitions	Directionality
Firearms ownership controls	• Ownership restrictions (e.g., background checks, waiting periods, etc.)	• Relaxed or tightened?
	• Training requirements	• Relaxed or tightened?
Firearms prohibitions	• Classes of firearms designated as restricted or prohibited	• More or fewer classes?
Firearms registrations	• Classes of firearms requiring registration	• More or fewer classes?
Firearms offences	• Number of firearms offences	• More or fewer offences?
	• Penalties for firearms offences	• Tougher or more lenient penalties?

will also examine qualitatively how much new or proposed policies strengthen or relax each factor.

Data and Cases

To test the explanatory power of an RCI-based approach, we used a diachronic case study (Gerring 2007) with six within-case comparisons. The six policy events represent the clearest attempts at legislative change to firearms policy in our time period[11] and provide variance on most of our key factors discussed below, including the outcomes. Table 4.2 summarizes the policy events in chronological order, starting shortly after the 1989 Montreal Massacre. For each policy event we collected evidence on our dependent variables using primary sources, such as official versions of bills from LEGISinfo and HeinOnline, and existing secondary sources.[12] The findings are detailed below.

Bill C-80

Bill C-80, the Mulroney PC government's initial attempt, in June 1990, to respond to the Montreal Massacre, was widely seen as very weak. The policy status quo had been laid out mainly in C-51, adopted by Pierre Trudeau's Liberals in 1977, which had significantly changed firearms regulation, although national registries for handguns and fully automatic weapons had existed since 1934 and 1951 respectively. Under C-51, all new gun owners required a Firearms Acquisition

Table 4.2. Summary of policy events

Policy Event	Government	Year	Maj/Min	Outcome
Bill C-80	PC (Mulroney)	1990–1	Majority	Failed
Bill C-17	PC (Mulroney)	1991	Majority	Successful
Bill C-68	Lib (Chrétien)	1993–5	Majority	Successful
Bills C-21, C-24	Con (Harper)	2006–8	Minority	Failed
Bill C-391	PMB/Con (Harper)	2009–11	Minority	Failed
Bill C-19	Con (Harper)	2011–12	Majority	Successful

Certificate (FAC) for any type of firearm purchase, but existing own-ers were exempted and a FAC holder could purchase an unlimited number of rifles and shotguns without giving any reasons (Friedland 1984, 118). FACs expired after five years. C-51 did not require safety training for a FAC, but provinces were empowered to create such re-quirements (RCMP 2016). An important change introduced in 1977 was the prohibition of fully automatic weapons, as well as a ban on private citizens carrying "restricted" weapons (primarily handguns and certain models of semi-automatics) to protect their property. C-80 proposed only incremental changes to this regime: adding a four-week waiting period for FAC applications but no other changes to licencing; additional bans on military and paramilitary weapons, high-capacity magazines, and semi-automatics converted from auto-matics (Bottomley 2004, 32); and restrictions on some semi-automatic models of assault weapons (notably not the one used by the Montreal Massacre shooter [Rathjen and Montpetit 1999, 57]). There were no changes proposed to registration, firearms offences, or gun crime sen-tencing, however.

Despite its limited scope, C-80 generated significant backlash within the PC caucus (Rathjen and Montpetit 1999; Brown 2012), particularly among its western and rural members. Rural MPs represented 60 per cent of the caucus, but Mulroney's majority government also relied heavily on representation from Quebec. The fifty-five Quebec PC MPs made up just over one third of the government party, the highest pro-portion in our study; notably, it had been even higher until May 1990 – only seven weeks before C-80 was introduced – when seven MPs led by Lucien Bouchard left the party to form the Bloc Québécois in protest over the failed Meech Lake Accord.[13] In the face of internal opposition, Justice Minister Kim Campbell – the first female to hold the post, and representing downtown Vancouver – referred the bill to committee, which recommended thirty-two amendments. Rather than invoking party discipline, Prime Minister Mulroney briefly prorogued Parliament on 12 May 1991, effectively killing C-80.

Bill C-17

Justice Minister Campbell tabled new firearms legislation in C-17 only two weeks after the demise of C-80. Both the substance and the outcome of this new bill differed considerably, as did the process followed. The licensing requirements were strengthened to include not only C-80's four-week waiting period but also mandatory safety training and more detailed background checks, as well as character references and potentially interviews with family, neighbours, social workers, and co-workers. C-17 also required judges to consider imposing firearm prohibitions as a condition of bail for those charged with violent or drug-trafficking offences, as well as a peace bond in domestic disputes. Firearm prohibitions for those convicted of drug trafficking were introduced, while existing bans for violent offenders were doubled, and made permanent for repeat offenders. As well, the minimum age to obtain a FAC was raised from sixteen to eighteen for those without parental consent. FACs would still expire after five years, however, and firearms purchases still would not require justification. C-17 included the main provisions of C-80 regarding banning the most powerful weapons but went further, moving about two hundred models into the prohibited and restricted categories (again, though, not the weapon used in the Montreal Massacre) (Brown 2012, 211). As well, large-capacity cartridge magazines for automatics and semi-automatics were banned (RCMP 2016). That said, existing owners of converted semi-automatics were grandfathered, and the power of the Justice Minister to reclassify weapons unilaterally was weakened by the introduction of a parliamentary oversight and reversal mechanism (Brown 2012). Penalties for firearms-related offences were doubled, and new firearms offences were created along with regulations governing the storage, handling, and transportation of firearms. While C-17 was certainly more ambitious than C-80 and contained some significant changes, they were essentially incremental rather than revolutionary.[14]

C-17 again sparked considerable internal dissent, especially when it came back from committee hearings strengthened (Rathjen and Montpetit 1999, 113–19). This time, however, PM Mulroney invoked party discipline, although many MPs continued to demonstrate their opposition by refusing to show up for the vote (Brown 2012, 209–11). The bill passed easily (189–14) on 7 November 1991 with widespread support from opposition parties and came into effect on 2 August 1992.

Bill C-68

C-17 had been incremental; C-68 (*Firearms Act*) amounted to a dramatic shift toward stronger gun control by Jean Chrétien's Liberal majority government. There were significant changes to licensing: the FAC regime was replaced with a mandatory Possession and Acquisition Licence (PAL) to own any firearms and ammunition (FACs had only been required for new purchases). A particularly controversial provision was that PALs were now required for models not classified as restricted or prohibited, including popular hunting rifles and shotguns. A PAL required the successful completion of the Canadian Firearms Safety Course (or provincial equivalent before 1995), as well as a special safety course to possess a restricted weapon; this effectively ended the exemption for many present-day gun owners under the FAC system. C-68 also required handgun owners to justify possession every five years and banned (rather than "restricted") many models of handguns and semi-automatic assault rifles, though without prohibiting either category completely. The biggest change, however, was the creation of a universal gun registry, the first in peacetime, with ownership of an unregistered firearm made a criminal offence. Sentences for serious gun crimes were also increased, with mandatory minimums.

The proposed changes were strongly supported by the BQ (the Official Opposition), but sparked dissent within the other parties, including the Liberals, whose rural members spoke openly against the bill and at least thirty of whom evaded party discipline by refusing to show up for C-68's second reading (Harper 1995). Even the Reform Party, which would quickly become the party most critical of the registry, was initially ambivalent, given that the party was committed to populism and many urban constituents, even in Alberta, favoured stronger gun control.[15] Prime Minister Chrétien's response to internal dissent was strict enforcement of party discipline, and three Liberal MPs who voted against C-68 at second reading were removed from their respective committee positions (Harper 1995; Docherty 1997; Pal 2003; Bottomley 2004).[16] The bill passed third reading easily (192–63) on 13 June 1995. In the Senate, there were concerns that the slim majority of PC senators might require substantial weakening of C-68 or reject it outright, but in the event, neither occurred,[17] and the bill received Royal Assent on 6 December 1995. Quebec MPs represented only about 11 per cent of the Liberal caucus (20 seats on 13 June 1995, mostly in the Montreal and

Outaouais areas), while rural MPs made up half of the Liberal caucus – a large proportion, and one that helps explain the internal dissent, but the lowest proportion of all the governments in this study.

Bills C-21 and C-24

The long run of Liberal governments came to an end with the election of Stephen Harper's minority Conservatives on 23 January 2006. The Conservative government was heavily rural (65% of caucus) but had only slightly fewer Quebec MPs (8.1%) than the Liberals during C-68 (see Tables 4.5 and 4.6 in Appendix).[18] The government introduced C-21 on 19 June 2006 with the sole purpose of ending the "long-gun" portion of the registry. Technically, it did this by eliminating registration (and the associated criminal offences for non-registration) for everything except restricted and prohibited weapons; that meant handguns, automatics, and many categories of semi-automatics were unaffected by C-21. This was a major change, as the vast majority of registered weapons – around seven out of eight million – were unrestricted long guns. The bill did not, however, try to reverse C-68's many other changes, including the PAL system and mandatory safety training, or change the sentences for firearms offences. The bill delivered on a key campaign promise made by the Conservatives and their predecessors in the Reform Party and Canadian Alliance, but it faced intense opposition from the BQ, the Liberals, and the NDP, who together constituted a majority in the House. C-21 died on the order paper when Prime Minister Harper prorogued Parliament in September 2007; it was reintroduced as C-24 in November 2007. C-24 made it no further than first reading when the House was dissolved in September 2008 for an election. C-21 and C-24 can thus be dealt with together, as they were identical and suffered essentially the same fate.

This policy event presents us with an important aspect of veto points, as represented here by the opposition parties in a minority government: they may operate via pre-emption rather than through formal exercise. Neither C-21 nor C-24 was voted down by the opposition parties; the Conservatives avoided that fate by refusing to move the bills to second reading, and ultimately both bills died by the Conservatives' own hand via prorogation and dissolution respectively. However, as a CBC report noted at the time, "all three opposition parties support the registry and would probably defeat any legislation that would dismantle it" (CBC News 2006). Further evidence of the pre-emptive effect of a hostile parliamentary veto point is provided by the government's efforts in May 2006 (just before the introduction of C-21) to weaken the registry via administrative changes (budget cuts, elimination of registration fees for long-gun owners, amnesties for non-registration, registry administration moved to RCMP) that did not need Parliament's approval.

Bill C-391

The October 2008 election returned another (albeit larger) Conservative minority government, this time equally rural and with no gains in Quebec.[19] The government did not propose any cuts to the registry; however, it vigorously endorsed several attempts by its MPs (mainly Garry Breitkreuz and Candice Hoeppner) to introduce private members' bills that were virtually identical to C-21 and C-24.[20] We focus on Hoeppner's C-391, which came the closest to adoption after being stalled by Prime Minister Harper's controversial 2009 prorogation to avoid a non-confidence vote by a Liberal/NDP coalition and the BQ (CBC News 2009). The bill had made it to second reading and referral to committee before prorogation, and after the government survived that scare, C-391 was reintroduced and proceeded to committee in mid-2010. Once there, however, the bill ran into stiff opposition from the other parties, which represented a majority, and the committee's formal recommendation in June 2010 was for Parliament to reject C-391. The Conservatives spent the summer visiting rural ridings campaign-style to promote C-391 (Ibbitson 2010), dispelling any illusions this was truly a private member's bill. The bill was narrowly defeated 153–151 on 22 September 2010 in a vote that saw some rural opposition MPs defy party discipline to support the bill (Mackreal 2013).

Bill C-19

Our final policy event is Bill C-19, the *Ending the Long-Gun Registry Act*, which finally delivered on the Conservatives' signature promise to the end the long-gun registry (Friesen and Ibbitson 2011). With only minor changes, the bill was effectively identical to those tabled as C-21, C-24, and C-391, and thus modest in scope beyond the registration issue. This was despite the fact that there was now a key difference, essential to C-19's success: the Conservatives had won a majority government in early May 2011. They moved to kill the registry only six months later with no internal dissent; this was formally accomplished in April 2012. In other respects, this government was similar to its immediate predecessors, if somewhat less rural (57%) due to successful forays into Ontario's suburbs ("the 905"), and even less reliant on Quebec (down to 3%, and only five MPs).

Figure 4.1. Direction and magnitude of proposed firearms policy changes, 1989–2021

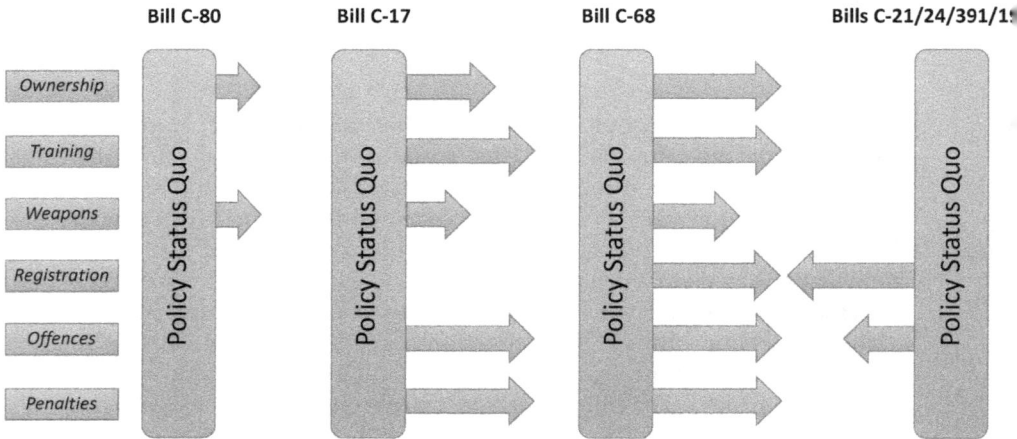

Figure 4.1 provides a visual comparison of the direction and magnitude of the proposed legislative changes, as captured by our composite dependent variable (y_2).

Discussion and Conclusions

The evidence reveals qualified support for the explanatory value of rational choice institutionalism for Canadian gun control policy from 1989 to 2012, at least as conceptualized here. The findings indicate that the veto player–based hypotheses concerning institutional constraints on the *capacity* to enact policy changes fared well, and better than those regarding the direction and magnitude of change. Table 4.3 summarizes the independent variables for our six policy events, and Table 4.4 provides an overview of how each of our four hypotheses fared.

Consistent with veto player theory, majority government alone did not explain robust policy change, as indicated by the PCs' failure to pass C-80. Party cohesion was indeed the key, as vigorous dissent went unwhipped in that period, while the prime minister intervened on both C-17 and C-68 to enforce party discipline and produced significant policy changes. Party cohesion was also very high in Prime Minister Harper's majority government – naturally, due to broad ideological agreement on gun control – and resulted in the major change of

Table 4.3. Variables by policy event

Event	Party	Majority	Unwhip dissent	Opp maj	% rural	% QC	Passed	Dir/Mag
C-80	PC	Yes	Yes	No	60	35	No	Minor pro-control
C-17	PC	Yes	No	No	60	35	Yes	Major pro-control
C-68	Lib	Yes	No	No	50	11.5	Yes	Major pro-control
C-21/24	Con	No	No	Yes	C-21: 65 C-24: 64	C-21: 8.1 C-24: 7.0	No	Major pro-gun
C-391	Con	No	No	Yes	64	7.7	No	Major pro-gun
C-19	Con	Yes	No	No	57	3	Yes	Major pro-gun

Table 4.4. Summary of hypothesis tests

H_1: Lower policy stability in majority government if party cohesion high	Strongly supported
H_2: Higher policy stability in minority government if low congruence between government and opposition parties	Strongly supported
H_3: Larger rural representation in governing caucus, less likely to adopt new restrictions on firearms / more likely to weaken gun control	Somewhat supported
H_4: Larger Quebec representation in governing caucus, more likely to adopt new restrictions on firearms / less likely to weaken gun control	Weakly supported

cancelling the long-gun registry and associated offences. The evidence thus supports the hypothesis that cohesive majority governments are the most likely to accomplish policy change. Similarly, the second hypothesis was decidedly confirmed, as periods of minority government with low congruence (C-21, C-24, C-391) could not pass new firearms legislation. Unfortunately, there is no natural experiment to examine a minority government with high congruence (e.g., Paul Martin's minority Liberal government did not pursue further restrictions on guns, despite sympathetic opposition parties in the BQ and NDP). That said, it is telling that in 2006 the Conservatives weakened gun control using administrative actions entirely within the jurisdiction of the executive branch, precisely because it could not relax firearms restrictions through legislation.

The findings regarding the magnitude, or "robustness," of policy change are somewhat more mixed. The first hypothesis predicts less robust (or no) change when party cohesion is low, and that is what we observe with the modest, and ultimately unsuccessful, reforms proposed in C-80. Conversely, cohesive majority governments in 1991, 1995, and 2011 proposed more significant reforms, as evidenced by C-17, C-19, and especially C-68's *Firearms Act*. As counter-evidence, however, C-19 – proposed by a cohesive majority government – was no more ambitious regarding loosening gun control than the series of bills proposed by the Conservatives while they were a minority government (C-21, C-24, C-391). All of the Harper-era Conservative bills in our study tried to do only one thing: eliminate the registration of roughly seven million unrestricted long guns and associated offences, with no changes to licencing, training, or weakening of firearms offences, although Harper's subsequent changes to regulations and the *Common Sense Firearms Licensing Act* (S.C. 2015, c. 27) weakened gun control. This may simply reflect an insufficiently nuanced view of gun control preferences in our model – after all, a party could be against firearms registration but support stronger screening of prospective gun users and punishment for misuse. The PC Minister of Justice, Kim Campbell, for example, explicitly rejected a national registry as too expensive, a counterproductive diversion of police resources from licence screening, and ultimately a firearms-counting exercise that "would have little effect on their use in crime, or on the number of deaths and injuries caused by suicides or accidents each year" (Parliament of Canada 1991, 1253). The approaches in some subsequent chapters (especially social constructivism and punctuated equilibrium theory) identify these finer distinctions more effectively. All of that said, it is puzzling that the Harper minority governments did not propose compromise bills that would have softened the cuts to the registry with stronger licencing requirements or harsher penalties. Such a strategy surely would have been more likely to attract opposition party support. That the Conservatives did not do so lends support to the view that the Harper government was less interested in passing these bills than in using the registry as a wedge issue to shore up support among the fervent pro-gun component of its base while vexing the Liberals and the NDP, both of which faced internal divisions on the issue (Giasson and Dumouchel 2012).

The two hypotheses predicting the direction of policy change (H_3 and H_4) have some support, although the evidence is mixed for both and stronger for the impact of rural over Quebec representation in caucus. It is the case that the least rural government – the Liberals in 1995 – proposed the most aggressive restrictions on firearms, and that the most rural ones – the Harper-era Conservatives – sought to weaken the gun registry. As well, the high level of rural representation within the Liberal caucus in 1995 and the PCs in 1990–91 was correlated with strong internal opposition to gun control that required the prime minister's direct intervention. While all governments during the period of our study had significant rural representation – a function of both rural overrepresentation in the electoral system and the brokerage efforts of winning parties – it is noteworthy that when the Liberals passed C-68, their caucus was significantly less rural (50%) than the Reform Party's (71%) and the NDP's (78%) (see Appendix for summary tables). But there is also contradictory evidence. The PC caucus that adopted new gun control measures in C-17 was almost as rural as those during the first two Conservative governments, and actually slightly *more* rural than the government that ended the long-gun registry. As well, the BQ was consistently pro-gun control despite having an even more rural caucus (64%) than the Liberals in 1995, which raises a question about whether the rural/urban distinction about gun control holds in Quebec. Finally, even with a heavily rural caucus, the Conservatives did not try to weaken gun control beyond the long-gun registry. This may well reflect the fact, noted earlier, that while many Canadian rural voters became highly critical of the registry, they did not reject gun control per se. Moreover, as Ibbitson (2010) observes, the only path to majority government for any federal party is through Canada's cities and suburbs, where support for gun control is very high.

There is only weak support for the explanatory power of Quebec representation in the government caucus. The Mulroney PCs had much more Quebec representation (35%) than any subsequent government, yet they initially failed to pass even modest gun control measures, even shortly after the massacre, with a majority, and in the middle of a constitutional crisis centring on Quebec. Given the context, one might have expected the PCs to be particularly sensitive to the prevailing attitudes in Quebec on gun control, but that does not appear to have been the case. Perhaps this outcome reflected the growing frustration within the party regarding Quebec and constitutional politics, which would ultimately decimate the PCs in the West and enable the rise of the Reform Party and BQ in the 1993 election. C-17 entailed more robust change, but as noted earlier, it required the direct intervention of Prime Minister Mulroney to pass over stiff caucus objection, with many Western and rural MPs abstaining. The expansive new restrictions in C-68 came from a Liberal government that had significant Quebec representation

(11.5%), but far less than the PCs in 1989–93 and only slightly more than the 2006 Conservative government (8.1%) that vowed to kill the long-gun registry. This suggests that the rural factor might be more relevant, since Conservative MPs from Quebec were from rural areas, where there was opposition to the registry. Still, the BQ's strong preference for gun control – even going so far as to vote for C-68 while the Official Opposition – provides some support for the directional influence of Quebec. Similarly, one has to wonder whether the fact the Reform Party in 1995 had no Quebec MPs, and no desire to acquire any, helps explain its vigorous opposition to C-68, despite considerable support for the gun registry in Western cities represented by Reform MPs. Conversely, the presence of Quebec MPs in Harper's 2006 minority government, and the need for the Conservatives to grow the party beyond its western and rural base to achieve majority status, may help explain the limited scope of the proposed changes in C-21 and C-24. There is also some anecdotal evidence that the Conservative position after 2008 was influenced by the party's electoral strategy regarding Quebec. Puddister and Kelly (2017) point to Conservative strategist Tom Flanagan's observation that after failing to break through in Quebec in 2008 the party "realized that Quebec would not be the route towards a majority government and shifted its priorities towards wooing ethnocultural minority voters. This change resulted in the government pursuing several policy changes that ran directly against the desires of most Quebec voters, such as its law-and-order criminal justice policy agenda that involved changes to the *Youth Criminal Justice Act* and the dismantling of the long-gun registry" (167). That said, between 2006 and 2008, when they were ostensibly still courting Quebec voters, the Conservatives had twice tried to eliminate the long-gun registry. Overall, then, there is only weak evidence that the level of Quebec representation in the government caucus influenced the direction of firearms policy change.

This first systematic test of RCI to explain Canadian firearms policy from 1989 to 2012 is encouraging and points to the need for further analysis. For example, one could assess the impact of rural and Quebec representation *in Cabinet*, since that is a more important source of government policy than the caucus. As well, the emphasis here has been on policy change, with no effort to explain *why* the various governments dedicated political capital to gun control; that is, there is no account of agenda-setting. Fleming (2012) undertakes such an analysis by looking at "focusing events," and Giasson and Dumouchel (2012) point to the concept of "wedge politics" to explain the Conservatives' fixation on ending the long-gun registry, and a more fulsome application of RCI (and especially game theory) to that issue is possible albeit beyond the scope of this chapter. It is also important to acknowledge what our application of RCI to explain gun control policy change did *not* try to incorporate, such as the role of civil society actors, or why governments chose to address firearms policy when they did, or the source of policy ideas (e.g., why a universal registry instead of bans or buy-backs?). Some of the chapters that follow address these issues more squarely, but it must be stressed that RCI could conceivably be adapted to offer hypotheses on these factors. More than anything else, RCI offers a perspective and a highly flexible conceptual toolkit that does not have any obvious scope conditions about the cases to which it can be applied. Moreover, we will see that the core tenet of RCI – that policy is shaped primarily by political actors making decisions based on their preferences but within institutional constraints – informs other policy theories.

APPENDIX

Table 4.5. Rural representation by party and policy event

Party	Percentage of Caucus (Number of MPs)				
	C-80, C-17	C-68	C-21, C-24	C-391	C-19
BQ	40.0 (4)	64.2 (34)	44.2 (23)	43.8 (21)	75.0 (3)
CON	n/a	n/a	**65.3 (81)**	**63.6 (91)**	**57.2 (95)**
LIB	48.8 (39)	**50.8 (90)**	30.4 (31)	21.1 (16)	31.4 (11)
NDP	68.2 (30)	77.8 (7)	31.0 (9)	38.8 (14)	35.3 (36)
PC	**60.4 (96)**	50.0 (1)	n/a	n/a	n/a
REF	100.0 (1)	71.2 (37)	n/a	n/a	n/a

Calculations by author. Government party **bolded**.

Table 4.6. Quebec representation by party and policy event

Party	Percentage of Caucus (Number of MPs)				
	C-80, C-17	C-68	C-21, C-24	C-391	C-19
BQ	100.0 (10)	100.0 (53)	100.0 (51)	100.0 (48)	100.0 (4)
CON	n/a	n/a	**8.1 (10)**	**7.7 (11)**	**3.0 (5)**
LIB	11.1 (9)	**11.4 (20)**	12.6 (13)*	8.0 (14)	20.6 (7)
NDP	2.3 (1)	0	0	2.8 (1)	51.5 (9)
PC	**34.8 (55)**	50.0 (1)	n/a	n/a	n/a
REF	0	0	n/a	n/a	n/a

Calculations by author. Government party **bolded**.
* Liberals 13% (13/100) for C-24 as 3 defections from caucus after vote on C-21.

5 Exploitation and Power: The Social Construction Framework

Rhetoric and pandering are ubiquitous in politics, yet most mainstream theories of the policy process overlook them completely. They are either dismissed as empty political theatre or derided as the distasteful underbelly of politics, as politicians play to the electorate's most base instincts. But what if rhetoric and pandering are, in actuality, an important substance of policy-making, the means through which policy elites construct social realities? What if the social groups affected by policies are not objectively or inherently "good" or "bad" and these labels are social constructions perpetuated by policy elites to secure political advantage? This is the perspective of the social construction framework (SCF), an approach that lifts the veil on political communication and explores how policy elites' constructions of social groups shape the policies affecting these groups. The SCF claims not only that social constructions are relevant in policy-making but also that there is a systematic linkage between different social constructions and policy designs. This chapter examines Canadian firearms policy from the SCF perspective, investigating how the SCF fares in explaining the three most substantial firearms policy changes between 1989 and 2012: Bill C-17 (1991), the *Firearms Act* (1995), and the *Ending the Long-Gun Registry Act* (2012).

The Social Construction Framework

The SCF is based on the fundamental insight that "much of the political world is socially constructed, drawing on emotional and value-laden images and symbols rather than objective representations of 'reality'" (Schneider, Ingram, and deLeon 2014, 106). Policy processes are part of the socially constructed political world, and policy outcomes are substantially shaped by the social constructions used by policy elites in these processes. In fact, the social constructions used by policy elites are crucial because different constructions lead politicians to different policy designs. It follows that policy outcomes can be explained in part by the prevalent social constructions within a policy process.

The SCF's emphasis on the social construction of reality has its roots in critical scholarship, but the SCF itself has a largely positivist orientation. The SCF was developed by two American political scientists, Anne Schneider and Helen Ingram, who laid out the general tenets of their approach in a 1993 article (Schneider and Ingram 1993) and expanded upon them in a 1997 book (Schneider and Ingram 1997). Schneider and Ingram drew from earlier scholarship in critical sociology, such as frame analysis and metaphorical framing, which stressed the social and linguistic construction of what we perceive as "reality" (Goffman 1974; Lakoff and Johnson 1980; Kuypers 2009). The most ardent social constructivists, informed by a post-positivist epistemology, argue that just about everything is socially constructed and that there is no objective or material reality, just individuals' unique and shared experiences of it. While drawing inspiration from this scholarship, Schneider and Ingram adopted an understanding of social constructions that is compatible with positivist precepts (Barbehön 2020, 140–1). As they put it, "the theory of social constructions that we embrace … is not one of strict constructionism in which there are no underlying material conditions; but is more of a contextual constructionism that recognizes that there are constraints and limits on the social constructions" (Schneider and Ingram 1997, 107). Schneider and Ingram further argued that there are patterns and regularities in policy elites' use of social constructions and that different social constructions lead to different policy designs. Over time, SCF scholars developed a number of empirically testable hypotheses to explain various aspects of the policy process, including policy change, and it is this emphasis on empirical hypothesis-testing that makes the SCF predominantly positivist, despite some of its critical origins (Pierce et al. 2014, 1–2). It also means that the SCF provides a distinctive framework for understanding policy processes and, based on this framework, a testable theory of policy change. In this section, we outline the tenets of that framework and describe the hypothesis on which the SCF theory of policy change is based.

The SCF holds that social constructions are especially important in "degenerative" policy-making systems "in which the social constructions of issues and target populations are strategically manipulated for political gain" (Schneider and Ingram 1997, 6).[1] Not all policy-making contexts are degenerative, but many are, particularly in the US, where Schneider and Ingram developed their theory. In degenerative contexts, there is little genuine effort to address social ills through public policy, and policies may exacerbate the problems they are ostensibly meant to solve (Schneider, Ingram, and deLeon 2014, 121–4). This happens because policy elites exploit policy debates for their own political gain, focusing on scoring political points rather than engaging in genuine attempts at policy analysis or policy learning. Policy elites score political points by playing into popular stereotypes and by providing assistance to good, deserving people while "getting tough" on bad, undeserving people (Schneider, Ingram, and deLeon 2014, 116). In this way, in degenerative contexts, policy elites manipulate and perpetuate prevalent social constructions in an effort to secure votes or other forms of political support, often at the expense of good public policy.[2]

Degenerative policy-making systems, as opposed to non-degenerative systems, have a number of characteristics, most of which could apply in Canadian firearms policy. As Schneider and Ingram describe it, "degenerative policy-making systems are characterized by an unequal distribution of political power, social constructions that separate the 'deserving' from the 'undeserving,' and an institutional culture that legitimizes strategic, manipulative, and deceptive patterns of communication and uses of political power" (Schneider and Ingram 1997, 102).

They also suggest that intense political or partisan competition in an issue area is an important feature of degenerative policy-making, a finding that has also been supported in Canadian studies of degenerative politics (Mondou and Montpetit 2010; Heinmiller, Hennigar, and Kopec 2017). Canadian firearms policy, with its heated rhetoric, emotive appeals, and intense partisanship (see chapter 3), seems a prime candidate for degenerative politics, meaning that the SCF and its hypotheses about policy-making in degenerative contexts should have application in this policy area.

In the SCF, the social groups affected by a policy are known as target groups (or target populations). Various aspects of policy design can affect target groups, and these are generally conceptualized as policy benefits and policy burdens. Policy benefits include such things as subsidies, tax breaks, and permissive regulations; policy burdens refer to things such as taxes, strict regulations, incarceration, and even state-sponsored execution (Schneider, Ingram, and deLeon 2014, 107). The mix of benefits and burdens in a policy design is typically treated as the dependent variable in SCF analyses of policy-making, so that the dependent variable is not just policy change, but policy design.

To explain policy designs, the SCF focuses on two independent variables: (1) the political power of the target group(s) affected by a policy, and (2) the social construction of the target group(s) affected by a policy (Pierce et al. 2014, 5). The political power of target groups is understood mostly as the "first face" of political power, which is the capacity to influence policy-makers. In more concrete terms, this can be understood as the size of a target group, its financial resources, its organization, its electoral influence, and its connectedness with policy elites (Schneider and Ingram 1997, 108). While power is a key variable in SCF explanations of policy-making, in practice, its operationalization and measurement are often neglected in SCF applications. The second independent variable is the social construction of target groups, the popular images or stereotypes of groups as deserving or undeserving of state assistance. Deserving groups are regarded positively as having "earned" the assignment of policy benefits and the avoidance of policy burdens, while undeserving groups are regarded negatively as having "earned" the assignment of policy burdens and the denial of policy benefits (106–7). As alluded to earlier, social constructions are found in the realm of political rhetoric, and SCF scholars often go to great lengths to operationalize and measure these constructions.

The intersection of political power and social construction creates a two-dimensional space in which four distinct types of target groups can be identified, as shown in Figure 5.1, with different mixes of policy benefits and burdens associated with each type. Advantaged groups are those with a high level of political power and a positive social construction, so they typically receive plenty of policy benefits and few policy burdens. Contenders are groups with lots of political power but a negative social construction. They also receive more policy benefits than burdens, but the benefits are often hidden from public view so as not to inflame public opposition, and the burdens are usually more superficial than real so as not to trigger backlash from these powerful groups. Dependents are those with little political power but a positive social construction, and these groups often receive benefits that are "heavy on rhetoric and low on funding," since policy-makers want to be seen helping them, but the groups lack political power to force policy-makers to follow through on their commitments. The final group, with low political power and a negative social construction, are the deviants, who are typically inflicted with all manner of policy burdens. Punishing deviants is an easy political score for politicians, who can take advantage of negative public stereotypes against groups who lack the political power to fight back effectively (Schneider, Ingram, and deLeon 2014, 110–13).

Thus, in the SCF, different types of target groups are associated with different policy designs, and this provides the basis for the SCF policy change hypothesis (H_1):

H_1: Types and patterns of policy change vary depending on the social construction and power of target groups (Schneider, Ingram, and deLeon 2014, 12).

Figure 5.1. Typology of target groups

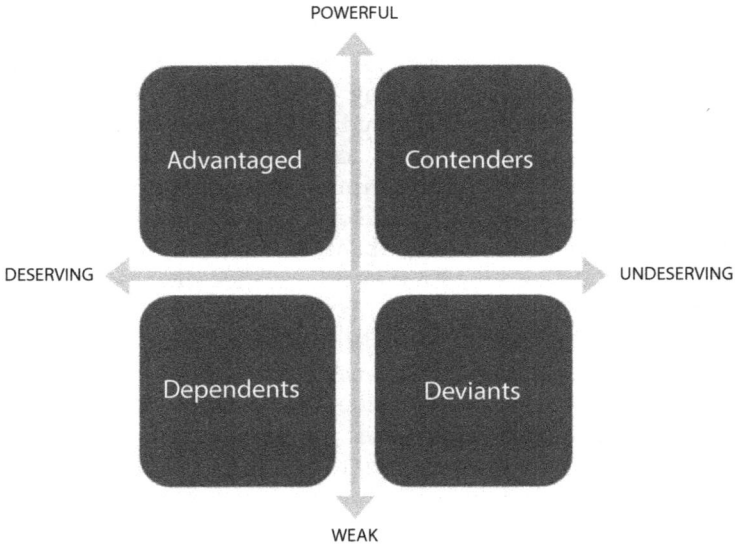

The SCF makes further claims about patterns of policy change over time, particularly with respect to policy designs affecting advantaged and deviant target groups. It posits that policies have "feed forward effects" that can politically empower or disempower the target groups they effect (116–17). Advantaged groups receive many policy benefits and few burdens, and policies tend to empower them so that they can effectively defend their policy benefits – and secure even more benefits – over time. Conversely, deviant groups receive so many burdens and so few benefits that they are disempowered in the policy process, making it likely that they will continue receiving burdens over time. In short, policies affecting advantaged and deviant groups tend to be self-reinforcing and path dependent so that advantaged groups tend to stay advantaged and deviant groups tend to stay deviant (129–30). Because the mixes of policy benefits and burdens assigned to contender and dependent groups are more varied, this sort of path dependency is not as prevalent in policies affecting these target groups.[3]

Six applications of the SCF are found in the Canadian public policy literature. The studies yield mixed results regarding the framework's capacity to explain Canadian policy-making. All of the applications are in the general realm of social policy. They include assisted reproduction policy (Montpetit, Rothmayr, and Varone 2005), poverty policy (Mondou and Montpetit 2010), midwifery policy (Marier, Paterson, and Angus 2014), immigration policy (Garon 2015), youth criminal justice policy (Heinmiller, Hennigar, and Kopec 2017), and the regulation of naturopathic medicine (Snow 2019). In this body of literature, two studies found the SCF adept at explaining Canadian policy-making (Montpetit, Rothmayr, and Varone 2005; Marier, Paterson, and Angus 2014), two studies found the framework adept in some cases but not others (Mondou and Montpetit 2010; Heinmiller, Hennigar, and Kopec 2017), and two studies found the framework's expectations to be inconsistent with actual policy outcomes (Snow 2019; Garon 2015), though the latter study may be subject to a contrary interpretation.[4] Overall, the jury is still out on the utility of the SCF in explaining Canadian policy-making, particularly on the question of the prevalence of degenerative politics in Canada, which is crucial to the SCF's applicability.

There is a considerable degree of methodological diversity in the Canadian SCF literature, especially given its relatively small size. Most of this diversity has to do with how social constructions are operationalized. Some studies take an illustrative, anecdotal approach (Marier, Paterson, and Angus 2014; Garon 2015), while others are more systematic, relying on public opinion data (Montpetit, Rothmayr, and Varone 2005) or content analyses of primary sources (Mondou and Montpetit 2010; Heinmiller, Hennigar, and Kopec 2017; Snow 2019). To obtain valid and reliable data on social constructions, the systematic approaches are preferable, and this chapter endeavours to undertake such an approach through a qualitative content analysis of Hansard debates about gun control legislation. Similar to the study conducted by Heinmiller, Hennigar, and Kopec (2017), Hansard transcripts are utilized because they allow direct observation of policy elites' rhetoric and their social constructions of target groups. This is an appropriate data source given the SCF assumption that it is social constructions by policy elites that matter most in policy development.

The content analysis identified MPs' assertions about various target groups (i.e., their target group assertions) and systematically coded those assertions to determine two things. First, the most prevalent target groups in each policy episode were identified inductively based on the target groups that MPs most often referenced in the House debates. These groups are identified in Table 5.1. Second, the social constructions of the most prevalent target groups, based on the proportion of assertions constructing each group as either deserving or undeserving, were also identified. As shown in Table 5.2, a clear social construction is said to exist if 80 per cent or more of the assertions construct a group as either deserving or undeserving. If, however, the assertions are less than 80 per cent consistent, the construction of that group is taken as contested, and there is no clear social construction. This high threshold is used in order to provide a clear and rigorous standard for identifying generally accepted social constructions. Much more detail on the content analysis research design is provided in the methodological appendix to this chapter, for those who are interested.

The second SCF independent variable – power – is operationalized using five standard measures of the "first face" of political power: target group size, wealth, organization, electoral influence, and connectedness with policy-makers (Schneider and Ingram 1997, 108). Table 5.3 provides summaries of these measures for the most prevalent target groups, with checkmarks (✓) indicating a high level of power and crosses (✗) indicating a low level of power on each measure. Target groups that score high on all measures are taken as powerful, while target groups that score high on one (or none) of the measures are considered as lacking power, with moderate levels of power between these two extremes. Measures were taken and tables were constructed for each policy episode, but the results did not vary across episodes, so the results in Table 5.3 summarize the results for all three policy episodes.

The dependent variable, policy design, is operationalized through analyses of policy documents to determine how burdensome/beneficial each policy was to the most prevalent target groups. Specifically, the analysis relied on the legislative summaries, produced by analysts in the Parliamentary Information and Research Service of the Library of Parliament, which translate hundreds of pages of arcane legislation into succinct descriptions of policy design. These policy designs were then compared against a standard of "burdensomeness" to determine how burdensome they were to target groups. The standard used was the extent to which policy designs inhibited the private ownership and use of firearms. The most burdensome policy possible would ban private gun ownership and confiscate all private weapons, while the least burdensome policy possible would have no regulatory controls at all on private ownership and use of weapons. Actual policy designs were placed on this ideal typical spectrum to determine their substantive burdensomeness.

The rest of this chapter investigates H_1 with respect to Canadian firearms policy. It does so in three sections, starting with Bill C-17, then the *Firearms Act*, and, finally, the *Ending the Long-Gun Registry Act*. Each section contains an analysis of the prevalent social constructions in the policy debates, the political power of the relevant target groups, and the policy designs actually produced. Ultimately, the expectations of H_1

are tested against the empirical findings, allowing us to draw some conclusions about the SCF's capacity to explain Canadian firearms policy.

Bill C-17

As shown in Table 5.1, two target groups dominated the House debates on Bill C-17: safe firearms users and unsafe firearms users.

Safe firearms users were the most prevalent target group, accounting for 60 per cent of target group assertions in the C-17 debates. This target group includes those who typically rely on long guns and who use them for socially approved activities such as farming, hunting, collecting, or sport shooting. This is an eclectic group with considerable internal diversity, but safe firearms users of various stripes have tended to organize and mobilize together, through organizations such as the National Firearms Association and the Canadian Shooting Sports Association. Through these organizations, they have sought common treatment by government, and many policy elites recognize and respond to them, making them a familiar target group in the firearms policy debates.

Unsafe firearms users were the second most prevalent group, being the subject of 31 per cent of target group assertions. This group includes violent criminals, gun smugglers, the mentally ill, and others. It is often associated with handguns, sawed-off shotguns, or military-style assault weapons rather than long guns. This parsing of firearms users into safe and unsafe target groups was prevalent in all of the firearms policy episodes analysed in this study and is a social construction that safe firearms users themselves labour to perpetuate. The Canadian Firearms Association, for example, emphasizes in its mission statement that it "exists to promote, support and protect all *safe* firearms activities" (Canadian Firearms Association 2017, 2, emphasis added).

Victims of firearms violence and those vulnerable to victimization were visible in the Bill C-17 debates, but they ranked far behind the safe and unsafe firearms users in overall prevalence, constituting only 5 per cent of target group assertions. This finding is somewhat surprising given that the Bill C-17 process, and the Bill C-80 process before it, were initiated by a public outcry over the Montreal Massacre, but it is a consistent finding across all policy episodes: victims are a mentioned target group but are a far less prevalent subject in policy debates than are firearms users.

Table 5.2 shows that safe firearms users were constructed as undeserving in 80 per cent of MPs' assertions about them. While the

Table 5.1. Prevalence (%) of target groups in House debates on gun control (percentage of total target group assertions)

House debates	Safe firearms users	Unsafe firearms users	Victims	Indigenous peoples	Law enforcement	Taxpayers	Business	Provinces
Bill C-17 (1991)	60	31	5	–	3	1	–	–
Firearms Act (1995)	49	33	6	5	4	1	1	–
Ending the Long-Gun Registry Act (2012)	45	16	12	–	14	–	–	8

construction was not unanimous, and there was some variance across the political parties, the overall tendency to construct safe firearms users in negative terms is clear.

In terms of political power, Table 5.3 shows that safe firearms users had all of the characteristics of a politically powerful target group. In 1992, it was estimated that about 26 per cent of Canadian households had at least one firearm, making safe firearms users a very large social group and giving them the power that comes with size (van Dijk, van Kesteren, and Smit 2007, 279). This group was well-organized politically through the National Firearms Association, which was well-resourced for political action from members' dues and donations. Moreover, safe firearms users were concentrated in rural, northern, and western ridings, giving them electoral influence that they could (threaten to) use to unseat candidates who supported gun control. Safe firearms users also had strong connections with the governing PC party, so much so that they had succeeded in splitting the PC caucus on Bill C-80 the year before. Altogether, given their large size, wealth, organization, electoral influence, and connectedness with policy-makers, safe firearms users should be regarded as having a high level of political power. With this political power, and their prevailing social construction as an undeserving group, safe firearms users fit the mould of a contender target group.

In contrast, unsafe firearms users can be categorized as deviants with an undeserving social construction and a low level of political power. As shown in Table 5.2, the undeserving social construction of unsafe firearms users was nearly unanimous: 97 per cent of the

Table 5.2. Social construction of prevalent target groups in House debates on gun control (percentage of deserving assertions without brackets; undeserving assertions within brackets)

House debates	Safe firearms users	Unsafe firearms users
Bill C-17 (1991)	20 (80) = Undeserving construction	3 (97) = Undeserving construction
Firearms Act (1995)	58 (32) = Contested construction	9 (91) = Undeserving construction
Ending the Long-Gun Registry Act (2012)	55 (35) = Contested construction	Not a prevalent target group

Table 5.3. Political power of prevalent target groups in gun control

Prevalent target groups	Size	Wealth	Organization	Electoral influence	Connectedness with policy-makers	Overall power
Safe firearms users	✓	✓	✓	✓	✓	High
Unsafe firearms users	✓	✗	✗	✗	✗	Low

assertions made by MPs about unsafe firearms users characterized them as undeserving, a result that was consistent across party lines. With respect to political power, unsafe firearms users have almost none of the attributes of a powerful group. If you could count all firearms-related criminals in Canada – both in and out of prison – they would constitute a sizeable group. However, they have limited wealth, they have little collective identity, and they have no political organization, apart from some prisoners' rights groups, which were not involved in the gun control debates. Unsafe firearms users are also spread out across the country, so they have little electoral influence in individual ridings, and they have no close connections to elites in any political party. In sum, unsafe firearms users have very little political power, which, in combination with their undeserving social construction, makes them a deviant target group in SCF terms.

Given the categorization of safe firearms users as contenders and unsafe firearms users as deviants, some policy design predictions can be made about Bill C-17 based on H_1. The hypothesis predicts that safe firearms users, being contenders, will receive policy burdens that are visible but largely superficial and/or that they will receive policy benefits that are substantial but hidden from public view. The SCF predicts that unsafe firearms users, being deviants, will be targeted with visible, substantial policy burdens and will receive no policy benefits. So, how well does H_1 predict the design of Bill C-17?

For safe firearms users, the design of Bill C-17 was consistent with SCF expectations. As described in chapter 2, Bill C-17 added a number of new regulatory controls on gun ownership, but none of those controls fundamentally challenged private gun ownership for safe users. Most of the new regulatory controls related to the acquisition and storage of firearms. The FAC process was strengthened by adding a mandatory training course, a detailed questionnaire, a reference check, and a twenty-eight-day waiting period for the issuance of gun permits. Gun owners were also required to store firearms and ammunition separately, to store firearms in an inoperable condition, and to hide and lock guns during transport (Dupuis, Kirkby, and MacKay 2011, 1). All of these regulatory controls are visible policy burdens that are inconvenient for safe firearms users, but they do not challenge private gun ownership and thus are consistent with safe firearms users' status as contenders. Moreover, safe firearms users received a substantive but largely invisible policy benefit in Bill C-17. The legislation contained a provision stating that any future regulations banning some classes of weapons or ammunition could be blocked by twenty MPs or 15 senators, thus forcing a parliamentary vote on the regulations (Brown 2012, 211). Given the safe firearms users' considerable political power, this amounted to a substantive procedural benefit for them, albeit a deferred benefit, obscured from public view. This too is consistent with safe firearms users' status as contenders, supporting H_1.

Unsafe firearms users, as deviants, are targeted with policy burdens in Bill C-17, and their ownership of firearms is challenged in fundamental ways. Unsafe users are closely associated with such weapons as handguns, sawed-off shotguns, and military-style assault weapons. Bill C-17 added about two hundred models of such weaponry to the prohibited and restricted weapons lists, thus banning or controlling their ownership. Furthermore, all of the regulatory controls on the acquisition of firearms created by the legislation were designed to "weed out" unsafe firearms users and prevent them from obtaining guns, so these controls were intended to be more burdensome on unsafe users than on safe users. All of this is consistent with H_1, which predicts that deviants will be targeted with substantive policy burdens, in this case the denial of firearms ownership.

Overall, H_1 is strongly supported in the case of Bill C-17. Safe firearms users (as contenders) and unsafe firearms users (as deviants) received the types of policy benefits/burdens predicted by the SCF. We now turn our attention to the development of the *Firearms Act* to determine whether the SCF successfully explains this case, as well.

The Firearms Act

The two most prevalent target groups in the *Firearms Act* House debates were safe and unsafe firearms users respectively. As shown in Table 5.1, safe firearms users were the subject of 49 per cent of target group assertions made by MPs in the debates, while unsafe firearms users were the subject of 33 per cent of target group assertions. Five other target groups were mentioned in the debates – victims (6% of assertions), Indigenous peoples (5%), law enforcement (4%), businesses (1%), and taxpayers (1%) – but none of them were nearly as prevalent as safe and unsafe firearms users. So, apart from the greater diversity of target groups mentioned in the debates, the results are similar to those found in the Bill C-17 debates, in which safe and unsafe firearms users were overwhelmingly the focus of discussion.

However, the social construction of the most prevalent target group, safe firearms users, was significantly different in the *Firearms Act* debates compared to the Bill C-17 debates. Whereas safe firearms users were constructed as undeserving in 80 per cent of assertions in the Bill C-17 debates, this number dropped to only 32 per cent in the *Firearms Act* debates. This indicates a remarkable improvement in safe firearms users' social construction from Bill C-17 to the *Firearms Act*, a period of barely four years. They went from having an undeserving social construction in 1991 to a contested social construction, leaning toward deserving, in 1995.

Safe firearms users remained a powerful group during the development of the *Firearms Act*; indeed, the factors underpinning their political power changed in only one substantial way. While they continued to be a large, well-organized, well-financed, and electorally influential group, the political party with which they had long been allied, the PCs, had been decimated in the 1993 election, which brought the Liberal Party to power. Nevertheless, they maintained some influence over policy-makers, for some rural, northern, and western Liberal MPs had close connections to gun advocacy groups and staunchly opposed further gun control within the Liberal caucus. The opposition Reform Party also took up opposition to further gun controls, ensuring that safe firearms users still had a voice in the House. Thus, safe firearms users remained a powerful group, though not as powerful as they had been during the previous PC government.

With a contested social construction and a high level of political power, safe firearms users can be categorized as somewhere between an advantaged and a contender group in the development of the *Firearms Act*. This ambiguity is unfortunate, but without a generally accepted social construction, it is impossible to choose between the advantaged and contender categories. The best that can be done is to examine the design of the *Firearms Act* to determine whether its mix of benefits and burdens matches the expectations of either of these target group types, which we will do shortly.

Unsafe firearms users were the other prevalent target group in the development of the *Firearms Act*, and all evidence indicates that they remained a deviant group. Over 90 per cent of assertions about unsafe firearms users constructed them as undeserving, which is a generally accepted, negative social construction. Relative to the Bill C-17 debates, the construction of unsafe firearms users improved slightly; this was most notable among BQ MPs, who emphasized the need to rehabilitate rather than punish violent criminals. Also notable was the position of Reform MPs in these debates: the Reform Party, despite being the third party in the House, made more assertions about unsafe users than any other party, and 100 per cent of these assertions were negative. Thus, there was some polarization between the opposition parties, both of them relatively new to Parliament, when it came to unsafe firearms users, but the overall construction of unsafe users was still resoundingly negative. In terms of political power, the position of unsafe firearms users did not change from 1991 to 1995; they remained a politically powerless group. The combination of an undeserving social construction and almost no political power made unsafe firearms users a deviant target group in 1995, just as they had been in 1991.

The categorization of safe firearms users as either advantaged or dependent, and unsafe firearms users as deviant, leads to a number of policy design predictions based on H_1. First, we would expect the *Firearms Act* to assign safe firearms users either substantial and visible policy benefits (if they are advantaged), or insubstantial and visible policy burdens (if they are contenders). Second, we would expect unsafe firearms users, as deviants, to be targeted with substantial and visible policy burdens.

Analysis of the design of the *Firearms Act* reveals that H_1 is not supported with respect to safe firearms users. The *Firearms Act* assigned a number of visible and substantial policy burdens on safe firearms users that were not in keeping with their status as either an advantaged or a contender target group. As described in chapter 2, new licensing systems were introduced for the acquisition and possession of all guns and ammunition, and all licences had to be renewed every five years. This replaced the less demanding FAC system, which entailed a one-time permit pertaining only to firearms acquisition. Universal firearms registration was also introduced, and a national firearms registry was created to allow authorities to track all firearms in Canada. Possession of an unregistered gun was made a criminal offence, and police were given increased powers to enter and search premises that had ten or more registered guns (Bartlett 1995). Altogether, the *Firearms Act* significantly increased regulatory controls on private gun ownership, made no efforts to disguise these controls, and applied these controls to all firearms users, safe and unsafe alike. These types of policy burdens are not predicted for advantaged or contender groups, so H_1 cannot explain the treatment of safe firearms users in the *Firearms Act*.

However, H_1 is supported with respect to unsafe firearms users. The *Firearms Act* prohibited additional classes of weapons that are typically associated with criminal activity, such as assault weapons with barrels 105 mm or less in length and .25 and .31 calibre handguns. Importantly, the new legislation also amended Part III of the *Criminal Code* to introduce stiffer penalties for those convicted of serious gun crimes (Bartlett 1995). These measures, which were designed to inhibit and disincentivize gun ownership and use by unsafe firearms users, constitute visible and substantial policy burdens for this target group. Since this is the sort of treatment expected for deviant groups, H_1 is supported in this instance.

It is also interesting that during the development of the *Firearms Act*, the Reform Party made a motion to split the bill into two parts, one part dealing with tougher sentences for gun crimes, which Reform would support, and one part dealing with the universal gun registry, which Reform would oppose (Parliament of Canada 1995a, 10363). This was a clear effort by Reform to use the legislative process to subdivide the bill between safe and unsafe firearms users, so that it could prevent the assignment of policy burdens to the former and heap further policy burdens on the latter. Take, for example, the comments of Reform MP John Duncan, who spoke in support of the motion to split Bill C-68: "*Anyone can see that splitting the bill will focus the wrath where it should be, at those individuals who use firearms in the commission of crimes and who continue to make our streets unsafe for law-abiding citizens*" (Parliament of Canada 1995b, 11156).

Even though the effort to split the bill failed, this attempt to isolate a deviant target group and subject it to additional policy burdens is consistent with SCF expectations of policy-making in degenerative contexts.

In sum, H_1 is only partly successful in explaining the design of the *Firearms Act*: it explains the policy burdens received by unsafe firearms users but does not explain the policy burdens received by safe firearms users. The hypothesis's failure with respect to safe firearms users is problematic in a number of ways. Safe firearms users were the most prevalent target group in the *Firearms Act* debates, and the bulk of the provisions in the legislation pertain to them, so the inability to explain these aspects of the policy is a significant explanatory shortcoming. Moreover, we were unable to categorize safe firearms users in the SCF typology with much specificity – that is, they could have been advantaged or contenders – with the consequence that policy design outcomes associated with either target type would have offered some support to H_1. In other words, the SCF hypothesis with respect to safe firearms users lacked specificity, so a greater number of policy design outcomes would have satisfied it, making it a relatively weak and easily supported hypothesis. Yet the hypothesis was still unsupported and did not make it over this relatively low bar.

The *Ending the Long-Gun Registry Act*

As with the House debates in the previous two policy episodes, the most prevalent target group in the *Ending the Long-Gun Registry Act* debates was safe firearms users. Table 5.1 shows that this group was the subject of 45 per cent of the target group assertions made during the debates. The remaining target group assertions were spread out among four other groups, including unsafe firearms users (16%), law enforcement (14%), victims (12%), and the provinces (8%). In contrast to the Bill C-17 and *Firearms Act* debates, unsafe firearms users did not feature prominently in the *Ending the Long-Gun Registry Act* debates. This finding is likely explained by the fact that the Conservatives had dealt with unsafe firearms users in other legislation, such as the *Safe Streets and Communities Act*, which introduced mandatory minimum sentences for many gun crimes (Barnett et al. 2011). Our analysis here is limited to the *Ending the Long-Gun Registry Act*, which had only one prevalent target group when it was being developed – safe firearms users – so H_1 will be tested according to the policy outcomes for this single target group.

The content analysis results in Table 5.2 show that the social construction of safe firearms users in 2012 had changed little from their social construction in 1995. In the 2012 debates, 35 per cent of the assertions about safe firearms users constructed them as undeserving, compared to 32 per cent in the 1995 debates. Thus, the construction of safe users was marginally more negative in 2012 than in 1995, and there was no significant shift in their construction. Nor was there a unanimous or generally accepted social construction of safe firearms users. Their construction was contested but leaning toward deserving, just as it had been in 1995.

Also, safe firearms users continued to be a very powerful target group, even more powerful than they had been in the previous two policy episodes. In 2012, safe firearms users were still a large, well-organized, well-resourced, and electorally influential group, as they had been in the past. Besides that, they enjoyed the advantage of being closely connected with policy elites within the governing Conservative Party. For example, Conservative MP Garry Breitkreuz, who was the party's point-person on firearms issues, also served on the board of directors of the Canadian Shooting Sports Association (Somerset 2016). Moreover, unlike in the 1991 and 1995 policy episodes, the Conservative caucus was unified in its opposition to stringent gun control. This meant that safe firearms users had access to governing elites and that most of these elites shared their views, giving safe users more influence on firearms policy than they had enjoyed in decades.

With their considerable power and contested social construction, safe firearms users can be categorized in SCF terms as somewhere between advantaged and contenders. Since their construction is contested, it is impossible to categorize them conclusively in either one of these groups, so we must consider the policy designs associated with both groups. The SCF predicts that if safe firearms users are advantaged, they should receive substantial policy benefits, whereas if they are contenders, they should be assigned substantial, concealed policy benefits and/or insubstantial, unconcealed policy burdens.

Not surprisingly, the design of the *Ending the Long-Gun Registry Act* reduced the policy burdens assigned to safe firearms users, generally in keeping with their advantaged/contender status. The Act did away with the requirement to register non-restricted firearms while maintaining the registration requirement for weapons in the restricted and prohibited classes, as described in chapter 2 (Dupuis, Kirkby, and MacKay 2011, 10). This was clearly an attempt to reduce burdens on safe firearms users, who are associated with long guns in the non-restricted class, while maintaining burdens on unsafe firearms users, who are associated with handguns and military-style assault weapons in the restricted and prohibited classes. It is important to note, however, that the *Ending the Long-Gun Registry Act* maintained some of the regulatory burdens on safe firearms users introduced in the *Firearms Act*. Instead of returning to the pre–*Firearms* Act situation, in which only firearms acquisition was licensed, the new legislation continued the *Firearms Act* requirement that all firearms possession, including non-restricted firearms possession, be licensed (Dupuis, Kirkby, and MacKay 2011, 10–11). Thus, safe firearms users had their policy burdens reduced in the *Ending the Long-Gun Registry Act*, but the private ownership of firearms was still regulated, and they were not relieved of policy burdens entirely. This sort of policy design is inconsistent with what is expected for an advantaged group, but it is somewhat consistent with what is expected for a contender group – that is, safe firearms users have been burdened, but not overly burdened, by the *Ending the Long-Gun Registry Act*.

In the case of the *Ending the Long-Gun Registry Act*, there is some evidence in support of H_1, but the hypothesis itself is not particularly strong. In this policy episode, the first difficulty was in trying to categorize the single prevalent target group – safe firearms users, for whom there was no generally accepted social construction. Using H_1, this resulted in a broad policy design prediction incorporating two target group types rather than a precise prediction based on one target group type. Nevertheless, the design of the *Ending the Long-Gun Registry Act* is in accordance with what would be expected of a contender group, which was one of the target group types identified in the hypothesis, so there is some evidence in support of it. This provides some confidence in the SCF hypothesis, but such confidence is qualified by the vagueness of the hypothesis itself.

Discussion

Based on the findings in this chapter, H_1 does well in explaining some firearms policy outcomes but not others. In this concluding section, we identify what the SCF does and does not explain well in the gun control case, and we probe some of the potential reasons for this uneven performance.

Across all policy episodes, the SCF did well in explaining the policy outcomes for unsafe firearms users. The evidence showed unequivocally that unsafe firearms users were a deviant target group in 1991 and 1995. Limited evidence suggests that they were also a deviant group in 2012, but they were not a prevalent target group in that policy episode. The policy design outcomes for unsafe firearms users in 1991 and 1995 were consistent with those predicted by the SCF hypothesis: in both instances, they received visible and substantial policy burdens, as expected for a deviant group. The SCF also predicts that, over time, deviant groups become locked in a self-reinforcing (or path-dependent) process in which they receive increasing policy burdens as they become increasingly alienated and disempowered in political processes. There is some evidence to support this contention with respect to unsafe firearms users in Canada. From Bill C-17 to the *Firearms Act*, to the *Safe Streets and Communities Act*, the penalties for criminal firearms offences became increasingly severe, and the target group affected by these increasingly harsh penalties was powerless to stop it. Overall, just about all of the policy outcomes predicted for a deviant target group were evident for unsafe firearms users, so the SCF did very well in explaining this aspect of Canadian firearms policy.

The SCF also did well in explaining the policy outcomes for safe firearms users in Bill C-17 (1991). In this policy episode, safe firearms users could be clearly categorized as a contender target group. Moreover, the policy outcomes assigned to this contender group matched the expectations of the SCF: they received insubstantial and visible policy burdens, as well as substantial but obscure policy benefits. Given that H_1 was able to explain the policy outcomes for the only two prevalent target groups in the Bill C-17 policy debates – safe and unsafe firearms users – the SCF explanation of policy design was supported in this particular policy.

But the SCF did not fare nearly as well in explaining policy design outcomes for safe firearms users in the *Firearms Act* (1995) or the *Ending the Long-Gun Registry Act* (2012). These shortcomings are substantial because safe firearms users were the most prevalent target group in the debates on both of these policies, and regulatory measures affecting safe firearms users constituted the bulk of both policy designs. H_1's inability to explain these important policy outcomes suggests that the explanatory power of the hypothesis may be limited in some way(s), and it is worth considering what these limiting scope conditions might be.

One limiting scope condition that may explain the SCF hypothesis's uneven performance in the Canadian gun control case is the presence/absence of degenerative politics. In their 1997 book, Schneider and Ingram imply that the SCF is meant to explain policy-making in contexts characterized by degenerative politics, which they define as a "form of politics in which the social constructions of issues and target populations are strategically manipulated for political gain" (Schneider and Ingram 1997, 6). This could make the presence of degenerative politics an important scope condition for the SCF hypothesis, though – to our knowledge – it has yet to be explicitly identified as such. This scope condition could explain why the SCF hypothesis explained some firearms policy outcomes but not others. For example, degenerative politics may have been present in policy-making for unsafe firearms users in 1991 and 1995 and safe firearms users in 1991, so the SCF hypothesis performed as expected.

But degenerative politics may not have been present in policy-making for safe firearms users in 1995 and 2012, so the SCF hypothesis would not have application in these cases and did not perform as expected. This explanation would rescue the SCF hypothesis in the gun control case, but its veracity hinges on the ability to identify degenerative politics situations readily, and this comes with its own challenges.

The (limited) Canadian literature on degenerative politics suggests that it is not unusual for degenerative politics to exist in some Canadian policy-making contexts and not others. Mondou and Montpetit (2010), for example, found evidence of degenerative politics in Quebec income assistance policy but not in Newfoundland income assistance policy. Heinmiller, Hennigar, and Kopec (2017) examined federal youth criminal justice policy and found evidence of degenerative politics in policy-making for violent young offenders but not for non-violent young offenders. So it is possible that some firearms policy-making situations may have been degenerative and others may not have been.

It is also possible to speculate on why some firearms policy-making situations may have been degenerative while others were not. For instance, policy-making for unsafe firearms users, in all policy episodes, may have been degenerative because this was a clearly deviant target group that provided politicians with an easy opportunity to score political points by heaping policy burdens on an undeserving group with little political power to resist or retaliate. Policy-making for safe firearms users in 1991 may also have been degenerative because it happened in the wake of the Montreal Massacre and all firearms users seemed, for a time, to be a deserving target for increased policy burdens. Then, as memories of the massacre faded in the 1995 and 2012 policy episodes, it is possible that policy-making for safe firearms users became non-degenerative. This claim is supported by the fact that safe firearms users had no clear social construction in either of these policy episodes, perhaps because politicians were not seeking to manipulate their social construction for political gain in a degenerative manner. If all of these claims are accurate – that policy-making for unsafe firearms users in 1991 and 1995 and for safe firearms in 1991 was degenerative and that policy-making for safe firearms users in 1995 and 2012 was not degenerative – this squares the SCF hypothesis with the empirical evidence in the Canadian gun control case. However, these claims are speculative and pinpoint one of the key challenges in using SCF theory: readily identifying situations of degenerative politics.

If SCF theory applies only in degenerative politics contexts, then identifying degenerative politics is crucial to the theory's utility. The definition of degenerative politics, as provided above, is clear and straightforward, but an equally clear and straightforward operationalization of degenerative politics has yet to emerge. Many studies have investigated the presence of degenerative politics, but most of these have relied on the same data that are used to investigate the SCF hypothesis, running the risk that both the scope condition and the hypothesis are observations of the same phenomenon. One challenge for SCF theory may be to develop a valid and reliable way of identifying degenerative politics so that cases meeting this key scope condition can be recognized. In the absence of this, we are left to speculate on when degenerative politics is and is not present, leaving us with little confidence in where the theory does and does not apply.

This represents an important frontier in SCF research and theoretical development. The Canadian SCF literature, including this study, suggests that degenerative politics is present in some cases of Canadian policy-making and that SCF theory has some utility in explaining policy outcomes in these cases. Yet the extent of degenerative politics in Canada remains unclear, as does the extent of SCF's explanatory reach, leaving important work to be done by Canadian SCF scholars.

APPENDIX: USING QUALITATIVE CONTENT ANALYSIS TO MEASURE SOCIAL CONSTRUCTIONS

Social constructions, one of two independent variables in the SCF, are best measured by analysing primary source materials that capture citizens' or policy elites' perceptions and descriptions of target groups. For example, Montpetit, Rothmayr, and Varone (2005) captured citizens' perceptions through surveys, Mondou and Montpetit (2010) examined policy elites' perceptions through an analysis of policy action plans, and Heinmiller, Hennigar, and Kopec (2017) captured policy elites' perceptions through an analysis of Hansard transcripts. The main reason for relying on primary sources is to measure social constructions of target groups by policy elites as directly as possible. In this chapter, Hansard transcripts were used as the data source for policy elites' social constructions. These transcripts were a good source because they captured – verbatim – the justifications that policy elites (i.e., MPs) used in support of various gun control measures, including justifications based on how they believed that various target groups should or should not be treated by government. Moreover, these justifications were explicit and public, capturing how policy elites may have exploited social constructions for their own political gain, as envisioned by the SCF. For our purposes, the English-language Hansard was used, which contained translations of other languages spoken in the debates, including French and Inuktitut.

To analyse the social constructions contained in the Hansard transcripts, a manageable sample of this material was needed. A sample was constructed using relevance sampling; that is, material was selected based on its relevance to the variable being measured (Krippendorf 2013, 120–1). The sample was limited to the House debates on bills C-17 (1992), C-68 (1995), and C-19 (2011), excluding Senate debates, since, in Canadian government, elected MPs better fit the definition of policy elites than do unelected senators. Relevance sampling was conducted to identify "target group assertions" within the House debates through keyword searches. A "target group assertion" is defined as an argument made by a policy elite about how a particular target group should (or should not) be treated by government. The debate transcripts from all three bills were converted to Microsoft Word files, and Word's Find function was used to search for five keywords that indicated an assertion (of some sort) in the text: "should," "ought," "must," "need," and "ensure." These searches yielded more than 2,000 hits, and each hit was reviewed to determine whether it met the definition of a target group assertion. If it met the definition, it was highlighted, given a unique identifier, and included in the sample; if it did not meet the definition, it was ignored and excluded. This procedure was undertaken by one coder, and verified by a second coder; ultimately, 844 potential target group assertions were identified in the debates.

The procedure did not identify all target group assertions in the transcripts, but it identified a large proportion of them. A control test was undertaken in which the first fifty pages of the 2011 transcripts were closely read and all possible target group assertions were identified. The test revealed that our procedure captured 57 per cent of all target group assertions and showed no systematic sampling biases based on political party, gender, or language originally spoken. Therefore, we concluded that our procedure captured a very large sample of target group assertions and was identifying them *as if* random, even though our procedure was not genuinely random. This gave us considerable confidence that the sample of target group assertions we identified was representative of all target group assertions in the Hansard debates.

To analyse the sample systematically, a qualitative content analysis was undertaken using "target group assertions" as the coding unit. Each target group assertion has three defining elements: (1) an identifiable target group, (2) a proposed policy benefit or burden for that group, and (3) an expression of support or opposition for the target group benefit/burden pairing. Textually, target group assertions may be as short as a phrase or as long as several paragraphs, making it a thematic coding unit rather than a mechanical coding unit (Schreier 2012).

To code the identified target group assertions, a three-level coding frame was developed, each level corresponding to one of the defining elements of target group assertions. The first level coded for types of target groups and had ten categories: safe firearms users, unsafe firearms users, victimized and vulnerable people, law enforcement, Indigenous peoples, provinces, businesses, taxpayers, other, and unclear. These categories had been inductively developed through a close reading of the data and a process of subsumption (Schreier 2012). The second level of the coding frame coded for policy benefits/burdens and had only four categories: policy benefit, policy burden, other, and unclear. These categories had been deductively derived from SCF theory but were inductively fleshed out as lists of example benefits and burdens were developed through a close reading of the data. Finally, the third level coded for support/opposition for a target group benefit/burden pairing. This level was deductively derived and included four categories: support, oppose, neutral, and unclear. The entire coding frame was subjected to a round of practice coding, which involved coding the first forty target group assertions from each of the three debates. The coding frame was then revised and improved based on these results.

The coding procedure itself involved two coders working independently but using the same coding guide. The coders reviewed the highlighted and numbered target group assertions in the Word files and recorded their coding decisions on an Excel spreadsheet. The coders' results were then compared to identify coding discrepancies and to measure inter-coder reliability. The coefficient of agreement between the two coders was 81 per cent, indicating an acceptable level of inter-coder reliability. The coders then reviewed and discussed each coding discrepancy in an effort to determine the correct coding decision and increase the amount of reliable data in the dataset. Whenever agreement could not be reached, the disputed coding decision was coded as unclear. This process ultimately produced a single dataset of coding decisions based on the agreement of two trained coders.

The dataset was then analysed in three steps to determine the prevalent social constructions in each debate.

First, the dataset was "cleaned" to remove any coding units that were coded as "other" or "unclear," since these coding units contained no useful information for our analysis. After the cleaning, 658 coding units remained in the dataset.

Second, the various combinations of benefits/burdens and support/opposition were dichotomized as either deserving or undeserving social constructions, in the following manners:

- benefits + support = deserving
- burdens + opposition = deserving

- benefits + opposition = undeserving
- burdens + support = undeserving

Third, using the newly created social constructions data, frequency tables were created for each debate. These tables, shown Tables 5.4, 5.5, and 5.6, tabulated the most frequently mentioned target groups as well as the proportions of assertions constructing each group as deserving or undeserving. Deserving constructions are shown without brackets; undeserving constructions are shown within brackets. These frequency tables provided the data for Tables 5.1 and 5.2, which appear in the chapter.

Table 5.4. Social constructions in the Bill C-17 House debates (%)

Target groups	PCs	Liberals	NDP	BQ	Reform	Totals
Safe firearms users	40 (60) n = 20	12 (88) n = 26	27 (73) n = 11	0 (100) n = 7	0 (100) n = 5	20 (80) n = 69
Unsafe firearms users	0 (100%) n = 17	8 (92) n = 12	0 (100%) n = 6	0 (100%) n = 1		3 (97%) n = 36
Victims	100 (0) n = 2	100 (0) n = 3	100 (0) n = 1			100 (0) n = 6
Law enforcement	100 (0) n = 2	100 (0) n = 1				100 (0) n = 3
Taxpayers				100 (0) n = 1		100 (0) n = 1

Table 5.5. Social constructions in the *Firearms Act* House debates (%)

Target groups	Liberals	BQ	Reform	NDP	PCs	Totals
Safe firearms users	63 (27) n = 59	21 (79%) n = 24	100 (0) n = 44	100 (0) n = 1	100 (0) n = 2	68 (32) n = 130
Unsafe firearms users	4 (96) n = 28	54 (46) n = 13	0 (100) n = 45	0 (100) n = 3		9 (91) n = 89
Victims	92 (18) n = 13	100 (0) n = 2	100 (0) n = 1	100 (0) n = 1		94 (6) n = 17
Indigenous peoples	100 (0) n = 9	0 (100) n = 1	0 (100) n = 3		100 (0) n = 1	71 (29) n = 14
Law enforcement	100 (0) n = 2		89 (11) n = 9	100 (0) n = 1		92 (8) n = 12
Business	0 (100) n = 1	0 (100) n = 3				0 (100) n = 4
Taxpayers	0 (100) n = 1	100 (0) n = 1				50 (50) n = 2

Table 5.6. Social constructions in the *Ending the Long-Gun Registry Act* House debates (%)

Target groups	Conservatives	NDP	Liberals	BQ	Green	Totals
Safe firearms users	73 (27) n = 96	38 (62) n = 24	0 (100) n = 3		100 (0) n = 1	65 (35) n = 124
Unsafe firearms users	0 (100) n = 38	25 (75) n = 4	0 (100) n = 1	0 (100) n = 1		2 (98) n = 44
Law enforcement	100 (0) n = 10	100 (0) n = 23	100 (0) n = 5			100 (0) n = 38
Victims	100 (0) n = 7	100 (0) n = 18	100 (0) n = 6		100 (0) n = 1	100 (0) n = 32
Provinces	0 (100) n = 6	100 (0) n = 12	100 (0) n = 3		100 (0) n = 1	73 (27) n = 22
Indigenous peoples	100 (0) n = 1	100 (0) n = 4				100 (0) n = 5
Taxpayers	100 (0) n = 3		100 (0) n = 2			100 (0) n = 5
Business		0 (100) n = 3				0 (100) n = 3

6 Policy-Making as a Team Sport: The Advocacy Coalition Framework

Policy-making is rarely a solitary affair. Instead, it usually involves a large cross-section of social actors, including interest groups, social movements, journalists, scientists, public servants, political staffers, and elected politicians. Among these actors there is often a considerable diversity of perspectives and beliefs, creating an almost bewildering complexity of actors and motivations in policy development. So, how does one make sense of this complexity? The advocacy coalition framework (ACF) argues that the actors in policy development typically organize themselves into one or more advocacy coalitions – that is, teams of actors with similar policy beliefs and goals who are motivated to work together to see their beliefs enacted in government policy. Thus, policy-making can be understood as a contest between advocacy coalitions, which compete and sometimes cooperate in their efforts to influence policy decision-makers and shape public policy. Moreover, the fortunes of advocacy coalitions rise and fall with changing political, economic, and social circumstances in ways that open and close pathways for policy change. In this chapter we explore the development of Canadian firearms policy from an ACF perspective, investigating the presence of advocacy coalitions and testing the ACF hypotheses on major policy change.

The Advocacy Coalition Framework (ACF)

The ACF was developed, starting in the mid-1980s, by American political scientist Paul Sabatier (1986, 1988), later joined by another American political scientist, Hank Jenkins-Smith (Sabatier and Jenkins-Smith 1993). The ACF is a framework, and this framework has supported the development of three bodies of theory: a theory of the formation and maintenance of advocacy coalitions, a theory of policy-oriented learning, and a theory of major policy change. We focus in this chapter on investigating the theory of major policy change; however, we begin by describing the framework itself, so as to provide a fuller understanding of that theory. From the start, both the framework and the theory of major policy change have undergone several revisions as ACF scholars have responded to the growing body of empirical ACF research and have sought to expand the ACF's application in political systems beyond the US (Pierce, Petersen, and Hicks 2017, S14–S15). In this chapter, we utilize the current version of the framework and test the most recent ACF policy change hypotheses, dating to around 2007 (Sabatier and Weible 2007).

The unit of analysis in the ACF is the policy subsystem. The ACF assumes that policy subsystems are of central importance based on the sheer complexity of modern policy-making and the tendency of actors to specialize and concentrate their efforts on one (or a few) policy areas. The ACF further assumes that most policy development occurs within policy subsystems, so understanding the political dynamics of policy subsystems is essential to explaining policy change. Within each policy subsystem are the various actors, noted in the introduction to this chapter, who claim a stake in the policy area and who regularly participate in policy processes. The boundaries of any policy subsystem are defined by both a substantive focus and a geographic scope (Sabatier and Weible 2007, 193). In our case, the substantive focus is firearms regulation and the geographic scope is Canada, so our unit of analysis is the Canadian firearms policy subsystem. Some policy subsystems overlap with one another or are nested within one another, which can make their boundaries a bit fuzzy, and it is important to be aware of these complexities when undertaking ACF analyses.

The ACF assumes that actors are driven by their beliefs and by their desire to see their beliefs reflected in policy. The framework further assumes that actors' beliefs can be understood as operating at three levels of abstraction. At the deepest level are deep core beliefs, which are quite broad in scope, predominantly normative, and very slow to change in response to empirical contradiction. These beliefs are relevant across a broad range of policy subsystems and include such things as one's left/right ideological orientation. At the next-deepest level are policy core beliefs, which are intermediate in scope because they involve the application of deep core beliefs to a specific policy subsystem. In gun control, for instance, one's beliefs about the appropriate role of the state in regulating gun ownership and use would be important examples of policy core beliefs. Policy core beliefs are resistant to change "but are more likely to adjust in response to verification and refutation from new experience and information than deep core beliefs" (Weible, Sabatier, and McQueen 2009, 123). At the shallowest level are secondary beliefs, which are narrowest in scope and pertain to the details of various policy issues, such as preferred modes of policy implementation. Secondary beliefs are linked to policy core beliefs but are more empirically based and are thus more amenable to change (Sabatier and Weible 2007, 194–6).

Actor beliefs are important in the ACF because policy core beliefs, the mid-level beliefs described above, serve as rallying points for advocacy coalitions. Like-minded actors in policy subsystems often make common cause in pursuit of their policy goals simply because they are more effective working together than working in isolation. When a number of actors share a set of policy core beliefs and engage in a non-trivial degree of collective action, they form an advocacy coalition (196). The ACF hypothesizes – and research has largely confirmed – that advocacy coalitions tend to be relatively stable over time despite some turnovers in coalition membership, so that on most major controversies in a policy subsystem, there is a characteristic line-up of coalitions seeking to influence policy (Jenkins-Smith et al. 2014, 195). The number of advocacy coalitions in a policy subsystem ranges between one and five, with the exact number constituting an empirical question (Sabatier 1993). In the case of firearms regulation, our research found that there have been two advocacy coalitions in the Canadian firearms policy subsystem, a gun rights coalition and a gun control coalition, which have taken opposing positions on most firearms regulation issues since the early 1990s.

From an ACF perspective, policy development can best be understood as a contest between advocacy coalitions, such as that between the gun rights and gun control coalitions. Most policy subsystems have a dominant coalition – a "majority" coalition, in ACF terms – and one or more minority coalitions. Identifying the majority coalition and its policy-oriented beliefs is important in ACF research because the beliefs of the majority coalition have a strong influence on policy design. Moreover, if there is a power shift and a minority coalition suddenly becomes dominant, this can be a precursor of major policy change. The relative power of advocacy coalitions is usually evaluated with reference to six coalition resources: leadership, mobilizable troops, public opinion, information, financial resources, and formal legal authority to make policy decisions (Sabatier and Weible 2007, 201–4). Of these, Nohrstedt (2011, 480) found that "formal legal authority should enjoy unique status compared with other political resources because legislators are veto players whose agreement is needed for policy change to happen." Thus, the advocacy coalition with the most formal legal authority in a policy subsystem is likely to be the majority coalition, though the other resources can provide coalitions with substantial "soft" power that should not be overlooked (Heinmiller 2013, 2016).

In some circumstances, advocacy coalitions that normally compete with one another may negotiate and cooperate in an effort to achieve mutually acceptable policy goals. Sometimes this cooperation is facilitated by policy brokers. Policy brokers are actors who position themselves between competing advocacy coalitions, often attempting to bridge some of the differences between them. Policy brokers come in many different forms, but they usually have some credibility with all of the contending advocacy coalitions, can speak earnestly to all of them, and can serve as a conduit – and sometimes even a translator – between them (Ingold and Varone 2012). This can facilitate policy-oriented learning among coalitions and help coalitions reach negotiated agreements that can serve as the basis for policy change.

Policy subsystems are the unit of analysis in the ACF, but the framework recognizes that subsystems do not exist in isolation. Policy subsystems are affected by a variety of systemic and idiosyncratic forces, which fall into three groups: relatively stable parameters, external events, and long-term coalition opportunity structures (see Figure 6.1). The relatively stable parameters are features of the natural, social, and legal context that are relatively constant, such as the distribution of natural resources, fundamental sociocultural values, and a state's constitutional structure. External events refer to factors outside of policy subsystems that are more changeable than the relatively stable parameters but that can still have a significant impact on subsystems, such as changes in socio-economic conditions, changes in public opinion, changes in government, and policy decisions within other policy subsystems. Long-term coalition opportunity structures refer to "relatively enduring features of a polity that affect the resources and constraints of subsystem actors," such as policy decision rules, participation norms, and underlying social cleavages such as class, race, and gender (Sabatier and Weible 2007, 200). All three sets of factors are important because significant changes in any of them can strongly impact policy subsystems, creating the conditions for a major policy change.

The ACF has a distinctive conception of public policy that differentiates between major and minor policy change. In the ACF, policies are assumed to be interpretations of and reflections of policy-oriented beliefs. Just as policy-oriented beliefs have core and secondary aspects, so too do public policies. Core aspects of a policy have to do with its overall direction and goals, and a change in the core attributes of a policy is considered a major policy change. The secondary aspects of a

Figure 6.1. A diagram of the advocacy coalition framework

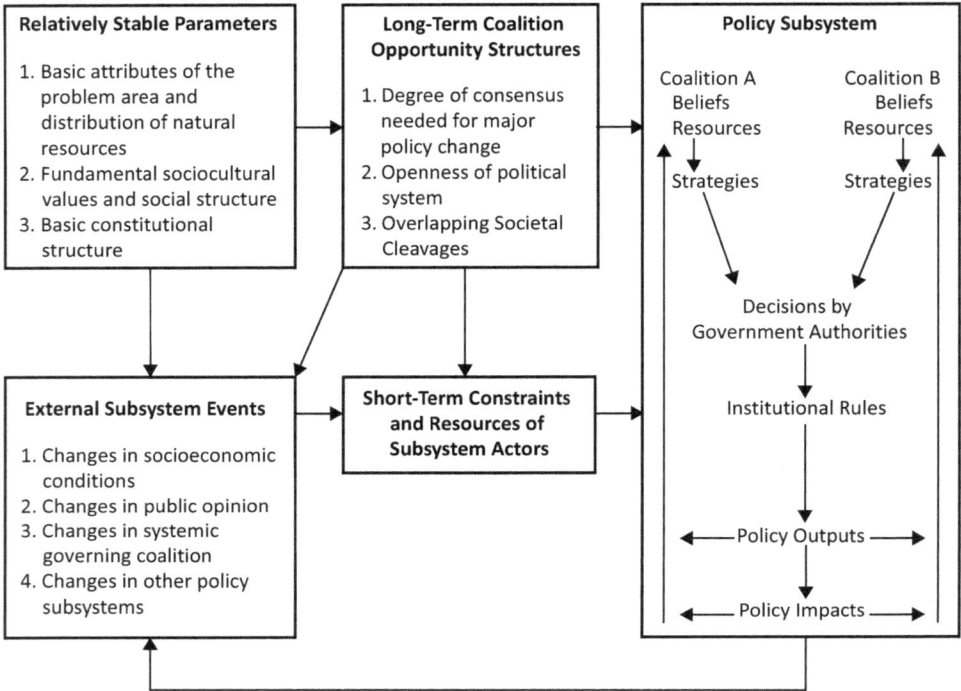

Source: Weible et al. (2011, 352)

policy pertain to the implementation of core goals, and a change in the secondary attributes of a policy is considered a minor policy change (Jenkins-Smith et al. 2014, 201). The core attributes of firearms policy, for example, relate to the balance between individual freedom and state control of firearms use, and any policy that substantially shifts this balance in either direction is a major policy change. The secondary attributes of firearms policy relate to the implementation of an existing balance, such as new curricula for firearms training courses, new regulations for firearms transportation or storage, and so on.

Importantly, the ACF theory of policy change is a theory of *major* policy change. Minor policy changes are assumed to result from dominant advocacy coalitions accepting new secondary beliefs – sometimes reluctantly – and translating these beliefs into policy, but there is no explicit ACF theory of minor policy change. The ACF theory of major policy change consists of two distinct but interrelated hypotheses, each specifying a necessary condition, that together provide an explanation of major policy change. This makes the ACF a deterministic theory, as it is the only theory of the policy process that specifies necessary or sufficient conditions for major policy change.

The first hypothesis (H_1) holds that at least one policy change pathway must be present for a major policy change to occur. It states:

> H_1: Significant perturbations external to the subsystem, a significant perturbation internal to the subsystem, policy-oriented learning, negotiated agreement, or some combination thereof are necessary, but not sufficient, sources of change in the policy core attributes of a governmental program (Jenkins-Smith et al. 2018, 147).

In other words, H_1 specifies four possible policy change pathways: a shock external to a policy subsystem, a shock internal to a policy subsystem, policy-oriented learning, or negotiated agreement between coalitions (Weible, Sabatier, and McQueen 2009, 124). The presence of one or more of these pathways is considered necessary for major policy change to occur.

The second ACF policy change hypothesis (H_2) focuses more directly on advocacy coalitions and the balance of power between advocacy coalitions within a policy subsystem:

> H_2: The policy core attributes of a government program in a specific jurisdiction will not be significantly revised as long as the subsystem advocacy coalition that instated the program remains in power within that jurisdiction – except when the change is imposed by a hierarchically superior jurisdiction (Jenkins-Smith et al. 2018, 147).

Put differently, H_2 claims that in order for major policy change to occur, the coalition that introduced the status quo policy must no longer be "in power," presumably because this loss of power means they have lost the ability to block major policy change. The only exception to this is when policy change is imposed from above by a hierarchically superior jurisdiction.

There is a sizeable ACF literature on Canadian policy development, contributing to all three lines of ACF theory. With respect to ACF theory on the existence and nature of advocacy coalitions, a number of studies have investigated the presence of advocacy coalitions in Canadian policy development, including Stritch's (2015) work on federal labour policy, Heinmiller's (2016) book on Alberta water policy, Montpetit,

Lachapelle, and Harvey's (2016) study of Quebec and BC fracking policy, and Heinmiller and Pirak's (2017) work on Ontario land use policy. With some notable caveats, all of them have found strong evidence that advocacy coalitions are present and active in Canadian policy-making, suggesting that the framework's central concept has application in Canada. In his cross-national studies of biotechnology policy, Montpetit (2009, 2011) has also made important contributions to ACF theory on policy-oriented learning, particularly with respect to the role of scientists in policy development.

The bulk of Canadian ACF studies address policy change, but most use the framework to construct explanatory narratives rather than to explicitly test the ACF policy change hypotheses. Falling into the former category are studies by Mawhinney (1993) on Ontario education policy, Lertzman, Rayner, and Wilson (1996) on BC forestry policy, Litfin (2000) on climate change policy, Jegen and Audet (2011) on Quebec wind energy policy, Bratt (2012) on federal and provincial nuclear policy, Heinmiller on Alberta water policy (2013), Swigger and Heinmiller (2014) on Ontario mental health policy, Anderson and MacLean (2015) on New Brunswick forestry policy, and Montpetit, Lachapelle, and Harvey (2016) on BC and Quebec fracking policy. The only study to explicitly test the ACF policy change hypotheses in Canadian policy-making is Heinmiller's (2016) book, but it tests a modified version of H_2, so it is not a straightforward test.

In sum, the ACF work to date indicates that the advocacy coalition concept is portable to Canada and that the framework can be used to fashion explanations of policy development in a wide range of Canadian policy areas. Yet there is little evidence specifically supporting or refuting ACF policy change theory, and that is this task we take up in this chapter.

Our investigation unfolds in three stages. First, we examine the central concept of the ACF – advocacy coalitions – and their presence in the Canadian firearms policy subsystem. Then we investigate the two necessary conditions for major policy change posited by ACF theory through a congruence analysis of the development of the *Firearms Act* and the *Ending the Long-Gun Registry Act*, the only two major firearms policy changes in our period of study. Finally, we draw conclusions about the strengths and weaknesses of the theory based on the results of our investigations.

Advocacy Coalitions in the Canadian Firearms Policy Subsystem

As noted earlier, a crucial premise of the ACF explanation of policy change is that actors on different sides of a policy issue tend to coalesce into one or more advocacy coalitions. So before we test the ACF policy change hypotheses, we must first investigate the presence of advocacy coalitions in Canadian firearms policy, for an absence of advocacy coalitions would effectively negate the ACF explanation of policy change.

We investigate the presence of advocacy coalitions through an organizational analysis focusing on the national and umbrella organizations that served as the focal points for political mobilization within the Canadian firearms policy subsystem during our period of analysis. As mentioned earlier, an advocacy coalition is a group of actors who share a set of policy core beliefs and who engage in non-trivial collective action to see their beliefs reflected in policy (Jenkins-Smith et al. 2018, 141). There are many degrees of collective action in advocacy coalitions, ranging from information-sharing at the low end to the creation of formal organizations at the high end (Stritch 2015, 446). The analysis here focuses on high-end, organization-based collective action, which does not provide a comprehensive picture of the advocacy coalitions but does provide confirming evidence of their existence. This organizational analysis is supplemented with organization name searches in Canadian major daily newspapers, which provide a general indication of each organization's level of activity in firearms policy development at various points in time. Altogether, our analysis confirms the presence of two advocacy coalitions, one based on beliefs about gun rights and the other based on beliefs about gun control.

The formation of a formal gun rights coalition predates our period of analysis. In the mid-1970s, the Canadian Wildlife Federation, the Shooting Federation of Canada, and the Firearms and Responsible Ownership group from Alberta banded together to form the Canadian Association for Sensible Arms Legislation (CASAL) (Brown 2012, 177–8). CASAL was formed to oppose new gun control legislation then being proposed by the federal government, but it proved unstable and dissolved just a few years after it was formed, mostly due to infighting over what gun control measures the group could accept (190–4). This sort of instability would be a persistent feature of the gun rights coalition; over the next four decades, successive national and umbrella organizations formed, grew, and dissolved.

By the early 1990s, when our analysis begins, two new organizations had emerged as the face of the gun rights coalition: the National Firearms Association (NFA) and Safeguard. The NFA was formed in 1978 with aspirations to become the Canadian version of the US National Rifle Association (NRA), but it folded only two years later due to lack of funds and damaged credibility. The NFA was reconstituted in 1984 at the initiative of Dave Tomlinson, and the success of the organization became closely tied to Tomlinson's leadership (Somerset 2016). During the debates on Bills C-80 (1990) and C-17 (1991), the NFA was the single largest gun rights organization in Canada, claiming 1,000 members from various gun-related organizations (Weston 1989); it was also the most frequently mentioned gun rights group in Canada's major daily newspapers.[1] Safeguard was formed in early 1989 as an umbrella group for around two hundred gun groups, collectors' groups, and hunting organizations, claiming to represent about 70,000 people (Weston 1989). The NFA was based in Edmonton, Safeguard in Toronto; they were rival organizations in the gun rights movement even though they shared many objectives (Weston 1989). Safeguard was active during the C-80 and C-17 debates, but after 1992 there are no further mentions of it in Canada's major daily newspapers. It seems that the organization faded into obscurity, leaving the NFA as the sole national gun rights organization for a time.

During the mid-1990s, the gun rights coalition displayed more organizational unity than at any other time in its history. This was partly because of the unchallenged national prominence of the NFA, but it was also due to the galvanizing effect of the proposed *Firearms Act*. In the early and mid-1990s, membership in the NFA ballooned, and at its peak, it claimed to represent more than 100,000 people (Brown 2012, 222). The NFA was also a founding member of a new umbrella organization of gun rights groups known as the Coalition of Responsible Firearm Owners and Sportsmen (CORFOS). CORFOS was created to stop the *Firearms Act*, an objective that all gun rights groups could support whatever their other differences, and it generated a high degree of national unity in the gun rights movement (Brown 2012, 222n66). The NFA and CORFOS also developed close ties with the Reform/Alliance Party, best illustrated by the Alliance's adoption of the NFA's "Practical Firearms Control System" as official party policy in 2000 (Foot 2000). As indicated by their newspaper mentions, both the NFA and CORFOS were very active during the *Firearms Act*'s passage and implementation. CORFOS, for example, acted as an intervenor in the unsuccessful Supreme Court challenge to the *Firearms Act* in 2000. Shortly thereafter, however, both organizations went into decline: when Tomlinson stepped down from the NFA's leadership, the CORFOS coalition seemed to drift apart. After 2006, CORFOS is barely mentioned in Canada's major daily newspapers, and it is not mentioned at all after 2009.

By the time the Conservatives came to power in 2006, the gun rights coalition had once again become fractious. The lead organization was no longer the NFA; instead it was the Canadian Shooting Sports Association (CSSA) (Somerset 2016). Tomlinson had returned as NFA president in 2005 but had been unable to restore the organization to its former stature, and his death in 2007 set it back even further.[2] Into this organizational void stepped the CSSA. Formed in 2000 through a merger of the Ontario Handgun Association and the Ontario Smallbore Federation, the CSSA quickly grew from its Ontario roots into a large national organization representing gun enthusiasts of various stripes (Canadian Shooting Sports Association 2018). It also formed close connections with the federal Conservative Party; indeed, the Conservatives' point-person on the firearms file, MP Gerry Breitkreuz, sat on the CSSA board of directors (Somerset 2016). The CSSA also forged alliances with like-minded interest groups such as the Canadian Firearms Institute, the Canadian Unlicensed Firearms Owners Association, and the Canadian Taxpayers Federation, all of which opposed the long-gun registry for various reasons (Hepburn 2010). During the various Conservative efforts to repeal the long-gun registry, the gun rights coalition was effectively led by the CSSA (Somerset 2016).

So there is confirming evidence that a gun rights advocacy coalition has existed in Canada – in various forms – since at least the mid-1970s. The coalition was most unified during the mid- and late 1990s, when the NFA was the pre-eminent national gun rights organization and was working with other gun rights groups under the umbrella of COR-FOS. Otherwise, the gun rights coalition has been rather fractious, as illustrated by the rivalries between the NFA and Safeguard in the early 1990s and the NFA and CSSA in the 2000s. This fractiousness continued even after the long-gun registry was repealed, with a splinter group abandoning the NFA in 2015 to form yet another national gun rights group, the Canadian Coalition for Firearms Rights (Somerset 2016). Despite this fractiousness, the level of collective action among gun rights advocates – which has, at times, included gun enthusiasts, gun collectors, sport shooters, hunters and trappers, taxpayers' organizations, Indigenous peoples, western provincial governments, territorial governments, academics, and right-wing politicians – has consistently risen well above the non-trivial threshold. The result has been a readily identifiable gun rights advocacy coalition in Canadian firearms policy development.

Regarding its policy core beliefs, the gun rights coalition believed that firearms were an essential part of many Canadians' livelihoods and pastimes and that only minimal government controls on firearms were necessary. They also believed that law-abiding gun owners were being unfairly targeted by government regulations and that the focus of firearms policy should be on the small percentage of individuals who use firearms for criminal purposes. Thus, they consistently argued for harsher penalties for those who commit gun crimes, while stringently opposing measures such as the registration of long guns, which they saw as an inappropriate and ineffective burden on law-abiding Canadians (National Firearms Association 1999; Bernardo 2011).

On the gun control side of the policy debate, the formation of an advocacy coalition can be traced to the Montreal Massacre in December 1989. Prior to this, various politicians (such as Liberal MP Warren Allmand) and various interest groups (such as the National Firearms Safety Council) had advocated for stricter gun control measures, but there was no organized gun control movement (Brown 2012, 180). This changed after the Montreal Massacre as Wendy Cukier formed Canadians for Gun Control in Toronto and Heidi Rathjen, a massacre survivor, formed a similar group in Montreal. After working together informally for several months, the two groups formally merged to create the Coalition for Gun Control (CGC) in April 1991 (Coalition for Gun Control 2005). The CGC was the first gun control advocacy coalition in Canada, and it would remain the nucleus of this coalition throughout our period of analysis.

Besides being a national gun control organization in its own right, the CGC was an umbrella organization for Canada's other gun control groups. After forming the CGC, Cukier and Rathjen built it into a professional research and advocacy organization, at the same time forging alliances with like-minded groups across Canada. The CGC was very much at the centre of this broad coalition of interests and was quite entrepreneurial in building and maintaining the coalition (Rathjen and Montpetit 1999). In addition to its thousands of individual members, the CGC had hundreds of group members representing gun violence victims, women, police, chiefs of police, lawyers, doctors, hospitals, public sector unions, private sector unions, spiritual groups, and municipal governments, among others (Coalition for Gun Control 2005) (Bottomley 2004, 22–3). The CGC also had ties with sympathetic politicians in the PC, Liberal, NDP, and BQ parties, though these parties were not as unified in their support for the gun control coalition as the Reform/Alliance/Conservative parties were in their support of the gun rights coalition.

Throughout our period of study, the CGC was the organizational platform for the gun control coalition, and it was very active in all instances of firearms policy-making. In daily newspaper coverage, the CGC and its predecessors were consistently presented as the voice of the gun control movement, and they received large numbers of mentions in the coverage of all gun control legislation, from Bill C-80 in 1990 to the *Ending the Long-Gun Registry Act* in 2012. However, the CGC was not a static entity, and it had three stages in its development. The first stage, in the early 1990s, was the formation and development stage, during which the organization was created, developed its research and advocacy capacity, and began to forge alliances with other groups. Rathjen and Montpetit (1999) observe that most of the people involved in the CGC lacked political experience, and the early fights over Bills C-80 and C-17 taught them important lessons in this regard. The second stage, in the mid-1990s, was the zenith of the CGC's influence, when its membership was at its largest and its coalition was at its broadest. This was also when the gun control coalition scored its biggest policy victory, the passage of the *Firearms Act*, and for many, it seemed as if the gun control battle had been fought and won (Rathjen and Montpetit 1999). The third stage was from the late 1990s onward, when the CGC struggled to retain its influence and preserve its policy victories. With the gun control fight seemingly won, CGC membership and donations went into decline, and after the universal gun registry lost credibility during its scandalous implementation, the CGC was unable to recover its former level of influence (Rathjen and Montpetit 1999). Nevertheless, it maintained its presence and carried on the gun control fight, as indicated by its persistent presence in newspaper coverage.

In sum, there is confirming evidence of a gun control coalition in the Canadian firearms policy subsystem since the early 1990s, in the form of the CGC. Under CGC leadership, the gun control coalition exhibited a high degree of organizational stability, even though the coalition's membership waxed and waned. There is no question that the CGC qualifies as an advocacy coalition since its collective action efforts, even in its early days, went well beyond the "non-trivial" level.

The gun control coalition had several policy core beliefs, all centred around the belief that guns were dangerous – in anyone's hands – and needed to be closely regulated by the state. Among other things, they argued that gun ownership was a privilege and not a right, that ownership and use of military and paramilitary weapons should be prohibited, and that regulations regarding firearms purchases, ammunition purchases, and firearms storage should be more stringent (Rathjen and Montpetit 1999, 72–3). Most importantly, for our purposes, the gun control coalition believed that a national registry of all firearms was essential for making firearms owners more responsible and for combating firearms crime (73). While all of these core beliefs were relevant, it was universal registration that became the crux of the gun control coalition's conflict with the gun rights coalition between 1989 and 2012.

All of this means that during our period of study, firearms policy development in Canada has featured two advocacy coalitions competing for policy influence: a gun rights coalition and a gun control coalition. This confirms the central concept of the ACF, a concept that is premised in ACF policy change theory.

Investigating ACF Policy Change Theory

With the presence of advocacy coalitions established, we now turn our attention to ACF policy change theory. ACF theory is a theory of major policy change, so we focus our investigation on the only two major policy changes evident in our period of study: the *Firearms Act* and the *Ending the Long-Gun Registry Act*. Thus our approach treats Canadian firearms policy as a diachronic case study with a temporally defined within-case comparison (Gerring 2007). Moreover, this within-case comparison examines two major policy changes that were in opposite directions – one increasing gun control, the other decreasing it – thereby testing the theory across a range of policy outcomes.

The two necessary conditions of ACF theory are investigated here using the congruence method. The congruence method "begins with a theory and then attempts to assess its ability to explain or predict the outcome in a particular case" by ascertaining the values of the posited causal factors and causal outcome and evaluating whether the empirical values are consistent with the theorized values (George and Bennett 2005, 181). We employ the congruence method by operationalizing the causal factors in both of the ACF policy change hypotheses, collecting evidence of them in both instances of major policy change, and then determining whether the empirical evidence in each case is consistent with the hypotheses. The causal factors are operationalized at the nominal level because, logically, necessary/sufficient factors are either present or absent. In operationalizing the hypotheses, we draw evidence from a wide range of sources: previous studies of Canadian firearms policy change, biographies of process participants, interviews with process participants, newspaper accounts, websites, Hansard transcripts, government reports, public opinion polls, election results, and others.

In H_1, the causal factors are the four policy change pathways, any one (or combination) of which is sufficient to satisfy this necessary condition. Each pathway was defined according to its usage in the ACF literature and operationalized using observable indicators specific to Canadian firearms policy. The definitions and operationalizations of each pathway are listed in the bullets below:

- External shocks are "events outside the control of subsystem participants (in terms of their ability to influence underlying causes and triggers) and involve change in socioeconomic conditions, regime change, outputs from other subsystems, and extreme events such as some crises and disasters" (Jenkins-Smith et al. 2018, 145). Generic examples of external shocks can be found in the External Subsystem Events box of the framework diagram in Figure 6.1. Based on these, the events most likely to confirm the presence of an external shock in Canadian firearms policy are a drastic swing in public opinion or a change in government.

- Internal shocks are events that occur within the territorial boundaries and topical area of a policy subsystem (Jenkins-Smith et al. 2018, 142). The events most likely to confirm an internal shock in Canadian firearms policy are a dramatic mass shooting, a substantial increase in gun crime, or a significant firearms policy failure.
- Policy-oriented learning refers to "relatively enduring alterations of thought or behavioral intentions that result from experience and/or new information and that are concerned with the attainment or revision of policy objectives" (Sabatier and Jenkins-Smith 1999, 123). The presence of policy-oriented learning is confirmed when an advocacy coalition revises some of its policy core beliefs in response to new research or policy experience.
- Negotiated agreement occurs when "agreements involving policy core changes are crafted among previously warring coalitions" (Sabatier and Weible 2007, 205). Evidence confirming the presence of negotiated agreements includes face-to-face policy negotiations between representatives of different advocacy coalitions in the lead-up to policy change and a new policy design that shows evidence of compromise between different coalitions' core beliefs.

The causal factors in H_2 are when the advocacy coalition that instituted the policy status quo is no longer in power or when policy change is imposed by a hierarchically superior jurisdiction; either is sufficient to satisfy this hypothesis. As with H_1, these causal factors were defined based on their usage in the ACF literature and operationalized by identifying indicators specific to Canadian firearms policy:

- The advocacy coalition that instituted the policy status quo is no longer in power when it loses the ability to block major policy change in the policy process. Research by Nohrstedt (2011) and Heinmiller (2016) has shown that a coalition's dominance is closely tied to its formal legal authority to make policy decisions. In Canada's centralized parliamentary system, described in chapter 3, formal legal authority to make policy decisions is concentrated in the hands of the governing party, especially in majority government situations. Accordingly, a status quo coalition is no longer in power in Canadian policy-making when the political part(ies) with which it is allied lose the ability to block legislation in Parliament.

- Policy change is imposed by a hierarchically superior jurisdiction when a government or court with higher-level constitutional authority forces policy change on a government with lower-level constitutional authority. Since we are investigating federal firearms policy, and the federal government is the highest level of government in Canada, only the courts have the constitutional authority to impose policy changes on the federal government in this policy area. Thus, a court decision forcing federal firearms policy change confirms the presence of policy imposition.

In the next two sections, we describe our empirical findings for both major firearms policy changes and whether these findings are congruent with the ACF hypotheses. We begin with the *Firearms Act* before shifting focus to the *Ending the Long-Gun Registry Act*.

The Firearms Act

In ACF terms, the passage of the *Firearms Act* in December 1995 was a major policy change because it changed the core attributes of Canadian firearms policy. Prior to this legislation, the firearms policy regime contained some attributes supporting individual freedom in firearms use and some attributes supporting state control of firearms use, the best illustration being the differential treatment of non-restricted, restricted, and prohibited weapons, as described in chapter 2. By requiring that all firearms be registered, including those previously designated as non-restricted, the *Firearms Act* shifted away from individual freedom in favour of significant state control. Because of this shift in core attributes, the *Firearms Act* was a major policy change; importantly, it was also a major policy change that embraced the policy core beliefs of the gun control coalition.

Accordingly, ACF theory would predict that in the adoption of the *Firearms Act*, two necessary factors must have been present: (1) at least one of the four policy change pathways; and (2) either the gun rights coalition falling out of power in the policy subsystem, or policy change being imposed by the courts. Based on the evidence described below, both necessary factors were evident in the lead-up to the *Firearms Act* and ACF theory is empirically supported in this case.

Let's begin with the policy change pathways of H_1. There is confirming evidence of no fewer than four shocks to the Canadian firearms policy subsystem between 1989 and 1995 – three internal and one external.

The first internal shock was the Montreal Massacre in December 1989 in which fourteen people were killed and thirteen were wounded. As described in chapter 2, this was the deadliest mass shooting in modern Canadian history, and it was made even more shocking by the gunman's purposeful targeting of women and feminists. As he opened fire, the shooter yelled, "You're a bunch of feminists. I hate feminists!" (Rathjen and Montpetit 1999, 12) The shooting garnered massive and sustained media and political attention; it also sparked the creation of the first organized gun control movement in Canada – the Canadian Coalition for Gun Control (Brown 2012). In several respects, then, the Montreal Massacre was a turning point in Canadian gun control politics.

The second internal shock happened two and a half years later. This one also involved a mass shooting at a Montreal post-secondary institution. In August 1992, a disgruntled faculty member at Concordia University opened fire on campus, killing four people and injuring one. This event was traumatic because it felt like a replay of the Montreal Massacre and came at time when Canadian gun crime rates were higher than they had been in more than a decade (Cotter 2014, 8; Perreault 2013, 5). This seemed to re-emphasize that Canada had a problem with gun violence and that government action was needed.

The third and final internal shock involved a series of shootings that happened in quick succession in early 1994. These included the random drive-by shooting of Nicholas Battersby in Ottawa, the murder of Joan Heimbecker in Hamilton, and the murder of Georgina Leimonis during a robbery attempt in Toronto (Fleming 2012, 121). These shootings graphically illustrated the problem of gun violence, garnered a lot of media attention, and put pressure on policy-makers to act. In fact, then Justice Minister Allan Rock specifically identified these shootings as one of the impetuses for the government's subsequent gun control efforts (Rock 2019).

The sole external shock was the 1993 federal election. That election was a shock because it replaced a gun control–reluctant parliament with the most gun control–friendly parliament in Canadian history. At the time of the Montreal Massacre, the Progressive Conservative (PC) party was in power, and its caucus was divided on the gun control issue. In response to the public outcry, the PCs made one unsuccessful attempt at minor firearms policy reform (Bill C-80 in 1990), and one successful attempt (Bill C-17 in 1991), but it could do little else. The 1993 election was transformative because it swept the PCs from office, reducing them to a rump of only two seats, and brought in a Liberal majority government that was much friendlier to gun control reforms. The 1993 election also installed the Bloc Québécois (BQ), a Quebec-based separatist party, as the Official Opposition, and the BQ was even more strongly in favour of gun control than the Liberals. The only clear anti–gun control party was the Reform Party, a western-based conservative-populist party, but they were the third party in Parliament. For the first time in Canadian history, both the government and the Official Opposition were pro–gun control, and this substantially shifted the politics of the Canadian firearms policy subsystem (Bottomley 2004).

The Canadian firearms policy subsystem was subjected to a series of internal and external shocks between 1989 and 1995. However, there is no evidence of other policy change pathways present.

The most likely policy-oriented learning about a universal firearms registry would have come from experience with Canada's existing firearms registry, the Restricted Weapons Registration System (RWRS). By late 1992, the RWRS had been transformed from a manual card system into a computerized system and included about 1.2 million restricted firearms (Wade and Tennuci 1994). Computerization lent a universal registry the appearance of a more viable policy option; however, it was well-known that the RWRS was incomplete and rife with errors, as documented in a technical report to the government in 1994 (Wade and Tennuci 1994). Ultimately, the lessons drawn from the RWRS seemed to reinforce actors' pre-existing beliefs about universal registration rather than changing them: gun control advocates used the RWRS to argue that universal registration was technically viable (Ford 1995; Cukier 1995), while gun rights advocates held up the RWRS as an unnecessary, expensive, and ineffective state intrusion (Thom 1995; Tomlinson 1995). Thus, there is no confirming evidence of policy-oriented learning in the adoption of the *Firearms Act*.

The same is true of the negotiated agreement pathway. At no point in the development of the *Firearms Act* did representatives from gun control and gun rights organizations sit down face-to-face to negotiate a policy compromise. However, there was some negotiation between members of these coalitions within the governing Liberal Party. In 1994 a special caucus committee was struck that included members (and co-chairs) holding both gun control and gun rights beliefs, and that committee developed a gun control policy proposal that gained the grudging support of both sides. Yet the Liberal leadership ignored most of the compromises forged by that committee to mollify gun rights advocates in the Liberal caucus and instead brought forward stringent gun control legislation (Delacourt 2000). Thus, the most obvious example of inter-coalition negotiation that took place during the development of the *Firearms Act* did not substantively impact the legislation's design, so there is no confirming evidence of the negotiated agreement pathway.

Altogether, there is confirming evidence of two policy change pathways (internal and external shocks) but no confirming evidence of two other pathways (policy-oriented learning and negotiated agreement). The presence of the internal and external shocks is sufficient to satisfy H_1, so it is empirically supported in this case.

With respect to H_2, there is confirming evidence that the gun rights coalition was no longer in power after the 1993 election, but there is no confirming evidence of policy imposition.

Prior to the 1993 election, the caucuses of both major parties had been split by the issue of gun control. As a consequence, both parties found it very difficult to implement major gun control measures while in government, as the Liberals' experience in 1977 and the PCs' experiences in 1990 and 1991 can attest. After the 1993 election, however, there was a partisan realignment on the gun control issue. The PCs had been decimated during that election and found themselves displaced by two regionally based opposition parties, one strongly supportive of gun control (BQ) and the other strongly opposed (Reform). The Liberals were back in government, and their electoral base was largely in Ontario and Quebec, where gun control was most popular; indeed, the new Liberal leadership was itself pro–gun control. Some Liberal MPs representing rural ridings were opposed to further gun control; even so, in 1994 the Liberals decided to embrace it: the Liberal leadership believed in it, it was popular with the Liberals' electoral base, it was a means to distinguish the Liberals from the Reform Party, and it was an issue the BQ would support in the House, more than offsetting any lost votes from Liberal dissidents (Pal 2003; Bottomley 2004).

The Liberals' commitment to gun control strengthened throughout 1994. At the Liberal policy convention in May, the party adopted Resolution 14, which called for a range of new gun control measures, perhaps to include "a national system of registration for all firearms" (Liberal Party of Canada 1994). The following day, Prime Minister Chretien committed himself to introducing major gun control reforms in Parliament by the fall (Wills 1994b). Over the summer, Justice Minister Rock engaged in cross-country consultations on gun control, and in November, the government released its *Action Plan on Firearms Control*, in which it committed itself to the universal gun registry it had been hinting at for several months (Government of Canada 1994). In February 1995, the *Firearms Act* was introduced in the House.

By committing the party to the gun control cause, the governing Liberals effectively allied themselves with the gun control coalition and decisively shifted power in its favour. The Liberals had a majority government and, as such, had effective control of the formal legal authority to make policy decisions. Even if some Liberal MPs voted against gun control, the government could expect the BQ to vote with it, ensuring the bill would pass. The Liberals were three seats short of a majority in the Senate, but the unelected Senate uses its veto power very rarely, and several PC senators made it clear that they supported the legislation, so the Senate was not a serious political obstacle (Bottomley 2004). With only the Reform Party clearly supporting them, the gun rights coalition had no political allies who could block major gun control reforms in Parliament, which effectively meant they were no longer in power in the firearms policy subsystem. Thus, there is evidence confirming this causal factor in H_2.

As for policy imposition by the courts, there is no evidence to support this. The *Firearms Act* was not imposed on the Liberal government by a court decision, and no court decisions had any substantive influence in the Liberals' decision to pursue a universal gun registry. Accordingly, the presence of this factor is not confirmed.

Nevertheless, the gun rights coalition's loss of power is enough to satisfy H_2, and we conclude that it is empirically supported in this case. This means that both ACF hypotheses are supported in the *Firearms Act* case, suggesting that ACF theory is effective in explaining this particular major policy change.

The *Ending the Long-Gun Registry Act*

Like the *Firearms Act* in 1995, the *Ending the Long-Gun Registry Act* in 2012 was a major policy change because it altered the core attributes of Canadian firearms policy. By ending the registration requirement for long guns (see chapter 2), the *Ending the Long-Gun Registry Act* moved away from state control and toward individual freedom in the use of long guns, the most widely owned type of firearm in Canada. This restored individual freedom as a core attribute of Canadian firearms policy, much as it had been prior to 1995. So this was a major policy change, one that aligned with the policy core beliefs of the gun rights coalition.

The *Ending the Long-Gun Registry Act* is explained by ACF theory as resulting from two necessary conditions: (1) the opening of at least one policy change pathway, and (2) either the gun control coalition falling out of power in the policy subsystem, or policy change imposed by the courts. The evidence presented below shows that both necessary conditions were present and that ACF policy change theory is empirically supported in this case.

In terms of policy change pathways, there is confirming evidence of two internal shocks and two external shocks in the development of the *Ending the Long-Gun Registry Act*.

The first internal shock relates to a serious policy scandal within the firearms policy subsystem. After the *Firearms Act* was passed in 1995, the universal gun registry was put into action through the Canadian Firearms Program. That program quickly ran into trouble. Problems with it dated from the late 1990s, but the signature event was the auditor general's report in December 2002. That report documented massive cost overruns due to poor planning, poor leadership, poor program design, technological failures, resistance from firearm owners, and refusals by some provinces to participate in the registry's implementation. The cost overruns were so severe that the program, which had initially been estimated to cost $85 million, was now projected by the auditor general to cost more than $1 billion by 2005. It also became clear that the Liberal government had not been forthcoming about the program's costs in Parliament, which deepened the scandal (Auditor General 2002). Ultimately, the manifold problems with the Canadian Firearms Program shocked the policy subsystem by making the registry itself a policy problem, by turning public opinion against the registry (Brown 2012, 233), by offering the opposition parties an easy way of attacking the registry, and by making it difficult for the gun control coalition to defend its signature policy achievement.

The second internal shock was a noticeable increase in gun violence starting in 2005. Between the early 1990s and 2004, the Canadian homicide rate trended downward, so that by the early 2000s, gun violence was not regarded as a serious social issue (Cotter 2014, 8). Then 2005 saw a sudden spike in homicides and gun violence (8), particularly in Toronto, where the media dubbed 2005 "the year of the gun" (Powell and Huffman 2005). The increase in gun violence was vividly illustrated by a series of high-profile shootings. In March 2005, four RCMP officers were slain in Mayerthorpe, Alberta; on Boxing Day 2005, one person was killed and six others injured in a shooting on Toronto's Yonge Street; and in September 2006, two people were killed by a shooter at Dawson College, in yet another shooting at a Montreal post-secondary institution. Although the increase in homicides proved temporary and homicide rates resumed their decline a few years later, gun violence attracted unprecedented media attention in the mid-2000s, as shown in Figure 8.1 (in chapter 8). It also became an important political issue, so much so that Paul Martin's Liberals campaigned on a handgun ban during the 2006 federal election.

The two external shocks had to do with the election of Conservative governments: a minority government in 2006, then a majority government in 2011. Between late 1993 and early 2006, the Liberals enjoyed an uninterrupted period in government, partly because Canadian conservatives had fragmented among multiple competing parties. In 2003, these competing parties merged to form the Conservative Party of Canada, and in 2006, the Conservatives won their first election, forming a minority government. This was a shock to the firearms policy subsystem, because the Conservatives had campaigned on dismantling the universal gun registry and ending the registration requirement for long guns (Conservative Party of Canada 2006). The Conservative government cut funding to the registry, declared an amnesty for those who had not yet registered their long guns, and refunded the registration costs for those who had registered their long guns; however, the opposition parties banded together to block legislation that would have ended the long-gun registry entirely. This situation continued after the Conservatives won another minority government in 2008 – the government kept trying to end the long-gun registry, and the opposition parties kept blocking these attempts – so the election of a second minority Conservative government was not particularly shocking. The election of a Conservative majority in 2011, however, *was* a shock to the subsystem because it gave the Conservatives a free hand to introduce their desired firearms policy reforms, which they had been promising since the party's formation in 2003.

As for the other two policy change pathways, policy-oriented learning and negotiated agreement, there is no confirming evidence of either in the development of the *Ending the Long-Gun Registry Act*.

One might argue that lessons learned from the implementation failures of the Canadian Firearms Program constituted policy-oriented learning, but there is no evidence that actors in either advocacy coalition altered their policy core beliefs in response to this experience. For those in the gun rights coalition, the problems with the Canadian Firearms Program were a vindication, amounting to proof that a universal gun registry was an unworkable and unviable policy option, as they had long argued (Bernardo 2011; Farrant 2017). Conversely, actors in the gun control coalition argued that, notwithstanding its start-up problems, the registry was a useful tool for law enforcement, for it facilitated the tracking of weapons during criminal investigations and enhanced the safety of peace officers who were executing warrants and pursuing suspects (Cukier 2011; Harel 2011). Thus, the lessons actors took from the program generally coincided with pre-existing beliefs about the universal registry, and there is no confirming evidence of policy-oriented learning in this case.

As with the *Firearms Act*, there is no evidence of negotiated agreement in the development of the *Ending the Long-Gun Registry Act*. There were no face-to-face negotiations between the two advocacy coalitions, nor were there any within the Conservative caucus, whose members held gun rights beliefs almost exclusively. Moreover, the act's design does not reflect any kind of inter-coalition compromise; instead, it amounts to a one-sided victory for the gun rights coalition. Thus, there is no confirming evidence of negotiated agreement in this case.

In sum, there is confirming evidence of two policy change pathways (internal and external shocks) in the *Ending the Long-Gun Registry Act* case, but there is no confirming evidence of the two other pathways (policy-oriented learning and negotiated agreement). The presence of the shocks is sufficient to satisfy H_1, so it is empirically supported in this case.

As for H_2, it posits that either the gun control coalition was no longer in power after the 2011 election or that there was policy imposition by the courts. As described below, there is confirming evidence of the former but no confirming evidence of the latter.

The crucial event in the gun control coalition losing power in Canadian firearms policy was the election of a majority Conservative government in 2011. The Conservatives and their antecedent parties had been allied with the gun rights coalition since 1994, when the Reform Party made opposition to the gun registry an official party policy. This party policy continued when Reform evolved into the Canadian Alliance in 2000 and was retained when the Canadian Alliance merged with the Progressive Conservatives to form the new Conservative Party in 2003. When the Conservatives formed minority governments in 2006 and 2008, the gun control coalition lost some influence, but its political allies were still able to block gun rights policy change in Parliament, so it remained in power in the policy subsystem. This was evident in the Conservatives' five attempts to repeal the long-gun registry during their minority governments: Bill C-21 (2006), Bill C-24 (2007), Bills C-301 and S-5 (2009), and Bill C-391 (2010). On each occasion, the opposition parties banded together to vote down the repeal bills and preserve the status quo. However, after the Conservatives won a majority government in 2011, the opposition parties lost the ability to block gun rights legislation, and less than a year later, the *Ending the Long-Gun Registry Act* was passed. This provides confirming evidence that the gun control coalition was no longer in power, supporting this part of H_2.

As for policy imposition by the courts, there is no evidence that this took place. In the late 1990s, the gun rights coalition pursued this strategy by challenging the constitutionality of the *Firearms Act* on the basis that it intruded on provincial jurisdiction. They hoped that the courts would strike down the legislation and thereby force a major policy change. However, in 2000, the Supreme Court of Canada ruled that the *Firearms Act* was a valid exercise of the federal government's criminal law powers and declared it constitutional (Supreme Court of Canada 2000). This effectively closed off any efforts at court-imposed firearms policy change and disconfirms the presence of policy imposition in the *Ending the Long-Gun Registry Act* case.

With respect to H_2, the evidence confirms that the gun control coalition was no longer in power in the development of the *Ending the Long-Gun Registry Act* and disconfirms the presence of policy imposition, which is sufficient to support H_2. Since both H_1 and H_2 are empirically supported, we conclude that ACF theory does well in explaining the adoption of the *Ending the Long-Gun Registry Act*.

Discussion

This chapter has investigated ACF policy change theory as an explanation for Canadian firearms policy between 1989 and 2012. Because the theory is designed to explain only major policy change, the analysis was restricted to the adoption of the *Firearms Act* (1995) and the *Ending the Long-Gun Registry Act* (2012). We began by investigating the presence of advocacy coalitions within the Canadian firearms policy subsystem and found confirming evidence of a gun rights coalition and a gun control coalition, both of which were politically active throughout our period of analysis. This confirmed the presence of the ACF's core concept – advocacy coalitions – in Canadian firearms policy development, making it feasible to test the ACF theory of policy change.

ACF theory posits two necessary conditions for major policy change, and both conditions were empirically present in the two cases examined here. In the development of the *Firearms Act*, there is confirming evidence of one external shock and three internal shocks, satisfying H_1. There is also evidence that the coalition defending the policy status quo, the gun rights coalition, was no longer in power in the policy subsystem after the 1993 election, satisfying H_2. Similarly, the lead-up to the *Ending the Long-Gun Registry Act* showed confirming evidence of two external and two internal shocks, supporting H_1. Evidence was also found that the gun control coalition – the coalition defending the policy status quo this time – was no longer in power after the 2011 election, thereby supporting H_2. Thus, the posited necessary conditions of ACF theory were present in both cases, empirically supporting the theory.

Although ACF policy change theory does well in explaining Canadian firearms policy – better than many of the other theories examined in this book – it is important not to overstate these findings. We examined only two cases of major policy change in this chapter, and it is possible that the posited necessary conditions of ACF theory may not be present in other cases of major policy change not examined here. The findings in this chapter add to the growing body of cross-national evidence that shows "strong support" for H_1 and "strong to partial support" for H_2 (Jenkins-Smith et al. 2018, 148). However, this study is the first one to explicitly test the hypotheses in a Canadian case, so further Canadian applications are clearly needed before firmer conclusions can be drawn about the applicability of ACF theory to Canadian policy-making. It is also important to keep in mind that ACF theory has a limiting scope condition that restricts its application to cases of major policy change, so it is not, as yet, a universal or general theory of policy change.

The analysis in this chapter also points to a limitation of ACF policy change theory, even though the theory is empirically supported by our cases. This limitation relates to the causal blank space between some of the theory's causal factors and the outcome of major policy change. The theory is somewhat vague, for example, about how the policy change pathways lead to major policy change (Zohlnhöfer 2009, 110). This was evident in the *Firearms Act*, where four internal/external shocks were present but the causal linkages between each shock and the major policy change that resulted are not entirely clear. It was even more evident in the *Ending the Long-Gun Registry Act*, where one of the internal shocks – the increase in gun violence in the mid-2000s – probably pointed to a need for more gun control but the ensuing major policy change resulted in less gun control. ACF scholars have recognized this limitation of ACF theory and have filled the blank space between cause and effect with a variety of "secondary components," a lengthy list of factors that connect the policy change pathways with major policy change. Pierce, Peterson, and Hicks (2017, 4–5) identify fourteen secondary components in their review of the ACF policy change literature, but the causal role of these factors remains undertheorized. Theorizing these factors and filling in the blank causal space between cause and effect is an important frontier of ACF policy change research, both in Canada and beyond.

7 Timing Is Everything: The Multiple Streams Framework

Introduction

Public policy-making often seems inherently chaotic. Policies are usually made in ambiguous circumstances by actors who lack compete information and who are subject to manipulation. Random events, charismatic personalities, and chance timing can significantly alter the trajectory of policy processes, sweeping away obstacles to policy change or erecting immovable ones. Given all of these contingent elements, policy processes may seem not just chaotic but unknowable. One theoretical approach has embraced the more chaotic aspects of policy development, fashioning a distinctive explanation of policy-making that incorporates important elements of contingency. This is the multiple streams framework (MSF), which has proven to be one of the most popular and enduring approaches to studying policy development.

First developed by American political scientist John Kingdon in the mid-1980s, the MSF is a framework for understanding policy processes and proposes hypotheses for explaining policy change. More recently, several scholars have noted shortcomings in the original MSF and have proposed modifications to the framework and developed new policy change hypotheses in attempts to increase the approach's explanatory power (Howlett, McConnell, and Perl 2015). One of these proposals, by Herweg, Huß, and Zohlnhöfer (2015), has been included in the MSF chapter of the fourth edition of *Theories of the Policy Process*, the leading textbook in the field. Accordingly, this proposal appears to enjoy the imprimatur of the leading MSF scholars, making it worth considering here. Using Canadian firearms policy, we investigate both the original MSF policy change hypothesis and the recent policy change hypotheses proposed by Herweg, Huß, and Zohlnhöfer. This allows us to investigate the efficacy of the MSF in explaining Canadian policy-making and to compare the two approaches to determine whether Herweg, Huß, and Zohlnhöfer's (2015) revisions offer an improvement over the original formulation.

We begin by describing Kingdon's framework and the policy change hypothesis derived from it. We then apply that framework to firearms policy adoption in Canada during our period of study, 1989 to 2012. This is followed by an account of Herweg, Huß, and Zohlnhöfer's proposed extension of the framework and an investigation of their revised policy change theory using the same set of cases. The findings do not support the original MSF hypothesis, but they do support Herweg, Huß, and Zohlnhöfer's more recent approach. These findings are tentative given that this study is the first application of the revised theory in a Canadian case and that many more applications will be required before firmer conclusions can be drawn.

Kingdon's Multiple Streams Framework

Much of MSF's appeal lies in an essential truth at the heart of the framework: policy-making is not an orderly, rational, and linear process, as it has often been portrayed, but an ambiguous, complex, and disorderly process in which personalities and chance events play a major role. This makes the MSF different from other mainstream policy process theories, which do not embrace ambiguity and disorder in the same way the MSF does. It also makes the framework intuitively appealing because just about everyone can recognize the role of charismatic personalities and chance events in policy development. The appeal of the MSF lies not only in its embrace of disorder but also in its effort to understand that disorder through a set of novel concepts and hypotheses that help make some generalizable sense of how and why policies are made. In this way, the framework walks a fine line between embracing disorder and explaining it.

The intellectual roots of the MSF can be traced to the "garbage can" model of policy-making developed in the early 1970s (Zahariadis 2014, 26–7). The garbage can model challenged the basic tenets of those process models that assume that policy-making is a relatively ordered and rational process akin to problem-solving in which a problem is identified, ideas to address the problem are investigated, and a policy solution is then selected. Garbage can proponents argued that such process models are far too linear to describe most policy-making. Instead, governments (and other large organizations) are more like a garbage can in which policy problems, policy solutions, and political opportunities are constantly swirling in an unordered mess; occasionally, an enterprising individual matches a problem with a solution during a political opportunity, yanking a policy output from the garbage can. It is difficult to theorize exactly how and when policy outputs are produced from the garbage can of government, because the entire process is ambiguous and subject to the exigencies of chance, timing, and personalities (Cohen, March, and Olsen 1972).

In creating his framework, Kingdon (1995) adopted many of the assumptions of the garbage can model and married them to a distinct conception of American government. He viewed government as comprising a central political system and a multitude of policy subsystems, each specializing in a different policy area. The central political system is dominated by the elected policy-makers of the executive and legislative branches, and this is where substantial policy decisions are made. The policy subsystems are comprised of bureaucrats, staffers, interest groups, journalists, scientists, and others who are engaged in the mundane but essential work of policy evaluation, research, and advocacy. Actors from just about every policy subsystem have policy problems they want addressed and policy solutions they want adopted, but the central political system can only accommodate a handful of these demands at any given time. Therefore, capturing the time and attention of policy-makers is crucial to getting an issue on the government's decision agenda. However, there is no established or straightforward path from obscurity in a policy subsystem to saliency in a political system, and it is this process that is characterized by the ambiguity and contingency captured by the garbage can model.

Kingdon created the MSF to explain agenda-setting; Zahariadis (2003) then extended it – without structural modification – to explain policy formation. Zahariadis argued that the original garbage can model was designed to explain decision-making, so extending the MSF to explain policy formation was in keeping with its fundamental assumptions. He also argued that the early stages of the policy process in which issues come to the fore, policy options are specified, and a policy decision is made are "normally examined as integral parts of the same process"; therefore, it is entirely appropriate to use the MSF to explain policy-making (11).

Until recently, most other MSF scholars implicitly accepted this claim, and the framework has routinely been applied to explain policy-making. However, in the past few years, several scholars have proposed extensions to the MSF to increase its explanatory power in policy-making (Howlett, McConnell, and Perl 2015). As described above, an emerging consensus seems to be forming around the proposal by Herweg, Huß, and Zohlnhöfer (2015), at which we will take a close look later in the chapter.

Kingdon's framework takes political systems as the unit of analysis and sets out to explain how policy ideas come to the fore, and are sometimes adopted, within those systems. The actors within this process are assumed to be rational, in the sense that they are calculating and strategic, whereas the system itself is assumed to be irrational, based on garbage can assumptions of ambiguity and contingency (Zahariadis 2014, 26–31). This does not mean that policy-making is inexplicable. Policy-making is complex and disorderly, but there are regularities that can be identified and used to construct a general explanation of policy change.

According to Kingdon, political systems can be understood as having three distinctive "streams" of policy-relevant activities: the identification and popularization of policy problems (the problem stream), the investigation and advocacy of policy ideas (the policy stream), and the opening and closing of political opportunities (the politics stream). These streams are ever-present, though the level of activity in the streams waxes and wanes. The streams provide a useful shorthand for identifying, sorting, and comprehending the relevant actors and activities in a policy area, but they are best regarded as heuristics rather than empirical concepts. There is no physical policy stream, for example, but the policy stream heuristic provides a conceptual category for identifying actors and activities related to the development and advocacy of policy ideas.

The streams play an important background role in policy-making as actors working in the streams prepare the ground for policy change. In the problem stream, actors seek to publicize economic, social, or environmental problems and to convince people that these problems are a priority that government must address. It often takes years of work by advocates to make a problem politically salient, though occasionally this can happen very quickly in response to a dramatic focusing event. In the policy stream, actors work in what Kingdon called the "policy primeval soup," developing, fine-tuning, and advocating ideas they would like to see adopted as policy (Kingdon 1995, 116). The policy stream is conceptualized as independent from the problem stream, which suggests only a tenuous link between prevailing policy problems and the purported policy solutions. Policy-making is characterized not only by problems in search of solutions but also by solutions in search of problems (Kingdon 1995). Finally, the politics stream is the domain of electoral, party, and bureaucratic politics, where changing circumstances, such as the election of a new government, can open and close opportunities. The politics stream is also conceptualized as independent of the other two streams, moving according to its own electoral and legislative cycles.[1]

Most of the time, the streams operate independently, but when a problem from the problem stream, an idea from the policy stream, and an opportunity from the politics stream are brought together – or "coupled," to use Kingdon's term – policy change becomes more likely. Coupling is viewed as a contingent process but not a spontaneous one, and the two factors that facilitate coupling are policy windows and policy entrepreneurs.

Policy windows are brief periods of time when circumstances align so that policy-makers become open to policy change. During policy windows, the policy problems and policy ideas that languish in the relative obscurity of policy subsystems have an opportunity to break through into the central political system where they can be addressed by policy-makers. Policy windows open because of significant developments in the problem or politics streams. An example of the former could be a mass shooting that tragically highlights the problem of gun violence; an example of the latter could be the election of a new government with a mandate for firearms policy reform. Policy windows provide opportunities for policy adoption, but these opportunities are fleeting so that it is not unusual for windows to close before a policy change has occurred as policy-makers' attention is diverted elsewhere (165–79).

Policy entrepreneurs are actors who are dedicated to a policy idea and who work persistently, sometimes for many years, toward its adoption. Policy entrepreneurs come from the policy stream and have cultivated enough credibility and political connections to gain a hearing for their ideas from policy decision-makers. When policy windows open, policy entrepreneurs try to exploit them through coupling: they advocate their favoured policy idea as a means of solving a prevailing policy problem in a way that is politically expedient. In so doing, policy entrepreneurs try to convince policy-makers of the utility and timeliness of a policy idea. This can be tricky. Coupling a policy idea with the wrong problem or the wrong opportunity can work against the idea and hurt its chances of adoption. Also, coupling must happen quickly, before a policy window closes and policy-makers move on to other priorities (172–84).

As mentioned earlier, Kingdon's framework for understanding agenda-setting was extended by Zahariadis to explain policy formation. The policy change hypothesis that emerged from this extension, and became the core of the MSF theory of policy change, can be expressed as follows:

H_1: The chances that a particular policy will be adopted are greater when all three streams are coupled by policy entrepreneurs during open windows of opportunity (Zahariadis 2003, 153).

The key independent variables in this hypothesis are policy entrepreneurs, who engage in stream coupling, and policy windows, which provide fleeting opportunities for policy change. When applied to Canadian firearms policy, the hypothesis posits that policy change should be more prevalent when policy entrepreneurs and policy windows are present and less prevalent when they are absent. The hypothesis is probabilistic rather than deterministic, in keeping with Kingdon's original agenda-setting explanation (Kingdon 1995, 225).

Compared to other theories of the policy process, the MSF has attracted a lot of followers from a variety of academic disciplines, resulting in a large number of Canadian applications. One of the earliest applications was undertaken by Howlett (1998), who studied agenda-setting and policy windows in six Canadian policy areas.[2] While Howlett restricted his MSF analysis to agenda-setting, subsequent Canadian studies have followed Zahariadis's lead and extended the MSF to explain policy-making. In fact, the MSF has been used to explain policy-making in a wide range of federal and provincial policy areas, including health care (Blankenau 2001), renewable energy (Rowlands 2007), water export (Bakenova 2008), drinking water (Schwartz and McConnell 2009), alcohol control (Bird 2010), tobacco control (Schwartz and Johnson 2010), homelessness (Macnaughton, Nelson, and Goering 2013), electoral reform (Alcantara and Roy 2014), drug control (Hayle 2015), education (Rexe 2015), forestry (Anderson and MacLean 2015), and Métis rights (Dubois and Saunders 2017). The framework has also been applied in a number of other governance situations such as emergency management in municipal government (Henstra 2010), program creation in a school board (Thompson and Wallner 2011), program changes in government organizations (Scodanibbio 2011), and priority-setting in a hospital (Smith et al. 2016). Few other policy process approaches can claim this breadth of application in Canadian scholarship, which speaks well to the general appeal and portability of the MSF and its concepts.

Just about all Canadian applications of the MSF have used it ideographically, to provide insights on policy development in isolated cases, and in doing so, they have relied on qualitative or interpretive research methods. Since our purpose is to investigate the MSF policy change hypothesis as a more general theory of policy change, a different methodological approach is warranted. The MSF hypothesis makes a probabilistic causal claim, and such a claim can only be evaluated by analysing a relatively large number of cases quantitatively. This is because a probabilistic claim is a claim about mean causal effects and a large number of cases is needed to evaluate such effects. Accordingly, we have adopted a quantitative approach to evaluating the hypothesis, using as many cases as we can, so that it can be evaluated on its own, probabilistic terms.

We defined our case set as all firearms-related bills proposed in Parliament in the period between the Montreal Massacre of December 1989 and the passage of the *Ending the Long-Gun Registry Act* in April 2012. Firearms-related bills were defined as any bill that sought to regulate the possession or use of firearms, including bills that addressed punishments for firearms crimes. Using Legisinfo and the House and Senate journals, a total of fifty-nine firearms-related bills were identified. (For those who are interested, more detail on how these bills were identified is provided in the methodological appendix at the end of this chapter). This provided a large enough case set for the statistical assessment of mean causal effects in Canadian firearms policy while keeping to our period of study. In the next section, we use the case set to analyse the original MSF policy change hypothesis (H_1); later on, we use it again to investigate Herweg, Huß, and Zohlnhöfer's (2015) revised MSF hypothesis (H_2).

Analysing the Original MSF Policy Change Hypothesis in Canadian Firearms Policy

H_1 identifies two independent variables – policy windows and policy entrepreneurs – both of which must be operationalized and measured in order to evaluate the hypothesis. Because the hypothesis treats both variables as either present or absent (i.e., there is no such thing as a policy window that is partly open or an actor who is "sort of" a policy entrepreneur), both variables were operationalized at the nominal level.

Policy windows were operationalized using an approach similar to that used by Blankenau (2001). According to Kingdon, policy windows open in the problem and politics streams, and he provides a further breakdown of where windows can originate in each of these streams. In the problem stream, windows may originate from indicators of socio-economic problems, feedback from past policies, or vivid focusing events. In the politics stream, windows may open due to administrative/ legislative turnover, changes in the national mood, or pressure group campaigns. These stream components were used as operationalizations of their respective streams. Each component was then investigated, for the entire 1989–2012 period, to determine whether, at any time, developments in that component created a strong impetus for gun control reform. The results of these investigations are summarized below.

Indicators. The indicators of most relevance to firearms policy are those pertaining to crime, violent crime, and firearms-related crime,

Figure 7.1. Homicides per capita, 1972–2012

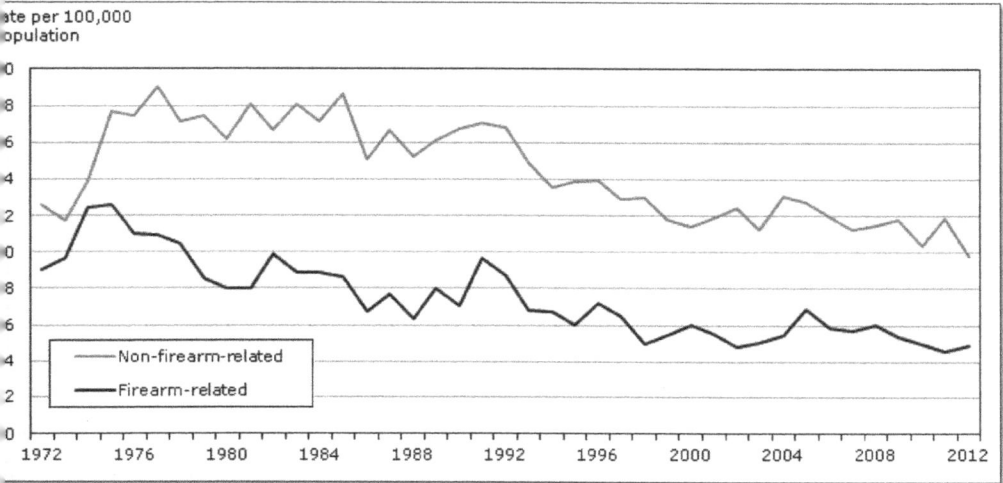

Source: Cotter (2014)

and none of these indicators provided the urgency necessary to open a policy window. The Canadian government statistics in Figures 7.1 and 7.2 show that the crime rate, the violent crime rate, the homicide rate, and the firearms-related homicide rate all spiked in the early 1990s but generally declined throughout the remainder of the study period. Furthermore, even when these rates were at their highest in the early 1990s, they were not particularly unusual or severe when viewed in longer historical context. Therefore, the indicators did not show that there was some sort of gun crime epidemic or public emergency during the period of study – in fact, the situation was improving for much of the time – and there is no reason to believe that indicators opened any policy windows.

Focusing events. In firearms policy, the most relevant focusing events are mass shootings that capture public and political attention. During the period of study, there were eleven mass shootings in Canada involving two or more victims. While all of these mass shootings qualify as focusing events, only one of them, the Montreal Massacre on 7 December 1989, clearly opened a policy window. The Montreal Massacre was different from the other mass shootings in two ways: (1) it had the largest number of victims, and (2) it was an explicit, premeditated attack on

Figure 7.2. Police-reported crimes per capita, 1962–2012

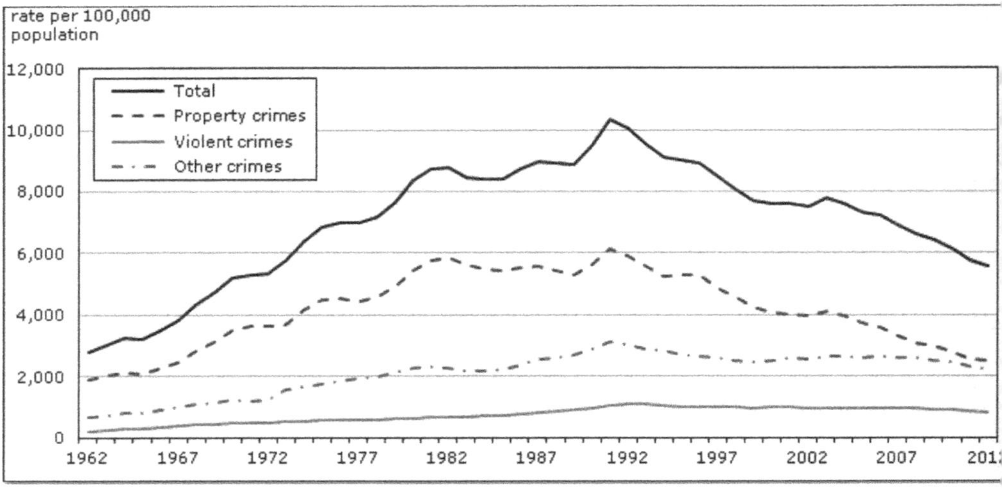

Source: Perreault (2013)

women (see chapter 2). Given these unique quantitative and qualitative features, the Montreal Massacre shocked the nation, attracting unprecedented and prolonged media coverage. It sparked the formation of an organized gun control movement and generated widespread and lasting calls for government action. All of this opened a policy window for gun control reform that other mass shootings had not.

Policy feedback. Policy feedback also can open policy windows, especially when evidence of dramatic policy failures comes to light. During the period of study, two consecutive gun control programs, the FAC program and the Canadian Firearms Program, came under critical scrutiny. In early 1993 the auditor general issued a report on the FAC program that chastised the government for extending it (through Bill C-17) without first having evaluated its effectiveness. While the report was newsworthy, there had been no dramatic policy failure and a policy window did not open because of it (Brown 2012, 217). In contrast, the auditor general's 2002 report on the Canadian Firearms Program documented vast cost overruns and all sorts of administrative errors in rolling out the program. A program that had been estimated to cost $85 million when proposed was estimated to cost almost $1 billion by the time it was completed. The opposition parties readily exploited this dramatic policy failure, demanding a response from the government, and this opened a policy window in the early 2000s (Brown 2012).

National mood. Changes in the national mood can open policy windows by creating sudden and overwhelming demands for policy change that policy-makers ignore at their peril. One way to gauge the national mood is through public opinion polls. The available data indicate that the national mood shifted noticeably during the study period. During the debates over Bills C-80 and C-17, the national mood strongly favoured tougher gun control measures: in the immediate aftermath of the Montreal Massacre, 72 per cent of Canadians wanted more restrictions on the purchase of deadly weapons, and even two years later, 79 per cent wanted tougher gun controls in general (Brown 2012, 204). When the debate shifted to a universal firearms registry, polls conducted in 1994, 1995, and 1998 found that a solid majority of Canadians supported the program (Department of Justice 2015). However, after the scandalous implementation of the registry, the national mood reversed itself, with polls in 2004 and 2006 showing that a slim majority of Canadians wanted it scrapped (Brown 2012, 233; SES Research 2006). All of this suggests that the national mood mirrored, and was probably affected by, events such as the Montreal Massacre and the gun registry scandal. But there is little evidence that the national mood, by itself, opened a policy window during the study period.

Pressure group campaigns. Pressure group campaigns can open policy windows by generating overwhelming public pressure or by capturing the support of key policy-makers. In Canadian gun control, it is difficult to identify any particular pressure group campaign that triggered a policy window on its own. One partial exception was the Coalition for Gun Control's 1993–94 campaign to have the Liberals adopt a universal gun registry as party policy. The Liberals did not campaign much on gun control in the 1993 election, and a gun registry was not mentioned anywhere in the Liberal platform, though the party was friendly to gun control. After some behind-the-scenes lobbying and manoeuvring by the CGC's leadership and some allies in the Liberal party, the Liberals voted to endorse the creation of a national registry at their May 1994 policy convention (Brown 2012; Rathjen and Montpetit 1999). Essentially, the CGC helped manufacture a policy window for a national gun registry where none existed before. However, this would not have been possible without the election of the Liberals in 1993, so the two events seem to have worked in concert to open this particular policy window.

Administrative and legislative turnover. Significant turnover in administrative and legislative actors can open policy windows by introducing new policy-makers with new mandates and priorities. This is especially true in Canada, where policy-making power is strongly concentrated in the centre of government (see chapter 3). In fact, turnover in the centre of government was responsible for most of the firearms policy window openings during the period of study. The most obvious policy windows are alternations in government between the Liberals and (Progressive) Conservatives, who tend strongly to line up on different sides of the gun control issue. Thus, the election of a Liberal government to replace a PC government in 1993 opened policy windows for gun control reform, just as did the election of a Conservative government to replace a Liberal government in 2006. The election of a minority Conservative government in 2008 and a majority Conservative government in 2011 also opened policy windows: in both elections the Conservatives had campaigned to eliminate the long-gun registry, so their election victories provided mandates to implement this reform.

Altogether, investigations of the various components of the problem and politics streams identified six policy windows during the study period: the Montreal Massacre in 1989, the Liberal election victory in 1993, the gun registry scandal in 2002, and the Conservative election victories of 2006, 2008, and 2011. These events were the starting points for the policy windows, and each window was assumed to have been open for a two-year period. Two years was selected as an appropriate window because this provided policy-makers with enough time to respond to an event with legislative change while recognizing that policy windows stay open for a limited time. The two-year period was also based on historical events. The Montreal Massacre opened an obvious policy window in December 1989 and sparked several attempts at legislative reform, until Bill C-17 was eventually passed almost two years later in November 1991. Using this as a guide, a two-year period seemed a reasonable maximum length for firearms policy windows. In the dataset, bills that had their final parliamentary vote within two years of one of the six window-opening events were coded as occurring inside a policy window, while bills that had their final parliamentary vote outside of these six two-year periods were coded as occurring outside a policy window. In total, 38 of the 59 bills in the dataset were recorded as occurring within a policy window.

The operationalization of policy entrepreneurs was also a multi-step process, beginning with the identification of actors who fit Kingdon's description of the concept. Policy entrepreneurs are located in the policy stream and are known to be deeply committed to a policy idea. We analysed the actors in the policy stream by identifying the leading proponents of policy ideas on both the pro- and anti-gun control sides of the policy debate, in this way creating a shortlist of potential policy entrepreneurs. The commitment of policy entrepreneurs to a policy idea is typically indicated by a lengthy track record of advocacy for the idea, and we examined all of the actors on the shortlist, according to this criterion, using actor biographies.

On the pro–gun control side, the policy entrepreneurs identified were Liberal MP Warren Allmand and CGC leaders Wendy Cukier and Heidi Rathjen. Allmand first took up the gun control cause as a backbench MP in the 1960s and eventually became the strongest voice for gun control in the Liberal caucus. This continued through the gun control battles of the 1970s, when as Solicitor General he was the person primarily responsible for the introduction of the FAC program, and in the wake of the Montreal Massacre, he continued to advocate for an expanded and strengthened FAC program (Brown 2012, 171–97). Cukier and Rathjen founded the Coalition for Gun Control and were its public face for almost two decades. They advocated for all forms of gun control and were the staunchest proponents of universal firearms registration, working tirelessly to introduce and later preserve this policy idea (Rathjen and Montpetit 1999).

Two other gun control actors were on the shortlist but did not make the cut because they lacked the requisite track records of advocacy. Justice Minister Kim Campbell was a key protagonist in the battles over Bills C-80 and C-17, but prior to being handed the Justice portfolio in the wake of the Montreal Massacre, she had no track record as a gun control advocate and was more intent on managing a divisive issue than on pushing for a particular policy idea. In describing her approach to gun control, she explains: "I wanted to send a clear signal that I was not captive of any one position on the issue. My goal was to improve public safety in Canada with legislation that would be effective and fair" (Campbell 1996, 152–3). Similarly, Justice Minister Allan Rock was an important figure in the adoption of the *Firearms Act*, but despite having strong convictions in favour of strict gun control, he had no prior history as a gun control advocate. In fact, after taking on the issue in 1994, he had to immerse himself thoroughly in the study of gun control to become versed in the nuances of the policy debates, which is not characteristic of a policy entrepreneur (Wilson-Smith 1995).

On the anti–gun control side, the two policy entrepreneurs identified were Dave Tomlinson and Gerry Breitkreuz. Tomlinson had a long track record of firearms rights advocacy, serving as NFA president from 1984 to 2000 and from 2005 to his death in 2007 (*Edmonton Journal* 2007). He was the main architect of the NFA's proposed "Practical Firearms Control System," which called for mandatory firearms licensing and the elimination of firearms registration (National Firearms Association

1999). He also advocated for tougher penalties for gun crimes, arguing that punishing offenders rather than regulating law-abiding gun owners was more just and more effective. Breitkreuz was first elected as a Reform MP in 1993 and quickly became one of the fiercest opponents of gun control, forming close ties with firearms advocacy groups and adopting their policy ideas of reduced regulation for owners and increased punishments for offenders. He was the gun control critic for the Reform/Alliance/Conservative parties while in opposition, and when the Conservatives formed government in 2006, he was put in charge of a government committee tasked with determining how to kill the long-gun registry as soon as possible (*Sudbury Star* 2006).

There were also several anti–gun control actors on the shortlist who, on closer inspection, did not fit the definition of policy entrepreneur. The various Conservative public safety ministers who handled the gun control file between 2006 and 2012 – Stockwell Day, Peter Van Loan, and Vic Toews – may appear to be policy entrepreneurs because they sponsored anti–gun control bills, as did Conservative MP Candace Hoeppner, who sponsored an anti-registry bill in 2009. But despite their clear opposition to the long-gun registry, none of them had a track record of firearms rights advocacy prior to assuming their ministerial or parliamentary roles, so they do not qualify as policy entrepreneurs. The same can be said of Prime Minister Harper himself, who was a strident critic of the registry and whose support was essential for repealing it. Yet Harper did not have a history as a gun rights advocate, and as a rookie Reform MP, he even voted in favour of the *Firearms Act*, citing his constituents' support for the legislation.

Having eliminated all of these potential candidates, our investigation was left with clear evidence of five policy entrepreneurs pushing various policy ideas: Warren Allmand (a strengthened FAC system), Wendy Cukier and Heidi Rathjen (a universal gun registry), David Tomlinson (no registration of long guns, licensing of gun owners, and increased penalties for gun crimes), and Garry Breitkreuz (no registration of long-guns, licensing of gun owners, and increased penalties for gun crimes).

With this list of policy entrepreneurs in hand, the remaining task was to determine which bills in the case set (if any) the policy entrepreneurs could have plausibly influenced through their advocacy. This was done in a three-step process.

The first step was to code each bill according to the policy idea(s) contained in it. This was done by reading Legisinfo summaries and/or parliamentary speeches for each bill. Through a process of open coding, the main policy idea(s) in each bill were identified and recorded in the dataset.

The second step was to identify whether the main policy ideas of each bill were advocated by a known policy entrepreneur. This was done by comparing the main policy idea(s) from each bill with the policy ideas advocated by each policy entrepreneur. When there were matches between the ideas in a bill and the ideas of an entrepreneur, the identity of the potential policy entrepreneur was recorded in the dataset. Cases in which the ideas in a bill did not match any of the policy entrepreneurs were recorded in the dataset as having no entrepreneur.

Finally, all cases in which the ideas in a bill matched the ideas of an entrepreneur were examined to determine whether the MP sponsoring the bill would have been receptive to the entrepreneur's ideas. It is well-known that Liberal and Bloc Québécois MPs have been more receptive to pro–gun control ideas, whereas PC, Reform, Alliance, and Conservative MPs have been more receptive to anti–gun control ideas. So in cases where the entrepreneur was pro–gun control and the bill sponsor was Liberal or BQ and in cases where the entrepreneur was anti–gun control and the bill sponsor was PC, Reform, Alliance, or Conservative, entrepreneurial influence on a bill was plausible, and in the dataset a policy entrepreneur was recorded as present. Conversely, in cases in which the pro/anti orientation of the entrepreneur did not match that of the bill sponsor, influence was deemed implausible and a policy entrepreneur was recorded as absent. For example, Liberal MP Warren Allmand advocated some of the ideas in Bills C-80 (1990) and C-17 (1991), but it is implausible that he was the influence behind the PC government's pursuit of these bills, so a policy entrepreneur was coded as absent in these cases. All NDP MPs who sponsored bills were treated as a special case. The NDP has long endorsed gun control as party policy, but individual MPs have frequently opposed it because they represent northern or rural ridings. Since their positions are influenced primarily by their constituents, it was assumed that they were not influenced by policy entrepreneurs on either side of the gun control debate, and bills sponsored by NDP MPs were recorded in the dataset as having no policy entrepreneurs present.

Essentially, the procedures for operationalizing the policy entrepreneur variable established a set of conditions that had to be satisfied in order for a policy entrepreneur to be present: the main policy idea(s) in a bill had to be advocated by a policy entrepreneur, and that entrepreneur had to plausibly be able to influence the bill's sponsor. Of the fifty-nine bills in the case set, forty-six met these conditions and were recorded as having a policy entrepreneur present.

For each bill in the case set, data on the presence/absence of policy windows and policy entrepreneurs were collected and compiled. As a measure of the dependent variable, policy adoption, data were also collected on whether each bill had been passed in Parliament and proclaimed into law. The resulting dataset was then analysed statistically to determine whether, in fact, the presence of policy windows and policy entrepreneurs increased the likelihood of policy change. Since all of the variables were operationalized at the nominal level, the analysis was done using cross-tabulations. Using SPSS, measures of statistical significance (Fisher's exact test) and correlation (Cramer's V) were calculated to describe the findings in the dataset.

Overall, the main finding was a lack of evidence supporting a correlation between policy windows, policy entrepreneurs, and policy change. When the two independent variables were cross-tabulated with policy change (see Table 7.1), the results were not statistically significant: the p value was .403, which is far above the .05 threshold that is typically regarded as the maximum allowable value for statistically significant results. The situation did not improve when each independent variable was cross-tabulated separately with policy change, as neither policy windows ($p = .643$) nor policy entrepreneurs ($p = .403$) came close to statistical significance. Failure to reach statistical significance means that the null hypothesis – which states that policy windows and policy entrepreneurs have no association with policy change – cannot be rejected. Thus, the data provide no support for H_1.

To test the hypothesis a second time, and potentially reach statistical significance, the dataset was restricted to government bills only; private members' bills were dropped from the analysis. This was done in recognition of the fact that in the Canadian parliamentary system, it is usually only government bills that stand a realistic chance of adoption. So it could be argued that in order to test H_1 fairly, only government bills should be included in the analysis. When this was done, the number of cases in the data set dropped from fifty-nine to twenty-three. Using this reduced data set, both independent variables were cross-tabulated with policy change (see Table 7.2). When this was done, the hypothesis did not fare any better: the resulting p value was .648, which is not statistically significant. So, again, the null hypothesis cannot be rejected and H_1 is not supported.

These results are interesting because they are at odds with the existing Canadian MSF literature. However, as noted earlier, just about all of the existing literature uses small "n" methods that are not well-suited to evaluating probabilistic hypotheses. These studies have shown that in specific cases, the MSF can work in describing how Canadian policy change takes place. The data presented here, in contrast, test the MSF as

Table 7.1. Cross-tabulation of policy entrepreneurs + policy windows and policy adoption (all bills) (numbers in parentheses are percentages)

	Policy adopted	Policy not adopted	Total
Policy entrepreneur present + Policy window open	5 (8.5)	26 (44.1)	31 (52.5)
Policy entrepreneur present + Policy window not open	0 (0)	15 (25.4)	15 (25.4)
Policy entrepreneur not present + Policy window open	1 (1.7)	6 (10.2)	7 (11.9)
Policy entrepreneur not present + Policy window not open	1 (1.7)	5 (8.5)	6 (10.2)
Total	7 (11.9)	52 (88.1)	59 (100)

Fisher's exact test = .403 (not statistically significant)

Table 7.2. Cross-tabulation of policy entrepreneurs + policy windows and policy adoption (government bills only) (numbers in parentheses are percentages)

	Policy adopted	Policy not adopted	Total
Policy entrepreneur present + Policy window open	5 (21.7)	10 (43.5)	15 (65.2)
Policy entrepreneur present + Policy window Not open	0 (0)	0 (0)	0 (0)
Policy entrepreneur not present + Policy Window Open	1 (4.3)	3 (13)	4 (17.4)
Policy entrepreneur not present + Policy window not open	1 (4.3)	3 (13)	4 (17.4)
Total	7 (30.4)	16 (69.6)	23 (100)

Fisher's exact test = .648 (not statistically significant)

a general theory, directly investigating the probabilistic MSF hypothesis, and the theory does not pass the test. None of the correlations predicted by H_1 were statistically significant, whether we considered all firearms-related bills proposed in Parliament or just those proposed by the government, so there is no evidence to support the hypothesis.

We believe the likely reason for this is the MSF's origins as a theory of agenda-setting rather than a theory of policy-making. Kingdon was primarily concerned with how issues come to the attention of government, and it is easy to see how policy windows and entrepreneurs can play a role in this process. For example, our data show that 52.5 per cent (31 of 59) of firearms-related bills that made it onto the parliamentary agenda involved both a policy window and a policy entrepreneur. Another 11.8 per cent (7 of 59) had a policy window and no entrepreneur, and a further 25 per cent (15 of 59) had an entrepreneur and no window. In total, 89.8 per cent of proposed bills involved policy windows and/ or policy entrepreneurs in some combination. Some caution must be exercised in interpreting this as support for Kingdon's theory of agenda-setting,[3] but at the very least, policy windows and entrepreneurs were prevalent factors in firearms-related bills that made it onto the parliamentary agenda.

However, many factors can intervene between agenda-setting and policy adoption, and one cannot assume that the factors that help a policy get onto the agenda will also help it get adopted. Viewed from this perspective, it is less surprising that there is no evident correlation between policy windows, policy entrepreneurs, and policy change. Recent MSF scholars have noted the causal distance between agenda-setting and policy adoption and have made several proposals to revise and extend the MSF to cover this theoretical gap. The most widely accepted of these proposals is the one by Herweg, Huß, and Zohlnhöfer (2015), and we now turn to an examination of their work to determine whether it provides a better theory of policy-making.

Herweg, Huß, and Zohlnhöfer's Extension of the Multiple Streams Framework

Herweg, Huß, and Zohlnhöfer's extension of Kingdon's framework begins with the insight that agenda-setting and policy decision-making should be treated as two distinct processes, contrary to Zahariadis's earlier claim that the two processes can be analysed as one. They further argue that there are actually two coupling processes rather than one: one coupling process at the agenda-setting stage, as Kingdon described, and one at the policy decision-making stage, which has been largely overlooked in the MSF. The former they label "agenda coupling" and the latter "decision coupling." Decision coupling is only initiated after agenda coupling has been successfully completed and a worked-out policy proposal has made it onto the policy agenda. During decision coupling, the focus is on building the necessary support to get a policy proposal passed through the legislative process and adopted as government policy (Herweg, Zahariadis, and Zohlnhöfer 2018, 31). The inclusion of decision coupling is important because it explicitly brings policy decision-making into the MSF without fundamentally altering its structure or assumptions.

In typical MSF fashion, decision coupling is facilitated by *windows* and *entrepreneurs*, but of a different sort than in agenda coupling. Herweg, Huß, and Zohlnhöfer label these *decision windows* and *political entrepreneurs* to distinguish them from the agenda windows and policy entrepreneurs at work in agenda coupling. Decision windows open in the policy stream after a policy proposal has made it onto the policy agenda. Essentially, a decision window refers to the window of opportunity available for a policy proposal to get through the legislative process and become adopted as policy. Shepherding a proposal through this process is a political entrepreneur. Political entrepreneurs come from the politics stream, and their main task is to build enough support among elected officials that a policy proposal can pass. Sometimes, but not necessarily, the same person acts as both policy entrepreneur (in agenda coupling) and political entrepreneur (in decision coupling). Often, political entrepreneurs are assigned this task by their party leadership, as was the case with Kim Campbell in the development of Bills C-80 and C-17 and with Allan Rock in the passage of the *Firearms Act*. Neither minister had any history in gun control advocacy that would have qualified them as policy entrepreneurs, but when tasked with the passage of gun control bills, they fought hard to get their bills through the legislative process, making them clear political entrepreneurs.

According to Herweg, Huß, and Zohlnhöfer, decision coupling is dominated by the politics stream, meaning that political factors strongly influence whether a policy proposal is ultimately adopted as policy. It matters, for instance, whether the policy problem a proposal is meant to solve is salient with voters. Policy proposals that address salient problems are more likely to be adopted because legislators fear the electoral consequences of (the appearance of) inaction on salient issues. Also, in building majorities to get bills passed, political entrepreneurs may have to build legislative coalitions with actors who have different ideas about what policies should be adopted. Consequently, policy proposals that can combine and reconcile multiple policy ideas are more likely to gain majority legislative support and are, therefore, more likely to be adopted as policy.

Also, decision coupling is far more institutionally structured than agenda coupling. The agenda-setting process is difficult to explain precisely because there are few institutions structuring this process, making it contingent and disorderly, as Kingdon tried to capture in his framework. Decision-making processes, in contrast, take place within well-established, highly structured institutions with institutionalized procedures and decision rules that actors are obliged to follow. This means that decision coupling is constrained by institutions and that institutional factors influence whether policy proposals are adopted. For instance, a policy proposal that is advanced by a political entrepreneur who occupies a leadership position in government stands a much better chance of adoption than a proposal sponsored by a backbench legislator with little influence in the legislative process. Similarly, a policy proposal that is supported by a governing party (or coalition) that controls all veto points in the legislative process is more likely to pass than a proposal put forward by a governing party that can be vetoed by the opposition.

Herweg, Huß, and Zohlnhöfer collect these various insights about the political and institutional factors that affect decision coupling and integrate them in a theory of policy change based on the following hypothesis:

> H_2: Policy adoption is more likely, if (a) the proposal is put forward by political entrepreneurs who hold an elected leadership position in government; (b) the proposal was put forward by a governing party or coalition that is not constrained by other veto actors; (c) different viable alternatives embraced by different parties can be combined in one package; and (d) the problem that the policy is supposed to solve is salient among the voters (Herweg, Huß, and Zohlnhöfer 2015, 446).

Like Kingdon, Herweg, Huß, and Zohlnhöfer formulate their hypothesis in probabilistic terms, identifying factors that make policy adoption more probable once a policy proposal has made it onto the policy agenda. Yet the four independent variables they identify to explain the likelihood of policy adoption bear little resemblance to those specified by Kingdon and represent a new and distinctive MSF explanation of policy change.

Herweg, Huß, and Zohlnhöfer's extension of the MSF is relatively new, yet it has already attracted at least two dozen applications in a wide variety of policy areas around the world – but none in Canada. What follows, then, is the first application of H_2 in a Canadian policy process, one that serves as a test case to begin determining its suitability in explaining Canadian policy-making. The application uses the same case set used to investigate H_1, allowing us to draw comparisons between the old and new MSF and to ascertain whether Herweg, Huß, and Zohlnhöfer have extended the theory in a useful direction.

Analysing Herweg, Huß, and Zohlnhöfer's Extension of the Multiple Stream Framework in Canadian Firearms Policy

H_2 specifies four independent variables affecting the likelihood of policy adoption once a policy proposal reaches the policy agenda: whether the political entrepreneur(s) advocating a proposal occupy a leadership position in government; whether the political entrepreneur(s) face a veto in the legislative process; whether the policy proposal combines different policy ideas supported by different parties; and whether the problem the proposal is meant to solve is politically salient. All of these independent variables are nominal in the sense that they are considered either present or absent (e.g., a problem is either salient or not salient). It is also possible to conceive these variables as ordinal (e.g., a problem is more or less salient by degrees) or interval (e.g., the number of vetoes facing a policy proposal), and this may be a frontier for further theoretical development. However, our task here is to investigate the hypothesis in its current form, so we have operationalized all four independent variables at the nominal level.

The first independent variable operationalized was whether a bill combined different policy proposals together in a single package in an effort to draw support from different parties and increase its chances of adoption. To operationalize this variable, we looked at the legislative history of each bill in the case set to identify any bills that had been merged with others in the legislative process. The legislative histories were found using a combination of Legisinfo and the House and Senate journals. This analysis of legislative histories failed to find a single case in which bills had been merged, but it did find one case in which a bill had been split (Bill C-15 in 2001). The absence of merged bills indicates that this is not a common strategy in Canadian policy-making and that this independent variable is probably not useful in explaining Canadian policy adoption, so it was not considered further in our analysis. Yet it is possible that in the Canadian legislative process, the merging of different viable policy proposals takes place during the pre-parliamentary drafting of bills; if so, our operationalization would not capture this. Future research should investigate this possibility and consider more thoroughly the role this variable may play in Canadian policy-making.

The second independent variable operationalized was whether the problem addressed by a policy proposal was salient among voters. This variable was operationalized in a four-step process:

1 Each bill was coded to determine what policy problem(s) the bill was meant to address. This involved a process of closed coding in which there were four coding options: a bill was meant to address the problem of gun violence; a bill was meant to address the problem of regulatory burden on gun owners; a bill was meant to address both of these problems; or a bill was meant to address neither of these problems. Coding decisions were made based on a reading of the legislative summaries found in Legisinfo or in the parliamentary speeches introducing a bill.
2 Using newspaper article analysis (see chapter 8), data on the public salience of firearms issues were generated. The newspaper analysis in chapter 8 identifies articles from the *Globe and Mail* from 1985 to 2015 covering firearms issues. These data on newspaper coverage could be used as a proxy for the public salience of firearms issues because they indicate how much public attention was being focused on firearms problems. The coverage data were analysed by, first, counting the number of *Globe and Mail* articles covering firearms issues for each year. These annual frequencies were then compared to a ten-year rolling average: years that were above the rolling average were those in which firearms issues were judged as salient; years below the rolling average were those in which firearms issues were judged as not salient. A rolling average, rather than a total fixed average, was used in order to compensate for any possible changes in reporting practices, over time, that could have resulted in less or greater coverage of firearms issues in absolute terms. Public opinion data were also considered as a possible indicator of firearms salience, but there were too many gaps in the available polling data to make this viable. Ultimately, the newspaper coverage analysis revealed three periods during which firearms issues were publicly salient: 1989–95, 2003, and 2005–9.
3 The specific firearms problems that were salient in each period were identified by contextualizing the periods of public salience. Each salient period was contextualized with historical events and other indicators to determine whether it was gun violence or the regulatory burden on gun owners that was the salient problem at the time. The 1989–95 period, for example, was initiated by the Montreal Massacre, saw an uptick in violent gun crime (see Figure 7.1), and was dominated by various legislative efforts to

strengthen gun regulations, so it is very likely that gun violence was the publicly salient problem at the time. The year 2003 was just after the release of the auditor general's report on the Canadian Firearms Program, and the issue coverage data in Figure 7.2 show that government actions made up a large proportion of the firearms activities reported, so it is the regulatory burden on firearms owners that was likely the salient problem at this time. Finally, the 2005–9 period saw an increase in violent gun crime after more than a decade of steady decline, and newspaper coverage of firearms was overwhelmingly focused on public health and safety activities, so it is likely that gun violence was the salient problem during this time. Based on this analysis, we concluded that gun violence was a publicly salient problem in 1989–95 and 2005–9 and that the regulatory burden on firearms owners was a publicly salient problem in 2003; years outside of these salient periods were judged as having no salient firearms problems.

4 Finally, the coding from step one (about the policy problem each bill was meant to solve) was cross-referenced with the coding from step three (about the prevailing problems that were salient). If the codes matched, then a bill was judged as meant to solve a salient problem; if the codes did not match, then a bill was judged as not meant to solve a salient problem. Of the fifty-nine bills in the dataset, twenty-three were identified as meant to address a publicly salient firearms problem.

The final two independent variables in H_2 were about political entrepreneurs and whether they, at the time they proposed a bill, occupied a leadership position in government and faced a veto in the legislative process. Both variables presume the identification of a political entrepreneur, so this concept was operationalized first. Quite simply, political entrepreneurs were identified as the MPs sponsoring each bill. Whether it is a cabinet minister sponsoring a bill on behalf of the government or a backbench MP sponsoring a bill on their own accord, it is the bill sponsor that typically takes the lead in trying to shepherd it through Parliament, so this operationalization was straightforward. Using Legisinfo and the House and Senate journals, all of the bill sponsors were identified.

Having identified the political entrepreneurs, we could then determine whether they occupied a leadership position in government and whether they faced a veto in the legislative process. The leadership position of political entrepreneurs was operationalized by determining whether a bill sponsor was a member of the Cabinet: if so, they were coded as a leader; if not, they were coded as not a leader. The vetoes facing a political entrepreneur were operationalized by considering whether the political entrepreneur was sponsoring a government bill on behalf of a majority government. If so, the governing majority controlled the legislative process and the political entrepreneur was not facing a veto. In all other scenarios, political entrepreneurs faced a veto: bills sponsored on behalf of a minority government faced a veto from the opposition parties, and bills sponsored by a backbench MP faced a veto from the government. So, bills sponsored by a majority government were coded as not facing a veto, and all other scenarios were coded as facing a veto. Information on the leadership positions of political entrepreneurs and the governments they represented (if any) was taken from Legisinfo and the House and Senate journals.

During the course of operationalization, it became apparent that these two variables were correlated and needed to be combined in a single interaction variable. The correlation between leadership position and veto presence occurs – in the Canadian parliamentary system, at least – when a political entrepreneur does not occupy a government leadership position. Non-leaders automatically face a veto from the government because they are proposing private members' bills rather than government bills, and private members' bills are regularly voted down in Canada's Parliament (or never even brought to a vote), even when sponsored by backbench MPs from the governing party. This means there is no realistic scenario in which a non-leader does not face a veto. This correlation between leadership position and veto presence is best treated by creating an interaction variable that captures the overall legislative influence of political entrepreneurs. This interaction variable has three potential outcomes:

- *Backbench political entrepreneurs.* A political entrepreneur does not occupy a leadership position in government and faces the prospect of a veto in the legislative process.
- *Minority government political entrepreneurs.* A political entrepreneur occupies a leadership position in a minority government and thereby faces a potential veto from the opposition parties in the legislative process.
- *Majority government political entrepreneurs.* A political entrepreneur has a leadership position in a majority government and does not face a veto from other parties in the legislative process.

Using the data already recorded for whether a political entrepreneur occupied a government leadership position and whether a political entrepreneur faced a legislative veto, the outcome of the interaction variable was determined for each bill and entered into the dataset.

Ultimately, H_2 was investigated using two independent variables: whether the problem a bill was meant to solve was politically salient, and what influence a political entrepreneur had over the legislative process. The former variable had two possible outcomes (salient or not salient); the latter had three possible outcomes (backbench entrepreneur, minority government entrepreneur, or majority government entrepreneur). The remaining independent variable in H_2 – whether a policy proposal had different viable alternatives supported by different parties – was not included in the analysis because, as explained earlier, its operationalization revealed no evidence of this in any case in the dataset. Together, the two independent variables included in the analysis produced six causal scenarios that could be cross-tabulated with policy adoptions. As with the analysis of H_1, H_2 was tested for both statistical significance and correlation, using Fisher's exact test and Cramer's V, respectively.

When the data were cross-tabulated for all fifty-nine cases, the results were statistically significant and showed a moderate correlation between the independent and dependent variables (see Table 7.3). The p value for the analysis was .001, which is well below the maximum allowable threshold to establish statistical significance. Thus, we can reject the null hypothesis and conclude that a chance correlation between the variables is very unlikely. In terms of correlation strength, on a scale of 0 to 1, with 0 being no correlation and 1 being perfect correlation, the variables had a Cramer's V score of .459. This is typically regarded as a moderate relationship between variables (Davis 1971, 49), suggesting that H_2 does a reasonably good job in accounting for policy change in Canadian firearms policy.

To verify these results, a second cross-tabulation was conducted, but only on the twenty-three bills in the case set that were government bills (see Table 7.4). This analysis was conducted for the same reasons described above: it can be argued that because private members' bills rarely become policy, it is only government bills that are realistic policy proposals and it is only these bills that should be included in the analysis. Analysing only government bills affected the political entrepreneur variable because it removed all cases involving backbench political entrepreneurs. This is why the first cross-tabulation (in Table 7.3) shows six causal scenarios whereas the second cross-tabulation (in Table 7.4) shows only four. A statistical analysis of the second cross-tabulation produced results that were statistically significant, with a p value of .026, and showed a stronger correlation than the first cross-tabulation,

Table 7.3. Cross-tabulation of political entrepreneur legislative influence + problem salience and policy adoption (all bills) (numbers in parentheses are percentages)

	Policy adopted	Policy not adopted	Total
Majority govt. political entrepreneur + Problem is salient	4 (6.8)	1 (1.7)	5 (8.5)
Majority govt. political entrepreneur + Problem is not salient	1 (1.7)	2 (3.4)	3 (5.1)
Minority govt. political entrepreneur + Problem is salient	2 (3.4)	8 (13.6)	10 (16.9)
Minority govt. political entrepreneur + Problem is not salient	0 (0)	5 (8.5)	5 (8.5)
Backbench political entrepreneur + Problem is salient	0 (0)	8 (13.6)	8 (13.6)
Backbench political entrepreneur + Problem is not salient	0 (0)	28 (47.5)	28 (47.5)
Total	7 (11.9)	52 (88.1)	59 (100)

Fisher's exact test = .001 (statistically significant)
Cramer's V = .459 (moderate relationship)

with a Cramer's V score of .509. Such a score typically indicates a substantial relationship between variables (Davis 1971, 49) and lends additional empirical support to H_2.

In sum, our analysis of Canadian firearms policy provides qualified support for H_2. Whether we considered all firearms bills or just government bills, the results showed a statistically significant correlation between Herweg, Huß, and Zohlnhöfer's independent variables and the dependent variable of policy adoption. The strength of the correlation hovered around the substantial level of .500: just below this level when all bills were analysed and just above this level when only government bills were analysed. This suggests that, though it is not a complete explanation, H_2 captures some important dynamics of Canadian policy-making.

The only exception was the "different viable alternatives embraced by different parties" variable, for which there was no supporting

Table 7.4. Cross-tabulation of presence of veto actors + problem salience and policy adoption (government bills only) (numbers in parentheses are percentages)

	Policy adopted	Policy not adopted	Total
Majority govt. political entrepreneur + Problem is salient	4 (17.4)	1 (4.3)	5 (21.7)
Majority govt. political entrepreneur + Problem is not salient	1 (4.3)	2 (8.7)	3 (13)
Minority govt. political entrepreneur + Problem is salient	2 (8.7)	8 (34.7)	10 (43.5)
Minority Govt. political Entrepreneur + Problem is not salient	0 (0)	5 (21.7)	5 (21.7)
Total	7 (30.4)	16 (69.6)	23 (100)

Fisher's exact test = .026 (statistically significant)
Cramer's V = .509 (substantial relationship, barely)

evidence. However, this is not too surprising because it accords with the highly centralized, majoritarian nature of Canadian parliamentary government: governments tend to propose bills and rely on strict party discipline, rather than inter-party compromise, to get them passed. Although this variable is not particularly relevant to Canadian policy-making, it is easy to see how it might be important in other political systems that are more decentralized and have looser party discipline, such as the US. So the lack of supporting evidence in this study should not be used to jettison that variable from the theory. Instead, it illustrates how scholars may have to exercise some flexibility in applying H_2 in different political systems, emphasizing some causal factors over others depending on context.

Discussion

Over the past decade or so, the MSF has generated renewed interest, with some scholars applying the original MSF theory and other scholars seeking to extend that theory in new directions. This chapter has investigated the MSF as a theory of Canadian policy-making, analysing both the original MSF hypothesis (H_1) and Herweg, Huß, and Zohlnhöfer's new hypothesis (H_2) using the same case set of firearms-related bills in the 1989–2012 period. Because both hypotheses were formulated in probabilistic terms, both were evaluated using a relatively large "n" and statistical techniques suited to evaluating mean causal effects. The results of these analyses are informative.

While there is no evidence to support H_1 as an explanation of Canadian firearms policy change, there is evidence to support H_2. Given that Kingdon formulated his hypothesis to explain agenda-setting, and that it was only later extended to explain policy change, this is not a complete repudiation of Kingdon's MSF and may simply be a reminder that the scope of Kingdon's theory should be restricted to agenda-setting. This was the starting point for Herweg, Huß, and Zohlnhöfer's work as they set out to extend the MSF to explain policy decision-making in addition to agenda-setting. The findings in this chapter suggest that they have been somewhat successful in this effort, developing a hypothesis that does a much better job of explaining Canadian firearms policy change than the original MSF hypothesis.

Nevertheless, this finding comes with a couple of notable caveats. First, it is important to note that because the strength of the correlations hovers around .500, Herweg, Huß, and Zohlnhöfer's independent variables explain only about half of the total variance in the dependent variable, policy adoption. This leaves plenty of room for improvement, and MSF scholars should investigate other potential independent variables that can account for the (as yet) unexplained variance. Second, this study is only the first application of H_2 to Canadian policy-making, and many other applications are needed if we are to gain a fuller understanding of how well this hypothesis serves as an explanation of Canadian policy-making. This chapter should be regarded as the beginning, rather than the end, of investigations into Herweg, Huß, and Zohlnhöfer's hypothesis in Canada.

Finally, it is worth asking whether Herweg, Huß, and Zohlnhöfer's work is an extension of the MSF or a surrender to rational choice institutionalism. Herweg, Huß, and Zohlnhöfer are quite explicit about trying to bring formal institutions into the MSF as a means of shedding light on the decision coupling process, and their policy adoption hypothesis has a strong institutional flavour, in that it refers to causal factors such as government leadership positions and legislative vetoes (Zohlnhöfer, Herweg, and Huß 2016). The question is whether this approach remains true to the multiple streams ethos as outlined by Kingdon. Is it accurate to describe policy decision-making as a coupling process when building majority legislative support, not stream coupling, is the central task at hand? Do multiple streams assumptions regarding ambiguity and contingency still have application in more structured legislative environments? Are these assumptions reflected in Herweg, Huß, and Zohlnhöfer's hypothesis? At the least, Herweg, Huß, and Zohlnhöfer's work seems to be a synthesis of the MSF and RCI, but whether much of the MSF ethos survives this combination is an open question.

APPENDIX: CONSTRUCTING THE CASE SET

The first task in investigating the MSF hypotheses was to assemble a relatively large "n" case set of firearms-related bills. A large "n" case set was desired because the old and new MSF hypotheses both make probabilistic causal claims and such claims can only be evaluated by analysing a relatively large number of cases. This is because a probabilistic claim is a claim about mean causal effects, and we need a large number of cases to evaluate mean causal effects.

The case set was created by identifying all firearms-related bills proposed in Parliament during our period of study, from the Montreal Massacre in December 1989 to the passage of the *Ending the Long-Gun Registry Act* in April 2012. Firearms-related bills were defined as any bill that sought to regulate the possession or use of firearms, including bills that addressed punishments for firearms crimes; this definition included both liberal and conservative conceptions of gun control. Firearms bills proposed in Parliament were considered an appropriate case set because they represent known efforts to undertake policy change. To address the concern that, in the Canadian parliamentary system, only government efforts at policy change represent realistic efforts at policy change, the case set was narrowed, at times, to include only government bills.

The bills in the case set were identified using a combination of Legisinfo (visit www.parl.ca/legisinfo/Home.aspx?Language=E&Parliament Session=42–1) and printed House and Senate journals. Legisinfo covered all bills from the 35th to 41st Parliaments (1993–2012), and its search function allowed for a longlist of firearms-related bills to be identified: searching for the term "firearms" produced 113 results. For the 34th Parliament (1989–93), the indexes of the House and Senate journals were searched for the term "firearms"; this produced ten results, which were added to the longlist.

Each bill on the longlist was then investigated to verify that it aimed to regulate the possession or use of firearms in some way. About half of the bills on the longlist had an accessible and searchable Legisinfo legislative summary. The firearms provisions of these bills (if any) were investigated by searching for the word "firearm" and reading the paragraph(s) surrounding each search result. The bills that did not have a Legisinfo summary were investigated using House transcripts accessed through www.lipad.ca. Each bill's number and title were searched in order to find the parliamentary speech, by the bill's sponsor, introducing and describing the bill to the House. The speech was then searched for the word "firearm," and the paragraphs surrounding each search result were read to determine the bill's firearms provisions (if any). By following this procedure for all 123 bills on the longlist, we developed a shortlist of 59 bills that, we were confident, aimed to regulate firearms in some way. Those 59 bills became the case set of bills proposed in Parliament. The case set was reduced to 23 bills when it was limited to government bills only.

8 Small Steps and Giant Leaps: Punctuated Equilibrium Theory

In 1959, Charles Lindblom observed that most policies most of the time follow a pattern of incrementalism; that is, they change very little from year to year and most policy changes can be characterized as modest adjustments made in response to changing political or socio-economic circumstances (Lindblom 1959). Yet many other scholars noted that rapid, transformative policy changes also occur from time to time, and when they do, a long-standing policy can be completely turned on its head. This evidence of incrementalism alongside occasional radical policy change created a difficult theoretical puzzle for policy scholars to unravel: how can policy development display both long-term stability (i.e., incrementalism) and periodic instability (i.e., periodic radical change)? This question inspired the development of punctuated equilibrium theory (PET), formulated by Frank Baumgartner and Bryan Jones in the early 1990s. PET has since become one of the most popular theories of the policy process, and an impressive international data collection initiative known as the Comparative Agendas Project continues to support new PET research. PET has gained less traction in Canada than in the US, and with that in mind, we will investigate its potential here by undertaking a PET analysis of Canadian firearms policy.

Punctuated Equilibrium Theory

PET begins with the observation that public policies follow a pattern of punctuated equilibrium in which policies remain relatively stable (or at equilibrium) for extended periods of time but periodically undergo radical change (or punctuation). The empirical evidence that policies follow a punctuated equilibrium pattern, both in the US and elsewhere, is extensive and overwhelming, so it is not surprising that a body of theory has been developed to explain it. PET's effort to explain both extended periods of policy stability and brief periods of radical change make it different from other theories – such as the ACF and MSF – that focus mainly on explaining policy change. Also, PET studies are inherently longitudinal, sometimes covering periods of more than a hundred years in seeking to identify patterns of punctuated equilibrium and to account for both aspects of the punctuated equilibrium cycle.

PET's conception of policy development is based on assumptions of bounded rationality and is fundamentally concerned with how governments receive, process, and respond to information. First, PET distinguishes between the macropolitical institutions at the centre of a political system (such as Parliament) and the policy subsystems on the peripheries of a political system (such as the firearms policy subsystem). Macropolitical institutions are where the "big" policy decisions are made, but it is within the policy subsystems that actors specializing in various policy areas do the day-to-day policy work of government, making incremental policy adjustments in response to new information. There are a multitude of policy subsystems, each of which specializes in a different policy area; thus, from a system-wide perspective, policy subsystems process information in a parallel fashion and allow governments to make simultaneous incremental policy adjustments to keep most policies at equilibrium most of the time. When demands for "big" policy changes arise, these must be addressed by the macropolitical institutions at the centre of a political system, but the macropolitical institutions process information in a serial fashion, dealing with one issue at a time. The issue demands placed on a macropolitical institution are always greater than its supply of attention; this creates a bottleneck so that only the most serious or pressing issues are addressed at any given time – the rest must wait in queue. All of this means it is very difficult to capture the attention of a macropolitical institution and to get an issue on its policy agenda. For those pursuing major policy change, that is the main challenge (Baumgartner, Jones, and Mortensen 2018, 59–60).

According to PET, most policy issues are confined to policy subsystems for long periods of time because of the presence of policy monopolies. A policy monopoly involves "a monopoly on political understandings concerning the policy of interest, and an institutional arrangement that reinforces that understanding" (Baumgartner and Jones 2009, 6). In a policy monopoly, some actors and their policy ideas become dominant, and this dominance is reinforced by established institutions, such as administrative agencies and legislative committees, which service and protect the monopoly. The hallmark of a policy monopoly is the presence of negative feedback. In negative feedback, most actors are content with the existing policy, and they send signals to maintain or adjust the status quo in modest increments, much as a thermostat receives signals to maintain or adjust room temperature at a constant level (Baumgartner, Jones, and Mortensen 2018, 61). Policy monopolies generating negative feedback are the source of incrementalism and equilibrium. Policy issues are confined to the policy subsystem, conflicts are managed within the subsystem, and policies are modestly adjusted in small increments.

A policy monopoly can dominate a policy area for decades, but in the long run, all policy monopolies are vulnerable to break-up through the onset of positive feedback. Positive feedback usually starts with small things, such as protests or incidents that illustrate the shortcomings of a policy monopoly, but those small things trigger more dissent, which triggers even more dissent, in a process that snowballs and becomes self-reinforcing. As positive feedback builds, the attacked policy monopoly becomes unable to contain conflict within the policy subsystem, and issue expansion occurs – that is, the issue expands to the macropolitical institutions. Issue expansion is crucial, because only in macropolitical institutions is there potential for major policy change (Baumgartner and Jones 2009).

The onset of positive feedback and issue expansion is somewhat unpredictable, but when it happens, it can bring down an established policy monopoly, sometimes in relatively short order. In PET, two factors are identified as particularly important in positive feedback and issue expansion: policy images and venue shopping (Baumgartner and Jones 2009, 37–8).

A policy image is a shared notion of a policy's purpose and the values it serves. When there is one clear policy image that is shared by most actors in a policy subsystem, this helps reinforce a policy monopoly. However, policy images can be contested, and challenging an image can initiate positive feedback as one image challenge emboldens another challenge, and another, and so on. Policy images often become contested because new dimensions of an issue come to light and receive sudden emphasis. For example, Baumgartner and Jones show that in the first half of the twentieth century, pesticides had a positive policy image based on how they helped increase agricultural production and economic growth; but in the late 1950s, a series of pesticide-related problems shifted the focus to the health and environmental dimensions of pesticide use, which triggered further attacks from environmentalists in the 1960s and eventually shifted the policy image of pesticides from overwhelmingly positive to overwhelmingly negative (95–9). Such policy image shifts are important because they help break up policy monopolies and expand issues from policy subsystems to the macropolitical institutions where policy punctuations can take place.

The other important factor in issue expansion is venue shopping. A policy venue is defined as any institution that has the authority to make policy decisions concerning an issue (31). Venue shopping occurs when the opponents of a policy monopoly shift an issue out of its traditional venues, which are typically dominated by the policy monopoly, into new venues that are more receptive to dissent and reform. Baumgartner and Jones (2009) highlighted the importance of venue shopping with US institutions in mind; those institutions tend to be quite open and jurisdictionally fluid, providing plenty of opportunities to move issues between venues. Canada's political institutions are not as open or fluid as in the US, but plenty of research has shown that Canadian institutions still provide opportunities for venue shopping (Pralle 2003; Constantelos 2010; Boucher 2013). Shifting issues into new venues can contribute to positive feedback and generate opportunities for issue expansion; an established policy monopoly can thereby be subverted and destroyed.

Fundamentally, the PET explanation of policy stability and change is based on the tendency of governments to be disproportionate information processors. A proportionate information processor is one that receives information signals and, based on the seriousness or urgency of the signals, responds in kind. So a proportionate information processor responds to minor problems with minor adjustments and major problems with major adjustments, in a timely and measured way. Governments, however, do not work like this, according to PET. Because of the presence of policy monopolies and the difficulties involved in breaking them down, governments tend to underreact to problem signals when a monopoly is present, or overreact to problem signals when a monopoly breaks down. This results in the lurching policy responses that characterize punctuated equilibrium, where governments offer little policy change for long periods of time, only to introduce sweeping change when they finally respond to problem signals (Jones and Baumgartner 2005, 20–1).

Jones and Baumgartner have pushed this logic even further in their "general punctuation hypothesis." They have shown that disproportionate information processing is endemic to many governance situations, not just policy-making. They also show that different institutional designs possess varying levels of "institutional friction" that can moderate or amplify disproportionate information processing. Institutions with low friction impose fewer decision costs, making it easier to act and thereby moderate disproportionality. In these low-friction institutions, equilibria tend to be shorter and punctuations less pronounced. In contrast, institutions with high friction impose higher decision costs, making it difficult to act and amplifying disproportionality. In high-friction institutions, equilibria tend to be longer and punctuations tend to be more pronounced. So in the general punctuation hypothesis, a connection is drawn between institutions and punctuated equilibrium outcomes, adding an element not formally included in the original PET formulation.

PET has been used as a theory of both agenda-setting and policy change, though we confine our analysis to investigating its efficacy as a theory of policy change.[1] Unlike most policy change theories, PET does not have an explicit policy change hypothesis that makes point predictions about when policy changes will (or will not) occur. PET scholars argue that the point at which positive feedback results in policy punctuation is inherently unpredictable, so attempting to hypothesize when policy punctuations will occur is a futile exercise. Instead, PET is intended to explain patterns of policy stability and change over the long term, preferably using quantitative data, even if specific instances of policy change cannot be predicted (Baumgartner 2006, 25). Nevertheless, this has not precluded PET scholars from advancing an elaborate explanation of the processes underlying policy stability and change, as described earlier. This explanation is grounded in extensive empirical work, and it is this explanation that will be further investigated here in the case of Canadian firearms policy.

PET is a popular theory in the US, has developed a strong following in Western Europe, and has a growing number of applications in Canada. Canada is included in some large "n" cross-national PET studies, such as Martin and Streams's (2015) analysis of global health expenditures in seventeen countries and Jones and colleagues' (2009) study of budgets across twelve different governance systems. These studies have found that Canadian policy outcomes fit the general pattern of punctuated equilibrium. PET was also an important influence in Soroka and Wlezien's (2010) award-winning work on the linkages between public opinion and policy outcomes in Canada, the UK, and the US. Their "thermostatic model" posits the presence of negative feedback in policy-making, and they marshal a wealth of empirical evidence in support of this model (29).

There are also PET studies of entirely Canadian cases, though there are not many of them and most utilize some aspect of PET rather than applying the theory as a whole. Howlett (1997) conducted one of the pioneering Canadian PET studies in his analysis of nuclear energy and acid rain policies from 1977 to 1992, but his focus was on agenda-setting, not policy-making.[2] Other studies make use of PET concepts to construct narratives explaining policy change, but they are not fulsome applications of the theory. Included in this group are Pralle's (2003) study of BC forestry policy, Eidelman's (2010) analysis of Ontario land use policy, Hoberg and Phillips's (2011) study of Alberta oil sands policy, Ritchie and Jackson's (2014) article on Canadian and international sport policy, and Retallack's (2020) investigation of Ontario source water protection policy. Collectively, these studies illustrate the applicability of PET concepts for understanding Canadian policy development, but they do not provide a clear indication of how well the PET explanation of policy change and stability explains Canadian policy-making. In this chapter, we take a small step toward filling this void this by investigating PET in Canadian firearms policy.

Our investigation of PET is a two-step process. First, we investigate Canadian firearms policy to determine whether it has followed the punctuated equilibrium pattern of stability and change. We do so using quantitative data on the number of firearms registered in Canada over the past four decades and find that there is strong evidence of punctuated equilibrium in this policy area. Second, we investigate the PET explanation of punctuated equilibrium using congruence methods. Congruence methods identify the independent and dependent variables in an explanation as well as the expected relationship between them. The researcher "ascertains the value of the independent variable at hand and then asks what prediction or expectation about the outcome of the dependent variable should follow from the theory. If the outcome of the case is consistent with the theory's prediction, the analyst can entertain the possibility that a causal relationship may exist" (George and Bennett 2005, 181). In keeping with the PET explanation, we collected data on both the firearms policy image and firearms venue shopping in the years between 1985 and 2015 and assessed whether the patterns of policy stability and punctuation matched what was expected by the theory. The PET explanation is investigated twice, in two cycles of policy equilibrium and punctuation, one punctuation being the *Firearms Act* in 1995 and the other punctuation being the *Ending the Long-Gun Registry Act* in 2012.

Policy Equilibria and Policy Punctuations

Any PET application is based on the premise that over the long term, the policy being studied follows a punctuated equilibrium pattern. This means that the first step in any PET analysis is to investigate whether the policy is characterized by punctuated equilibrium. To do so, PET analysts rely on quantitative policy indicators using data collected over a long period of time, usually several decades, and that is what we undertake for Canadian firearms policy in this section.

Most PET studies, including Baumgartner and Jones's (2009) foundational work, rely on program spending as their preferred policy indicator, tracking spending over time to identify periods of equilibrium and punctuation. However, in the case of Canadian firearms policy, relying on program spending data is problematic because these figures became so highly politicized in the early 2000s that it is difficult to find reliable spending figures for the Canadian Firearms Program. The most credible figures come from the auditor general's reports, but these do not provide year-by-year spending breakdowns, so they are of limited use for our purposes. A more reliable quantitative indicator of firearms policy activity is the number of registered firearms in Canada each year. This number demonstrates the extent of the federal government's reach in firearms regulation; also, since Ottawa has been registering some types of firearms for decades, it allows for longitudinal tracking of Canadian firearms policy. To that end, Figure 8.1 charts the number of registered firearms in Canada from 1978 to 2016, both in absolute numbers and per capita to account for population change. The registration numbers are those recorded in the Restricted Weapons Registration System from 1978 to 2002 and the Canadian Firearms Registration System from 1999 to 2016;[3] the population numbers used in the per capita calculations are taken from Statistics Canada (2020).

An examination of Figure 8.1 readily shows that, based on firearm registrations, Canadian firearms policy has followed the punctuated equilibrium pattern. More specifically, Figure 8.1 suggests that during our period of study, there have been three periods of policy equilibrium interrupted by two policy punctuations: an equilibrium prior to 2000, a policy punctuation in 2001–2, a second equilibrium from 2002 to 2011, a second punctuation in 2012, and a third equilibrium since 2012. Even more importantly, the pattern of equilibria and punctuations in Figure 8.1 matches well with the legislative history of gun control during this period.

The first period of equilibrium was prior to 2000 and was shaped by legislation from 1969 requiring the registration of all firearms classified as prohibited and restricted. Figure 8.1 shows modest and incremental growth in firearm registrations during this period, from around 750,000 in the late 1970s to about 1.2 million in the late 1990s, most likely due to demographic factors such as population growth. However, no dramatic increases or decreases in registrations took place, not even after Bill C-17's passage in 1991, suggesting that Bill C-17 was a modest, incremental policy change, despite the high political drama surrounding it and its failed predecessor Bill C-80 at the time they were debated.

The first period of equilibrium was interrupted by the policy punctuation of the *Firearms Act* in 1995, though the effects of that Act were delayed and do not become evident in Figure 8.1 until 2001–2. As described in chapter 2, the *Firearms Act* required the registration of all firearms in Canada, thus extending the registration requirement from prohibited and restricted weapons to unrestricted ones as well. After several delays, the deadline for registering all firearms was set at 1 January 2003, resulting in a massive spike in registrations in 2001 and especially 2002 as firearms owners rushed to meet the deadline. By 2003, almost 7 million firearms were registered in Canada – a direct result of the *Firearms Act*, even though it had been passed eight years earlier.

With the introduction of universal firearms registration, Canadian firearms policy settled into a new equilibrium that lasted until 2012. During this equilibrium, registration numbers were in the 7 to 8 million range, showing only modest growth. Most of this growth is accounted for by stragglers and resisters who gradually came to terms with the new policy regime and slowly registered their weapons. The most notable feature of this period of equilibrium is its brevity. Policy equilibria are typically quite stable and enduring, with most lasting several decades, but this one was relatively short, lasting about seventeen years (if we count from 1995). Policy equilibria of this brief duration are not theoretically impossible, but they are somewhat unusual.

Universal firearms registration came to an abrupt end in 2012 as a result of a second policy punctuation, the *Ending the Long-Gun Registry Act*. This legislation returned registration requirements to a pre-*Firearms Act* state, so that prohibited and restricted firearms had to be registered but unrestricted firearms did not (see chapter 2). The effects of the *Ending the Long-Gun Registry Act* were immediate, because it was dismantling rather than creating a government program, and as a result, the number of registrations plummeted from just under 8 million in 2011 to only 767,757 in 2012. This is the largest year-on-year punctuation shown in Figure 8.1. Since then, the limited evidence available suggests that we have entered another period of policy equilibrium, with registrations growing slowly between 2012 and 2016.

The finding of punctuated equilibrium in Canadian firearms policy is consistent with the PET literature, which has found that all public policies follow the punctuated equilibrium pattern when studied over the long-term. Jones and colleagues (2009) even go so far as to suggest that in public budgets, punctuated equilibrium should be considered "a general empirical law." PET proponents argue that punctuated equilibrium

Figure 8.1. Registered firearms in Canada, 1978–2016

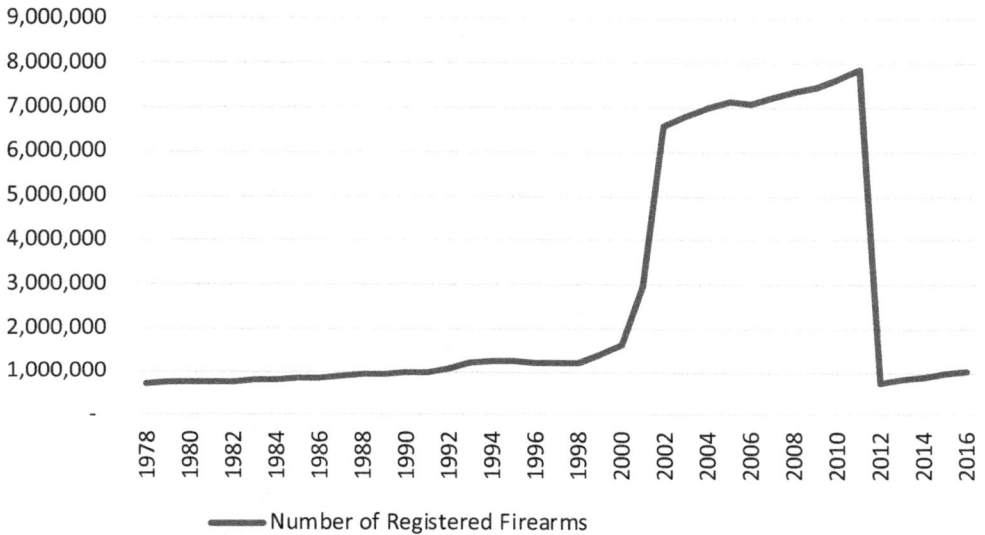

Number of Registered Firearms

Source: Hung (2006); Commissioner of Firearms (2003–16)

is universal "because it is rooted in the capacities of government to process information and allocate attention" (Baumgartner, Jones, and Mortensen 2018, 77–8). Institutional differences across political systems can affect the duration of equilibria and the intensity of punctuations, but the punctuated equilibrium pattern itself is universal (Jones and Baumgartner 2005). The presence of punctuated equilibrium in Canadian firearms policy is also important for our purposes because it allows for a test of the PET explanation of policy equilibria and punctuations using our selected case.

Explaining Policy Equilibria and Policy Punctuations

As outlined earlier, PET has an elaborate explanation of policy equilibria and punctuations. Periods of equilibrium are the result of policy monopolies characterized by policy image and institutional stability, producing negative feedback that keeps issues mostly contained within policy subsystems where only incremental policy changes can occur. Policy punctuations occur when policy image shifts and venue shopping break down policy monopolies, producing positive feed-back and expanding a policy issue into the macropolitical institutions where major policy change is possible. The key observable factors in this explanation are policy image and venue shopping. Accordingly, our investigation of the PET explanation in Canadian firearms policy focused on these two variables and whether they were consistent with PET expectations.

The firearms policy image was operationalized using Baumgartner and Jones's (2009) content analysis methodology. All articles relating to firearms, firearms use, firearms regulation, and the firearms industry were collected from the *Globe and Mail* between 1985 and 2015. The content analysis coded each article on three dimensions: (1) the type of firearms-related activity being reported (whether it was an economic activity, a public health and safety activity, a government action, or a court action), (2) the tone of the article (whether it was positive or negative to the firearms industry or firearms users), and (3) the location of the activity being reported (whether it was inside or outside of Canada). A full description of the coding frame and coding procedure is included in the chapter appendix. The types of firearms activities reported and the tone of this coverage were used as indicators of the firearms policy image, the data for which are summarized in Figures 8.2 and 8.3.

Some of the content analysis data were also used to identify instances of venue shopping. All of the articles coded as involving government or court actions were examined to identify the policy venues in which these actions took place. Given the federal government's clear jurisdiction over criminal law, the typical venue for firearms policy reforms is the federal Parliament. Thus, any efforts to shift the debate and challenge federal firearms policies in venues outside of Parliament, such as in municipal councils, provincial legislatures, or the courts, were counted as instances of venue shopping.[4]

During the first cycle of equilibrium and punctuation, which culminated in the passage of the 1995 *Firearms Act*, the policy image and venue shopping data are generally consistent with PET expectations and the PET explanation of policy stability and change is largely supported.

The media coverage data in Figure 8.2 show that prior to 1995, the firearms policy image did not experience a major change, but the prevailing policy image matched the policy reforms adopted in 1995. In most years between 1985 and 1995, less than 20 per cent of media coverage was positive, suggesting that the firearms policy image was predominantly negative. Without pre-1985 data, there is no way to know whether this negative policy image was a recent or long-standing development, but the presence of a negative policy image is clear. It is also notable that the firearms policy image was most negative in the aftermath of the 1989 Montreal Massacre, which is to be expected. Most importantly, the prevailing policy image matched the policy punctuation that eventually took place: the firearms policy image was negative and the *Firearms Act* reforms were negative for gun owners. Thus, a causal linkage between the two is plausible.

The data on government and court actions in the 1985–95 period are also consistent with the presence of venue shopping in the lead-up to the 1995 policy punctuation. Very few government actions related to firearms were reported in 1985 and 1986, and no government actions were reported at all in 1987 and 1988.[5] This suggests that firearms-related government activity, including venue shopping, was minimal during this time, which is consistent with a policy at equilibrium. After the Montreal Massacre, however, the situation changed. More government actions were reported in every year between 1989 and 1995 than in any year between 1985 and 1988. Although the vast majority of these reported actions were in the federal Parliament, some actions were also reported in provincial and municipal venues. The best examples of venue shopping were at the municipal level, where gun control advocates advanced their cause in the city councils of Canada's largest cities. In 1991–92, the Coalition for Gun Control persuaded eleven city councils across Canada to pass resolutions calling for stricter gun control (*Globe and Mail* 1992), and in 1994–95, the coalition again got endorsements from Canada's big city councils in support of universal firearms registration (Cernetig 1994). This is consistent with the PET expectation that reform-minded actors will chip away at a policy status quo in any venue that is friendly to their cause. It should be noted, however, that this kind of venue shopping was not as evident in provincial policy venues, as most provincial governments who spoke out on gun control during this time took stances against it, protecting rather than attacking the policy status quo (*Globe and Mail* 1995).

The overall levels of media coverage between 1985 and 1995 are also consistent with a policy issue that was initially at equilibrium but experienced positive feedback and issue expansion, culminating in a policy punctuation. From 1985 to 1988, there was little overall media coverage of firearms issues, and this coverage was not increasing, suggesting that firearms issues were contained in the low-profile policy subsystem and not generating positive feedback. From 1989 to 1995, however, coverage of firearms issues increased noticeably, and as shown in Figure 8.3, most of this coverage was focused on health and safety issues related to firearms and government actions intended to regulate firearms use. This increased media and political attention is consistent with the onset of positive feedback and the expansion of firearms issues from low-profile policy subsystem to a high-profile macropolitical institution. This finding is further corroborated by historical events: the increased media attention coincided with the Montreal Massacre, which was a key event in catalysing the pursuit of gun control reforms. The massacre sparked the formation of the organized gun control movement in Canada, which over the next several years would recruit thousands of supporters and pursue new gun control measures in a variety of policy venues, eventually achieving their greatest policy success in the 1995 *Firearms Act*. All of this is consistent with the onset of positive feedback between 1989 and 1995.

Altogether, the firearms policy image and venue shopping data in the first cycle of equilibrium and punctuation are consistent with PET expectations, so PET provides a plausible explanation for firearms policy outcomes during this period. After the 1995 policy punctuation, firearms policy settled into a new equilibrium based on universal firearms registration, also in accordance with PET expectations. Figure 8.2 shows that coverage of firearms issues dropped off significantly in the wake of the *Firearms Act*, and Figure 8.3 shows that few government actions were reported during this time, mostly because no new gun control legislation was proposed. Instead, firearms stakeholders were preoccupied with the implementation of the new universal gun registry, a process orchestrated by government administrators with input from various gun control and gun rights stakeholders on the Canadian Firearms Advisory Committee. The work of the committee was largely low-profile and technical, as is characteristic of issues confined to a policy subsystem (Pal 2003, 252). Thus, the period from 1996 to 2000 shows all of the expected hallmarks of a policy equilibrium.

As it happened, however, this period of equilibrium was relatively brief, interrupted by another policy punctuation with the passage of the *Ending the Long-Gun Registry Act* in 2012. In this second cycle of equilibrium and punctuation, the policy image and venue shopping data do not tell as clear a story as they do in the first cycle, and there are notable inconsistencies between the data and some aspects of the PET explanation.

The part of the PET explanation that is most clearly supported by the data is the presence of venue shopping and its role in discrediting universal firearms registration. The two most important instances of venue shopping were a constitutional court challenge and an auditor general's investigation. The former was an attempt by several provinces opposed to the universal gun registry to have the *Firearms Act* struck down by the Supreme Court as unconstitutional because it violated

Figure 8.2. Firearms-related coverage in the *Globe and Mail*, 1985–2015

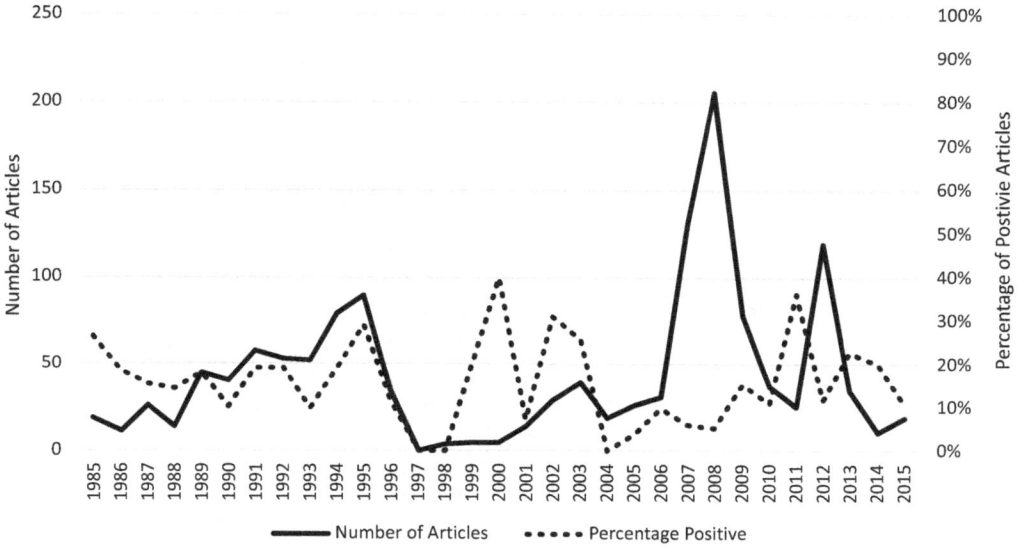

Figure 8.3. Firearms-related activities in the *Globe and Mail*, 1985–2015

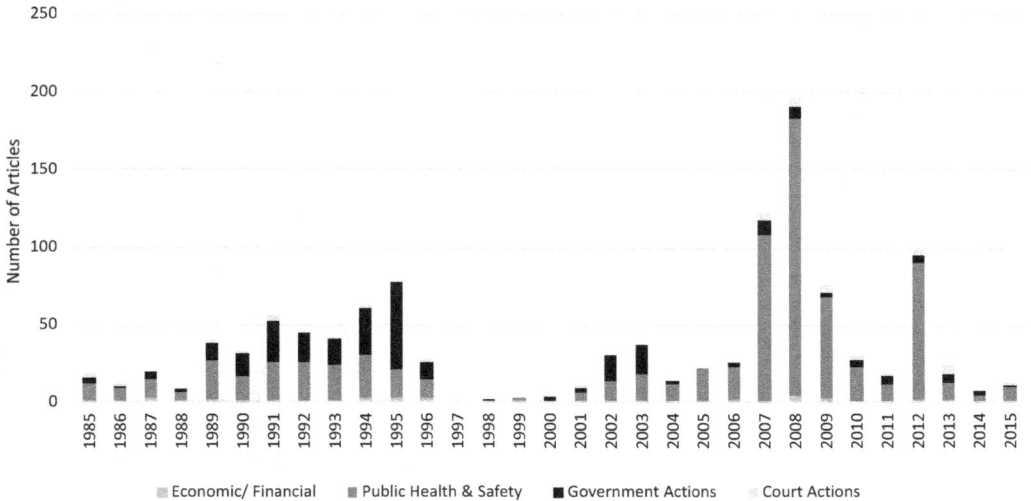

areas of provincial jurisdiction, an argument that was rejected by the Court in 2000 (*Reference re Firearms Act* 2000). The latter, which was far more consequential, was an attempt to shift the gun registry issue into a venue where the financial costs and implementation failures of the registry would be the focus. Problems with the implementation of the Canadian Firearms Program started coming to light as early as 1999. Around this time, gun registry opponents began attacking the government on the registry's problems, and in early 2001 they convinced the federal auditor general to do a full investigation (Auditor General 2002). This moved the gun registry issue into a venue the Liberal government could neither control nor suppress, one that focused primarily on public spending and accountability, two areas where the registry was vulnerable. The auditor general's scathing report in 2002 sharply undermined the integrity and popularity of the gun registry and presented a serious challenge to the prevailing policy monopoly.

When it comes to the policy image data, however, the PET explanation is not empirically supported. In the early 2000s, as problems with the gun registry surfaced and the Liberal government struggled to contain the fallout from the auditor general's report, the firearms policy image improved for a few years, as might be expected. But, as Figure 8.2 shows, positive coverage never exceeded 40 per cent and the firearms policy image did not improve to the point where a positive image prevailed. Then, in the mid-2000s, coverage became more negative again, as negative as it had been in the early 1990s. This is problematic for the PET explanation, for even though the firearms policy image was clearly negative, the policy punctuation that occurred in 2012 was clearly positive for firearms owners with the cancellation of universal registration. Thus, there is a mismatch between the prevailing policy image and the policy punctuation.

The overall coverage and types of coverage during this time also run counter to PET expectations. After 2005, overall coverage of firearms issues spiked to unprecedented levels. This could be interpreted as the onset of positive feedback; however, the focus of this coverage was overwhelmingly on health and safety issues, primarily gun violence. Increased coverage of these issues coincided with an increase in gun crime in Canada's cities and the designation of 2005 as the "Year of the Gun" by Toronto media (*Toronto Star* 2005). With this overwhelming attention on gun violence, and the prevailing negative firearms policy image, any onset of positive feedback would be expected by PET to result in a policy punctuation producing *more* gun controls, not fewer. A policy punctuation did in fact take place, but in the opposite direction to that anticipated by the theory.

Thus, the PET explanation is only partly supported in the second cycle of firearms policy equilibrium and punctuation. The policy image and venue shopping data are consistent with PET expectations during the equilibrium part of the cycle, but in the punctuation part of the cycle, only the venue shopping data are consistent with PET expectations. The policy image data, which show a negative firearms policy image even though the policy punctuation was positive for gun owners, are inconsistent with PET expectations. This is a substantial inconsistency, and the possible reasons for it – and their implications for the theory – are explored in the discussion section.

Discussion

Our investigation of PET in Canadian firearms policy focused on two aspects of the theory: whether firearms policy displayed the punctuated equilibrium pattern of stability and change, and whether the underlying factors identified as explaining stability and change acted as expected. Regarding the first aspect, the theory was clearly supported; regarding the second, it was partly supported.

The premise of PET, that policies experience long periods of equilibrium interrupted by occasional punctuations, is evident in this case. The data on firearm registrations summarized in Figure 8.1 clearly show a first period of equilibrium punctuated by the 1995 *Firearms Act*, followed by a second period of equilibrium punctuated by the 2012 *Ending the Long-Gun Registry Act*. This adds to the mountain of evidence already amassed by PET scholars demonstrating the pervasiveness of the punctuated equilibrium pattern in a range of policy areas across a variety of polities. The only caveat is the unusually short duration of the second equilibrium period in Canadian firearms policy, which lasted only seventeen years, in contrast to the decades-long equilibria more commonly found in PET studies.

Recent PET work on "institutional friction" may be instructive here. As noted earlier, institutional friction is the idea that some institutions offer less resistance to policy punctuations because they put up fewer institutional barriers to major policy change. Centralized institutions with few veto points – as existed in the Canadian firearms case (see chapters 3 and 4) – offer less institutional friction than decentralized institutions with many veto points. This is potentially relevant here because, if Canadian institutions offer little institutional friction, this may have facilitated efforts to scrap the long-gun registry, ending this policy equilibrium in relatively short order. Thus, low institutional friction may help explain why the policy equilibrium based on universal firearms registration lasted only seventeen years. Further research is needed to conclude this with certainty.

As for the PET explanation of the factors underlying policy stability and change, support in the Canadian firearms case is mixed. In the first cycle of policy equilibrium and punctuation, the policy image and venue shopping data are mostly consistent with PET expectations: there was a negative firearms policy image leading to a policy punctuation that was negative for firearms owners; there was evidence of venue shopping by reform-minded actors challenging the policy status quo; and there is some evidence of positive feedback and issue expansion in the run-up to the 1995 policy punctuation. However, in the second cycle of equilibrium and punctuation, only the venue shopping data are consistent with PET expectations, and the policy image data are contrary to them. The firearms policy image was predominantly negative in the years preceding it, but the 2012 policy punctuation was positive for firearms owners. Thus, there appears to be a disconnect between the prevailing policy image and the policy punctuation, which is problematic for PET. The reasons for this are not obvious, and it is worth exploring them as they could point to some unidentified scope limitations for the PET explanation of policy stability and change.

First, it is important to acknowledge that the PET's shortcomings in this case may not be a serious problem for the theory given its probabilistic tendencies. Although PET does not specify a policy change hypothesis that is explicitly probabilistic, its approach to identifying and understanding long-term patterns of policy stability and change seems implicitly probabilistic. That being so, the 2012 policy punctuation may be regarded as a deviant case for the theory – one that does not fundamentally challenge the theory so long as the PET explanation accounts for patterns of policy stability and change *on average*. However, even if the 2012 punctuation can be appropriately considered a deviant case, it is still worth asking *why* it is a deviant case.

One question, which other scholars have already raised, is whether the PET's conception of policy-making as a succession of policy monopolies is accurate in all cases. The mismatch between the negative policy image and the positive policy punctuation in 2012, for example, may reflect a reality in which the firearms policy image is highly contested and a policy monopoly simply does not exist. In these circumstances, the policy punctuation may have more to do with other factors, such as underlying partisan or interest group power dynamics, than it does with one policy monopoly displacing another.

This is reminiscent of PET work by Worsham (2006), who has argued that policy subsystems display different balances of positive and negative feedback and that these different feedback balances result in different coalition structures. Subsystems displaying predominantly negative feedback have a dominant coalition with a policy monopoly and are quite stable, while subsystems with predominantly positive feedback have a transitory coalition with a disintegrating policy monopoly and are ripe for punctuation. In between these extremes are subsystems with a relatively even balance of positive and negative feedback that feature competitive coalitions engaged in "protracted and regular competition," often between an industry and those seeking to regulate it (440). Given that the gun control and gun rights sides of the firearms issue are well-organized and highly mobilized and are relatively evenly matched, as found in the ACF chapter, it seems reasonable to conclude that the Canadian firearms policy subsystem has a competitive coalition structure, not a dominant or transitory one.

While dominant and transitory coalition structures seem readily compatible with the PET explanation of policy stability and change, the competitive coalition structure may not be. Dominant and transitory coalition structures fit with the PET notion of successive policy monopolies, as dominant coalition structures explain stable policy monopolies (and periods of policy stability) and transitory coalition structures explain unstable policy monopolies (and periods of policy punctuation). However, competitive coalition structures fit uneasily with the very idea of policy monopolies, as competitive coalitions are unlikely to achieve the levels of ideational consensus or institutional entrenchment necessary for a policy monopoly. So in competitive coalition contexts, policy punctuations may not be readily explained as a shift from one policy monopoly to another, and this may be why the PET explanation was unable to account for the 2012 firearms policy punctuation.

If this is the case, then the PET explanation of policy stability and change may need to be reconsidered in competitive coalition contexts. It may be that the veracity of the current explanation is limited to dominant and transitory coalition structures, and these may be defined as scope conditions for the explanation. Or it may be that the current explanation can be adapted to better explain equilibria and punctuations in competitive coalition contexts, allowing it to remain as a general explanation of policy-making. This represents a potentially important frontier in PET research as more research on the PET explanation in competitive coalition contexts is certainly needed, both to confirm the findings of this study and to determine the future course of the theory.

APPENDIX: CONTENT ANALYSIS METHODOLOGY FOR MEASURING
THE FIREARMS POLICY IMAGE

In their foundational book, Baumgartner and Jones measured policy images by undertaking content analyses of media articles, and the approach used here followed their methodology as closely as possible. The overall strategy is to analyse media coverage of a policy area to determine whether coverage of the industry – in our case, the firearms industry – is positive or negative toward the industry and whether this changes over time. Baumgartner and Jones assumed that most policy areas are multidimensional and that the media can choose to cover some dimensions and ignore others. Some of these dimensions are positive to the industry while others are negative. For example, in firearms policy, the media may choose to cover positive stories, such as growth in gun manufacturing or the popularity of firearms-based recreation, or they may choose to cover negative stories, such as gun violence and crime. The purpose of our content analysis was to generate data on such media coverage as a way of tracking the Canadian firearms policy image over time.

Baumgartner and Jones took samples of media articles from both periodicals and newspapers, but only the latter proved viable in this case. Baumgartner and Jones used the *Reader's Guide to Periodical Literature* to construct samples of US periodical articles, so we attempted to use the closest Canadian equivalent, the *Canadian Periodical Index Quarterly* (CPI.Q). Unfortunately, CPI.Q's coverage of Canadian periodicals prior to the mid-1990s is thin, so a viable sample of Canadian periodical articles could not be constructed. For their samples of newspaper articles, Baumgartner and Jones used the *New York Times*. As the closest Canadian equivalent, we selected the *Globe and Mail*. This was for several reasons: (1) it is an indisputably national newspaper, (2) it was published throughout our period of analysis (unlike the *National Post*), and (3) it has a centre-right editorial orientation. We acknowledge that relying on the *Globe and Mail* has some possible shortcomings, such as not capturing variations in the firearms policy image across regions or across ideological orientations. Relying on a sample of newspapers from across the country and across the ideological spectrum might capture such variations, but the sample would be so large as to be unmanageable. Moreover, the goal was to capture the (aggregate) *national* firearms policy image in a manner similar to how Baumgartner and Jones did it, and relying on the *Globe and Mail* allowed us to do that. Investigating the firearms policy image in other newspapers would be a worthwhile follow-up project to our study but is beyond the scope of our current analysis.

Using CPI.Q, we took a sample of firearms-related articles from the *Globe and Mail* spanning from 1985 to 2015. Following Baumgartner and Jones's lead, we constructed the sample using subject searches rather than keyword searches. The following CPI.Q subjects were included in the sample: firearms, firearms industry and trade, firearms owners, firearms ownership, gun control, gun violence, and gun laws. These subjects were selected in an effort to ensure comprehensive coverage of the firearms industry. The timespan 1985 to 2015 was selected in order to generate policy image data for the entire period of analysis in this book (1989–2012) and slightly beyond. Having applied the subject terms to the 1985–2015 period, we identified a total sample of 1,419 articles for the content analysis.

The content analysis was designed so that each article title served as a coding unit. This means that in most cases, it was the article titles that were read and coded by the coders. In cases where article titles were vague or unclear, coders could resort to the context unit, which was defined as the article body. The context unit (i.e., the article body) provided suitable context to enable the coders to make decisions about the coding unit (i.e., the article title).

Article titles were coded using a three-level coding frame, two levels of which were based closely on those used by Baumgartner and Jones.

The first level of the coding frame coded for activity type – that is, coders were asked to identify the type of firearms-related activity being reported in the article. They were also asked to select from among six coding options at this level: (1) economic and financial activities (such as firearms manufacturing, sales, and importing/exporting, or firearms-based livelihoods), (2) public health and safety activities (such as firearms crime, violence, or accidents, as well as firearms use for personal protection or recreation), (3) government actions (to regulate or control the manufacture, trade, distribution, or use of firearms), (4) court actions (related to firearms regulation or use), (5) other types of firearms-related activities, and (6) unable to determine the type of activity. These categories were based on those used by Baumgartner and Jones.

The second level of the coding frame coded for article tone: the coders were asked to determine whether the article was positive or negative to the firearms industry. In coding for tone, there were three coding options: (1) positive for the firearms industry (good things for the industry cast in a positive or neutral light and bad things for the industry cast in a negative light), (2) negative for the firearms industry (bad things for the industry cast in a positive or neutral light and good things for the industry cast in a negative light), and (3) unable to determine the tone for the firearms industry. Again, these codes were based on those used by Baumgartner and Jones. The coding guide included numerous examples of activities with positive and negative tones in order to guide the coders' coding decisions.

Finally, the third level of the coding frame coded for the location of the reported activity, something not contemplated by Baumgartner and Jones. This was added due to the coverage that American firearms issues receive in Canada. It was useful to know whether the policy image data being generated by our *Globe and Mail* analysis was based on coverage of Canadian firearms-related activities, foreign firearms-related activities, or some combination of the two. Baumgartner and Jones did not have to contemplate this in their analysis because US media are not affected by foreign influences in the same way that Canadian media are. Coding for activity location involved four options: (1) activities inside Canada, (2) activities outside Canada, (3) activities both inside and outside Canada (such as firearms smuggling and importing/exporting), and (4) unable to determine activity location.

The coding process involved two coders working independently from the same coding guide. The coding guide outlined the coding frame in detail, and two rounds of practice coding were undertaken to familiarize the coders with the coding frame. Each round of practice coding involved fifty different articles from the sample. During final coding, all coding decisions were recorded in Microsoft Excel spreadsheets, one for each coder.

The use of independent coders was important because it enhanced the reliability of the resulting data. The percentage of agreement between the coders was 94.4 per cent for activity type, 95.4 per cent for tone, and 98.7 per cent for activity location. These levels are a close match for those reported by Baumgartner and Jones and indicate a very high level of inter-coder reliability. All instances of coder disagreement were excluded from the final dataset, ensuring that all of the data included in the dataset were intersubjectively reliable.

Once the final dataset was assembled, it was analysed and summarized using Excel. The total *Globe and Mail* coverage of firearms-related issues and the tone of this coverage are summarized in Figure 8.2. Similarly, the types of firearms activities covered are summarized in Figure 8.3. These two figures served as the main data sources for our analysis of the Canadian firearms policy image and (in part) for firearms venue shopping as well. The location of firearms activities covered was also graphically summarized, but the data showed that the proportions of coverage related to Canadian firearms activities and foreign firearms activities were fairly consistent over time, so these data did not figure prominently in the analysis and were not included in the chapter.

9 Conclusion

Our goal in this book has been to test a group of leading theories of policy change in the Canadian context, using a single policy area that has been largely ignored by scholars in this field. The period of firearms policy from the 1989 Montreal Massacre to the cancellation of the long-gun registry in 2012 provided examples of both successful and failed reform attempts, high levels of political mobilization by advocacy groups and political parties, majority and minority governments of different parties, and a series of high-profile events (shootings and policy crises) that grabbed the attention of political leaders and the media. In this final chapter we review our findings through a series of thematic lenses informed by our adopted contradictory approach to multi-theoretical analysis (Cairney 2013). As stated in the introduction, our goal was not to develop a "super-theory" that synthesizes multiple approaches, nor was it to apply a variety of theories to gain a fuller understanding of Canadian firearms policy (though as we discuss later, that is a by-product of our study). Also, a direct comparison of theories was not possible, for they are often incommensurate – that is, they attempt to explain different things. Specifically, their units of analysis may differ, with some focusing on more macro-structural or environmental factors and others emphasizing subsystems of groups and institutions or even individual political actors. As well, various theories make different types of causal claims, some deterministic, some probabilistic, and others unclear. Theories also often have divergent "scope conditions," or internal limitations on when the approach should be applied. Thus, our contradictory analysis assesses each theory on its own terms to determine whether its explanatory factors or policy-making patterns were in fact present as expected, and then compares the results.

With this in mind, the summary questions explored in this chapter include:

- What causal story does each approach tell, and based on the evidence, how does each approach fare?
- What are the implications of our findings for each approach?

Finally, although our goal was not really to comprehensively explain the development of Canadian firearms policy in our period of study, we close the book by considering what we have learned in that regard and offer some thoughts on future research in this area.

Theory Summaries and Performance

Each of the theories we have examined in this book contains an explanation of policy change, usually in the form of a deductive hypothesis that can be tested against empirical evidence. Table 9.1 summarizes the key features of each approach, including its main focus, independent variables and concepts, the nature of the causal claim, overall performance in our applied tests, and scope conditions. The central difference between the approaches is ultimately the causal story they tell, so that will be our focus in this section, along with an assessment of how persuasive that story was in our case. The subsequent section will focus on the limits, including scope conditions, of each approach, and on what those suggest about how well the approach can "travel," so to speak, and areas for future development.

Rational choice institutionalism (RCI) is unique among the approaches included in this book in that it is more of a perspective and conceptual toolkit, one that allows a variety of approaches, which makes it highly adaptable. The core tenet of RCI is that policy change is explained by looking to the preferences of those individuals who have power, while also acknowledging how those actors are constrained by the institutional structures in which they operate. Moreover, RCI is premised on the deductive testing of (usually simplified) hypotheses drawn from existing literature or logical inference. We employed a well-established version of RCI, focusing on veto players (Tsebelis 2002) in the legislative process. That approach focuses on the number of veto players in the process, how closely their preferences align with one another ("congruence"), and, because our key actors are collective ones – political parties – how cohesive they are. RCI predicts that when the government party is highly cohesive and faces no veto points it can act decisively to implement its preferred policy changes. Conversely,

Table 9.1. Theory overview

	RCI	SCF	ACF	MSF	PET
Focus of approach	Political actors ("agents" with decision-making capacity and power); institutional incentive structures	Social constructions of groups targeted by policy	Policy sub-system: coalitions of civil society and state actors, with both issue-area and geographical boundaries	Kingdon: Central political system and policy sub-systems, with 3 streams: problem, policy, political. Herweg, Huß and Zohlnhöfer: 2 "coupling" phases, agenda and decision (policy change); explicit focus on actors who couple streams	Pattern of sudden and dramatic policy change (punctuation) due to events at macro-level, followed by long periods of policy stability (equilibrium) in subsystem
Independent variables/key concepts	In the veto players' variant of RCI: number of veto players; internal cohesion of veto players; congruence between veto players	Political power of target group; social construction of whether target group is "deserving" or "undeserving" of burdens and benefits	Presence of at least one policy change pathway (internal shock, external shock, policy-oriented learning, negotiated agreement). Advocacy coalition that instituted the policy status quo is no longer "in power" or policy imposition by a hierarchically superior jurisdiction	Kingdon: policy entrepreneurs and policy windows. HHZ: two phases: policy windows and policy entrepreneurs in agenda-setting phase, decision windows and political entrepreneurs in policy change phase; veto actors; packaging of viable alternatives; issue salience among voters	Policy monopolies; issue expansion; policy image: venue shopping; 'institutional friction'
Causal claim	Flexible: veto player theory is probabilistic, other RCI variants can be deterministic	Unclear	Deterministic	Probabilistic	Unclear, implicitly probabilistic

(Continued)

Table 9.1. Theory overview (Continued)

	RCI	SCF	ACF	MSF	PET
Performance	Mixed	Mixed	Strong, overall	Kingdon: failed Herweg, Huß and Zohlnhöfer: reasonably strong	Mixed
Scope conditions — Established	None	None	Only explains major policy changes	Kingdon: theory of agenda-setting, not policy change HHZ: none	None
Scope conditions — Potential	None	Presence of degenerative politics might be necessary for the SCF to apply	None	None	May not apply to policy subsystems with a competitive coalition structure
Future directions	Refine hypotheses concerning magnitude and direction of policy change Develop hypotheses to incorporate role of non-state actors	Develop reliable, non-tautological way to identify constructions and presence of degenerative politics Specify precise causal mechanisms Assess theory applicability when target group construction ambiguous	Investigate the intersections between advocacy coalitions and political parties in Canada Specify causal mechanisms to clarify the causal effects and intersections of the hypotheses	HHZ: Assess relative weight of causal factors	Specify causal mechanisms (currently, largely left to other theories) Develop testable hypotheses

if the government party faces veto points or is internally divided, then it is less likely that it will be able to enact its policy preferences. The exception is when the government's policy preferences are congruent with those of the other veto players, in which case policy change can still occur. RCI by itself offers no universal prediction on the direction of policy change, other than that it will reflect the preferences of decision-makers with the most power, such as the prime minister and their government. Tsebelis (2002), for example, takes the players' preferences as given without exploring where they might come from, while Zohln-höfer (2009) attempts to explicitly model the preferences of veto players using research on European political parties; both, however, are examples of RCI. In our application of the approach, we tested hypotheses of the government party's preferences regarding gun control based on the level of rural and Quebec representation in its caucus. While veto player theory, as used here, is essentially probabilistic, in some contexts it may be possible to construct RCI hypotheses that are deterministic – for example, a hypothesis that particular conditions are necessary and / or sufficient to cause policy change. Again, this reflects the inherent flexibility of RCI.

RCI enjoyed mixed success in our tests. The central expectations of veto player theory were confirmed: between 1989 and 2012, majority governments that faced no external veto players and that had high internal cohesion were able to make sweeping changes to firearms policy; most notably, the Liberals adopted the long-gun registry (among other changes) in 1995, and the Conservatives cancelled that registry in 2012. In contrast, internally divided governments were unable to act even with a majority of MPs, for the caucus functioned as a veto player. As well, our tests confirmed RCI's prediction that minority governments will be unlikely to enact their policy preferences when they are incongruent with those of other veto players – in the case at hand, the opposition parties in the House. In summary, RCI did well in explaining when governments would be able to enact policy change.

RCI fared less well in explaining the magnitude and direction of policy change, at least based on the factors we hypothesized. As expected, internally divided governments proposed only weak gun control measures, whereas cohesive majority governments in 1991, 1995, and 2011 proposed more ambitious reforms. However, we observed both minority governments and a cohesive majority government during the Harper era propose exactly the same fairly ambitious measure, contrary to expectations that the latter would be more ambitious. The two hypotheses predicting the direction of policy change had some support, although the evidence is mixed for both, and the impact of rural representation in caucus appears to matter more than representation from Quebec. While this particular test of RCI-based hypotheses therefore produced mixed results, it is important to remember that the approach could have been used to test other, perhaps more refined hypotheses. That flexibility and capacity for deductive hypothesis-testing means that RCI has significant potential for the study of policy change.

While RCI prioritizes individual or collective political actors in its causal story, the social construction framework (SCF) draws on work in critical theory, sociology, psychology, and metaphorical framing to argue that policy change is shaped by the social constructions and power of those groups that are a policy's target. Policy design, in turn, helps shape social constructions and often reinforces power dynamics. Individual state actors are still a key component in the SCF, however, because they want to be seen as doing good things for "good people" and punishing "bad people," often for electoral gain. The theory's proponents point to the role of political entrepreneurship: politicians may criticize or punish a socially maligned group (such as urban gangs), or reward a popular group (such as small business owners), to gain voters' favour. Moreover, the power of a target group is important because powerful groups can pressure politicians to make favourable policy decisions. The intersection of social constructions and group power generates four possible categories of target groups: "advantaged" groups with high power and deserving constructions; "dependents," who are low-power but positively constructed; "contenders," who are powerful but negatively constructed; and "deviants," who are both weak and negatively constructed. The SCF argues that policy design is associated with a target group's social construction and power but does not clearly specify whether this relationship is probabilistic or deterministic.

The performance of the SCF as an explanation for Canadian firearms policy was uneven. We found that unsafe firearms users, as a target population, were repeatedly constructed as deviants in the policy process and that the policy outcomes received by this group were consistent with SCF expectations. However, the construction of safe firearms users varied across policy episodes and was sometimes unclear. Moreover, the policy outcomes received by this group were inconsistent with SCF expectations in two of the three policy episodes investigated. Thus, SCF theory did well in explaining policy outcomes for one target population in firearms policy but did poorly in explaining policy outcomes for another target population. We speculate that this uneven performance has to do with an underregarded scope condition of SCF theory – the presence of degenerative politics. Schneider and Ingram (1997) regarded the presence of degenerative politics as a requisite condition for the operation of the SCF policy change hypothesis, and it may be that degenerative politics was present in policy development for unsafe firearms users but was not present in policy development for safe firearms users. Previous SCF research in Canadian cases has found the presence of degenerative politics in some policy-making contexts and not in others, so its varied presence/absence in firearms policy may not be that unusual. This may mean, however, that SCF scholars need to more explicitly recognize the presence of degenerative politics as a scope condition for SCF theory, and develop ways to readily identify the presence of degenerative politics, if SCF theory is to have useful application to Canadian policy-making.

The advocacy coalition framework (ACF) builds on the pluralist approach that sees the occurrence and nature of policy change as a reflection of the influence of those organized interests that have power in a policy subsystem. More specifically, the ACF's causal story is that policy change is driven by coalitions of civil society organizations – interest groups, businesses, unions, and so forth – and allies within the state, who are able to exploit some "policy change pathway," such as an internal or external shock, policy-oriented learning, or a negotiated agreement. Examples of the these pathways in our context include mass shootings like the Montreal Massacre, and the auditor general's report of spectacular cost overruns in the long-gun registry. While other approaches in this book share an explicit concern for how existing policies are disrupted – most notably PET and the MSF – the ACF stands out in that it makes deterministic causal claims. ACF theory is comprised of two conditions, both of which are necessary in the ACF causal story. The first is the presence of one of the four policy change pathways; any one, or any combination, of them satisfies this condition. The second is that either the coalition that introduced the status quo policy is no longer dominant in a policy subsystem, or a hierarchically superior jurisdiction imposes policy change on a policy subsystem (e.g., through judicial review). Either of these is sufficient for satisfying the second condition.

Among all the theories investigated in this book, it was the ACF that enjoyed the most unequivocal empirical support. Our investigation found sufficient evidence of two advocacy coalitions in Canadian firearms policy: a long-standing gun rights coalition and a more recently formed gun control coalition. There was also clear evidence of these advocacy coalitions at work, competing and pursuing their respective policy goals, in the two major policy changes investigated. More pointedly, the two necessary conditions posited in ACF policy change theory were empirically supported. In both instances of major policy change, there was evidence of at least one policy change pathway in the lead-up to policy change, as well as a coalition power shift such that the coalition that had instituted the policy status quo was no longer in power. Thus, ACF policy change theory is largely consistent with the empirical experiences of Canadian firearms policy change, bearing in mind that it is limited in scope to major policy changes only. It was also found that, although the theory was consistent with the evidence, the causal mechanisms at work in the theory – particularly the presence of multiple policy change pathways and the intersection of the two necessary conditions – were unclear, and further work could be undertaken to unpack this causal black box. Nevertheless, our findings suggest that ACF theory has considerable potential and is worthy of further investigation.

The multiple streams framework (MSF) tells a causal story in which high-profile events or changes in government create opportunities for policy change (i.e., windows), during which ideas for new policies, including those generated by organized interests or policy stakeholders, are taken up by those in power. The MSF especially embraces the chaotic nature of policy-making and "lucky breaks" associated with good timing, or having the right individual in the right place (politically) at the right time. The MSF was originally developed by Kingdon (1995) as a framework for understanding agenda-setting and was subsequently applied by Zahariadis (2003) and others to explain policy formation; more recently the framework has been refined by Herweg, Huß, and Zohlnhöfer (2015) to more conscientiously address the latter. In its original form the MSF conceived of political systems as composed of three streams: a problem stream (essentially, issues people want addressed), a policy stream (of ideas to solve those problems), and a political stream (of elections, and party and bureaucratic politics, which create opportunities for policy change). Two key concepts in Kingdon's version of the MSF are policy windows and policy entrepreneurs: windows provide fleeting opportunities for entrepreneurs to couple the three streams by advocating their favoured policy idea as a means of solving a prevailing policy problem in a way that is politically expedient. Kingdon saw this process happening fairly quickly, as windows usually open suddenly – for example, in response to some high-profile event like a mass shooting – and can quickly close again as the attention of the public, the media, and politicians moves on to something else.

The major refinement to the MSF by Herweg, Huß, and Zohlnhöfer was to reconceptualize the policy process as having two distinct phases of stream coupling: an agenda-setting phase that mirrors Kingdon's original version and a policy decision-making phase involving "decision" windows and "political" entrepreneurs. A decision window opens in the policy stream and is the window of opportunity that a policy proposal has to get through the legislative process and be formally adopted. Policy entrepreneurs in the agenda-setting phase come from the policy stream – such people typically have a long history of involvement in that area – whereas a political entrepreneur is typically a politician from the politics stream who guides a proposal through the legislative process, for example, by working to build support within caucus, across party lines, between chambers in bicameral systems, or between governments in federal or international systems. Agenda-setting is inherently unstructured; policy decision-making is more structured in that it involves the movement of a proposal through the formal law-making institutions, and here Herweg, Huß, and Zohlnhöfer incorporate some of the insights about veto players from rational choice institutionalism (RCI). Specifically, they argue that policy adoption is more likely – note the probabilistic rather than deterministic causal claim – if (a) the proposal is put forward by political entrepreneurs who hold an elected leadership position in government, (b) the proposal was put forward by a governing party or coalition that is not constrained by other veto actors, (c) different viable alternatives embraced by different parties can be combined in one package, and (d) the problem the policy is supposed to solve is salient among voters (Herweg, Huß, and Zohlnhöfer 2015).

Our investigations of the MSF found no empirical support for Kingdon's original version of the theory but moderate to substantial support for Herweg, Huß, and Zohlnhöfer's revised version. After constructing a case set of firearms-related bills between 1989 and 2012, and operationalizing policy windows and policy entrepreneurs as explanatory variables, we found no statistically significant relationship between the presence of these variables and firearms policy change. We speculate that this finding is simply due to the fact that Kingdon's theory was designed as a theory of agenda-setting and that agenda-setting should be regarded as the appropriate scope for this theory. When it is extended beyond this scope to explain policy-making, the theory loses its effectiveness. In fact, Herweg, Huß, and Zohlnhöfer developed their revised version of the theory based on the assumption that agenda-setting and policy-making are two distinct aspects of the policy process requiring two distinct explanations, and the evidence in Canadian firearms policy-making supports this assertion. Their version of MSF theory provided a statistically significant explanation of policy change in our case set, though one of their explanatory variables – different viable alternatives embraced by different parties and combined in one package – did not play a causal role in our case set, and the independent variables collectively explained only about half of the variance in the dependent variable. Thus, there is room for improvement in the revised MSF theory, but it shows potential.

Punctuated equilibrium theory (PET) starts from the observation that policies usually experience long periods of stability, or incremental change, interrupted by occasional punctuations of major change. PET's causal story emphasizes that the long periods of policy stability occur when policy issues linger in narrow policy subsystems, maintained by policy monopolies, and that policy punctuations only happen when these issues shift to the macropolitical system, where political leaders and legislatures have the constitutional authority to make such changes. Accordingly, a key part of any policy punctuation is "issue expansion," during which reformers expand the bounds of a political conflict and, in so doing, move an issue from a subsystem to the macropolitical arena. Such issue expansion involves what Baumgartner and Jones (2009) term "positive feedback," a self-reinforcing process whereby initial demands for reform catalyse more demands for reform until the process becomes an irresistible avalanche that sweeps aside all obstacles to change. Positive feedback is generated through venue shopping and shifts in policy image. Jones and Baumgartner (2005), applying the concept of institutional friction, further point to the importance of how well government institutions process the information they receive and translate that into policy adjustments, thus echoing some of the considerations shared by RCI and the revised version of MSF about how institutional designs affect policy change. Nevertheless, PET does not predict or explain when positive feedback will happen and holds that even minor events can unleash it. As such, PET contains a causal story but does not specify its hypotheses, nor does it take a stand on whether positive feedback is a necessary condition for radical change (deterministic) or merely makes radical change more likely (probabilistic). That said, it seems to be implicitly the latter – major policy change is more likely following issue expansion when there is evidence of positive feedback.

PET performed reasonably well in explaining Canadian firearms policy outcomes, with one important exception that may point to a limitation of the theory. Data on the number of registered firearms in Canada clearly showed that firearms policy has followed the punctuated equilibrium pattern of policy stability and change over time: an initial period of equilibrium was punctuated by the 1995 *Firearms Act*; this was followed by a second period of equilibrium punctuated by the 2012 *Ending the Long-Gun Registry Act*. In the first period of equilibrium and punctuation, the venue shopping and policy image data were consistent with PET expectations and the policy punctuation was congruent with the prevailing policy image. In the second period of equilibrium and punctuation, however, the venue shopping data were consistent with PET expectations but the policy image data were not. While the prevailing firearms policy image was negative, the 2012 policy punctuation was positive for firearms owners, indicating a mismatch between the policy image and the policy punctuation. We speculate that this mismatch, and PET's inability to explain this policy change, may be due to PET's reliance on successive policy monopolies as its underlying explanation for long-term policy change. In policy subsystems in which there are two or more highly competitive and evenly matched sets of interests, such as the Canadian firearms policy subsystem, the presence of a policy monopoly is questionable and thus seems unlikely to provide an explanation of policy change. This suggests there may be some unspecified scope conditions for the PET explanation of policy change, perhaps based on how interests are structured within a policy subsystem (Worsham 2006). This could be an important frontier in future PET work.

In summary, while some approaches clearly succeeded better than others on their own terms, we did not conclusively invalidate any of the theories' hypotheses or central assumptions, nor was this our intention. In the next section we consider what these findings tell us about the theories' scope conditions and how that could be useful in their ongoing development, and whether there are lessons for Canadian public policy scholars about which theories have narrow or general application in their current form.

Theory Limits and Implications

Weible (2014) observes that "theories are lenses designed to see some aspects of the policy process and ignore others" and warns that applying a theory outside its scope can provoke a kind of tunnel vision, where the researcher forces "observations into predefined categories, ignore[s] vital aspects of the policy process, and misinterpret[s] the magnitude and constancy of interactions" (394). He calls for researchers to openly recognize the scope conditions of the theoretical approaches they apply and to proceed cautiously when using an approach beyond those conditions. Following George and Bennett (2005), Gerring (2007), and Beach and Pedersen (2016), we define scope conditions as the class of cases to which a theory applies. In this section we dig more deeply into the scope conditions of our five approaches, both those that are widely acknowledged by the theory's proponents and some potential ones revealed by our tests. We also reflect on some other weaknesses or theoretical issues, such as abeyances or blind spots in the theories' casual stories, that were raised in our analyses and point to areas for future research. An analysis of theory limits also enables us to address how well the theories "travel," in three senses: (1) between countries (specifically, applying theories developed elsewhere to Canada), (2) between policy areas (applying a theory that was developed in a particular policy area to firearms policy), and (3) between stages of the policy process (e.g., using an agenda-setting theory to explain policy decision-making).

RCI

RCI does not contain any acknowledged scope conditions, and our tests did not reveal any potential ones. To reiterate our earlier point, RCI offers a perspective and toolkit that is highly adaptable, and we note that the insights of this approach have been adopted in other theories such as the MSF, PET, and ACF. RCI does have some assumptions hardwired into its ontology, such as the belief that political actors have goals and are procedurally rational about pursuing them, which includes having the ability to assess the incentive structures of major institutions. This does not mean that RCI assumes "perfect" knowledge or absolute preference-maximization; quite the contrary. But it does make the plausible assumption that political leaders understand the basic features of the political system, such as responsible government in a Westminster system. RCI also typically focuses on *known* institutional incentive structures (such as responsible government and the electoral system), as opposed to unknown private influences (such as bribery or personal connections). The most obvious limit that emerged from our tests was that the causal story in RCI was decidedly less fulsome than that offered by the ACF, the MSF, or even PET: there is no explanation, for example, of the background or macropolitical conditions that preceded policy change, and the roles of civil society actors are not contemplated. This narrower focus is both a shortcoming and an advantage of RCI. While it lacks a comprehensive account of policy change, RCI excels at testing for more precise causal relationships, for example, particular institutional arrangements such as majority versus minority government. And, it must be stressed, it is possible to build up RCI hypotheses to offer testable explanations of agenda-setting, policy design, and the role of other actors; for example, the entire field of game theory has been developed to explain decision-making outcomes when they are the product of interdependent actor decisions.

Not surprisingly given its inherent flexibility, RCI travels well in all three senses mentioned earlier. Our tests confirmed that the basic explanatory features of the veto player model can be readily applied to Canada's system, thus matching the common belief that majority governments in Canada's Westminster system can act decisively and make radical policy changes, despite formal bicameralism, when the governing party is cohesive and there are no major impediments in terms of federalism (jurisdiction) or constitutional rights. The hypotheses explaining the *direction* of policy change may not have performed as well, but overall, the findings suggest a need for further refinement rather than a rejection of the approach itself. RCI and veto player theory were not developed in a particular policy area but rather as a broader approach to the study of politics and especially comparative politics, so it has wide applicability to policy areas and different stages of the policy process.

SCF

The SCF has no clearly acknowledged scope conditions but only performed well consistently in our tests with regard to policy outcomes observed for the "deviant" group of unsafe firearms users. This may suggest a scope condition unacknowledged in previous applications of the SCF: that it only applies when degenerative politics is present. However, there is some ambiguity about precisely what degenerative politics is, given that it is sometimes referred to as a pattern of policy-making and other times discussed as a structural/cultural factor that shapes policy-making. The SCF's central insight is that all sociopolitical phenomena are, to a significant extent, products of value-laden social constructions and structural inequalities in the power of various groups. Individual political entrepreneurs play an important role in the timing of policy change, responding to pressure from powerful groups, and in exploiting existing social constructions, but how all of this shapes the fine details of new policies is not entirely clear. The SCF's leading proponents have in more recent years acknowledged this imprecision and have suggested combining the SCF with other policy theories that have more robust causal stories, such as the ACF, PET, and RCI (Schneider, Ingram, and deLeon 2014). Our application of the SCF highlights some additional areas for future development, the most significant being that it lacks a reliable way to identify the presence of degenerative politics. As well, we found that one of the target groups – safe firearms users – was difficult to clearly assign to one of the four SCF categories; moreover, this group received some policy burdens that the theory struggled to explain. This may suggest that target groups must clearly belong to a specific category for the SCF to apply.

The SCF does not appear to travel as well as some of the other approaches, at least in some respects. As shown here and in previous applications, it can be used in Canada despite being developed in the US. This is not surprising, since, like RCI, it was originally proposed as a broader approach within comparative politics and public policy theory (Schneider and Ingram 1988, 1993, 1997), and the central concepts of group power and social constructions have wide application. By the same token, the SCF is not implicitly tied to a particular policy area – despite its strong association with social welfare policy – and it travelled to gun control well only for some aspects of policy-making. Finally, although the SCF was developed to address all stages of the policy process, our sole focus was on policy decision-making, and here SCF's proponents acknowledge something we also found: on its own, the approach struggles to explain processes of policy change.

ACF

The ACF is constructed in such a way as to have wide application: it incorporates a fulsome set of conditions that create opportunities for policy change, and it focuses on a factor – the power of organized interests and their state allies – that can be observed in virtually any policy area. ACF theory nonetheless contains an important explicit scope condition: it seeks to explain *major* policy change – defined as "a change in the core attributes of a policy" such as its directions and goals – as opposed to "secondary" changes regarding the attainment of policy goals. We did not uncover any further potential scope conditions; however, our tests did reveal that advocacy coalitions relied heavily on government allies in Canadian firearms policy and on changes in which political party had formal legal authority. This points to some possible implications for using the ACF in the Canadian context, as discussed below. Also, the approach assumes that advocacy coalitions influence government decision-makers but the precise causal linkages are somewhat unclear. Without a more detailed account, the ACF cannot rule out the possibility that what appears to be causal influence is merely correlation; put another way, a government may be making policies in line with its own preferences, which happen to align with those of civil society groups but do not rely on the latter's support to exist or to be enacted. One could even argue that advocacy groups function more to legitimate government decisions than to influence those decisions. All of this said, our test found some evidence that the idea of universal gun registration emerged from the gun control advocacy coalition rather than from within government, which supports the causal assumptions made by the ACF.

The ACF was developed in the US to help explain how policy changes occur in a context characterized by multiple veto points, or in more familiar terms, the checks and balances associated with the republican separation of powers. Advocacy coalitions and their conceptual precursors in pluralism and what the Framers called "factions" are strongly associated with US politics. It has long been argued that lobbying and coordination by such groups, facilitated by the constitutional freedoms of association and free speech, help overcome the US system's structural impediments to policy change. As noted by many others historically, and as re-emphasized in the RCI section of this book, the Canadian Westminster system lacks many of these checks in periods of majority government, during which the party in power can act quickly and decisively. While the ACF clearly travels well to Canada, where lobbying by civil society organizations is pervasive, the Westminster system's centralization of power may help explain the finding above regarding how much advocacy coalitions in firearms policy relied on government allies, or more specifically on political parties that formed government. That centralization also suggests a caution when it comes to applying ACF in Canada, as the coordinating function of advocacy coalitions may not be needed, and governments are more able to act independent of civil society. Our findings also indicate that despite the ACF's origins in the field of environmental policy, it travels well to other policy areas where there are advocacy coalitions, such as gun control. As for the third sense of "travelling," the ACF was originally developed to explain three phenomena, each with its own distinctive hypotheses: the formation, maintenance, and dissolution of advocacy coalitions; policy-oriented learning; and policy change. As such, the theory was originally intended to address policy change and did not need to "travel" in this sense.

MSF

The only explicit scope condition in Kingdon's original version of the MSF was that it was a theory of agenda-setting and not of policy change, though others subsequently ignored that caveat. Herweg, Huß, and Zohlnhöfer's (2015) refinements attempt to expand the MSF into an account of policy change, so the most recent version of the approach effectively removes that scope condition. Their changes do raise some questions for future research, however. They hypothesize that policy changes are more likely to occur when they are salient among voters; moreover, consistent with the insights of RCI, policy changes are more likely when the political entrepreneur is in the governing party or coalition and government is not constrained by veto actors. But what are the relative causal weights of each of these factors? More theoretical development on this front would help the MSF better explain policy changes that have low public salience, or where the issue is highly salient (e.g., abortion rights) but so socially polarizing that any action the government takes would generate significant opposition. Or, policy changes that were proposed by opposition parties or private member's bills, which could conceivably pass without much input from government members, especially during minority governments.

As noted earlier, our findings support Kingdon's original scope condition, as his conceptualization of the MSF was unable to explain changes in Canadian firearms policy. This suggests that the original account of agenda-setting in the MSF does not travel well to the policy change phase of the policy process, despite many studies in the MSF literature that attempt to make just such a journey. Herweg, Huß, and Zohlnhöfer's efforts to address that problem are encouraging, as their approach fared much better in our tests. This suggests that the MSF has significant potential in the Canadian context, where the concentration of power in the political executive means that "political entrepreneurs" may find it relatively easy to combine the streams and enact policy change. Our successful application of the MSF to firearms policy follows a long line of scholarship that employs this theory in a wide variety of policy areas, thus further underscoring its portability.

PET

PET does not contain any acknowledged scope conditions, but our tests pointed to a potential one. The theory explains policy change in large part by pointing to the shift from one policy monopoly to another; however, some policy subsystems are marked by two or more competitive sets of interests where there is no clear monopoly for extended periods of time. This was the case in Canadian firearms policy and may explain why the PET struggled to explain some of the policy changes we examined. The presence of unambiguous policy monopolies may therefore represent an implicit condition for the successful application of PET. Additional limits within the theory that point to opportunities for further development concern PET's causal account. PET spells out a causal story, but as we noted, it does not lay out any explicit and testable hypotheses about policy equilibria or policy punctuations.

The pattern of long periods of incremental policy change punctuated by rapid and dramatic change has been observed in many countries and policy areas, so one might expect that it would travel well to Canada and firearms policy. That said, the theory has strong roots in the US, where the separation of powers is designed to frustrate government action and thus long periods of policy equilibrium are to be expected. PET arose as an attempt to explain why those barriers to dramatic change can sometimes be overcome. Canada's system of weak bicameralism, heavily concentrated power during periods of majority government, and federalism (including exclusive national government jurisdiction over criminal law) suggests that we shouldn't really expect the same barriers to dramatic policy change; indeed, a standard defence of the Canadian Westminster system is its capacity to act decisively. This may help explain PET's mixed performance in our study and the short period of "equilibrium" between the punctuations of creating and abolishing the long-gun registry. PET's mixed record explaining Canadian firearms policy may also be due to the potential scope condition noted earlier: the policy subsystem was persistently competitive rather than a series of policy monopolies. PET may therefore struggle when applied to other policy areas with this structure of interests in the policy subsystem. Finally, PET did not have to "travel" to this part of the policy process because it was originally designed to explain both agenda-setting and policy change.

Our findings thus suggest a variety of potential abeyances and scope limits for the theories we have investigated in this study. While these potential abeyances and scope limits suggest areas of concern in the established theories, and suggest that some prudence be exercised when applying the theories, they also point to exciting areas for further investigation and theoretical development. We leave it to the proponents of the various theories to investigate these potential abeyances and scope limits further; they might use our findings as a platform for advancing their theories. Moreover, our findings highlight the need for further theoretical investigation and testing, either to refute or to support our findings and, ultimately, refine or reject the theories based on a larger body of evidence. This study is not meant to be the final word in the development of any of the theories investigated here; instead, we hope it will help direct future research in the ongoing collective enterprise that is theoretical development. As well, it bears emphasizing that we are not suggesting that these are the only policy change theories worth pursuing, or that new theories and approaches won't emerge in the coming years.

At an epistemological level, this study also provides some lessons about the contradictory approach to multi-theoretical analysis. Our parallel investigations of multiple policy process theories in the same policy area proved useful in highlighting the potential abeyances and scope limits of these theories: as we contrasted the theories' divergent causal stories, and evaluated them empirically, the blind spots of each became that much more apparent. Thus, we would recommend that other Canadian public policy scholars take the contradictory approach, applying it in other policy areas where policy process theories can be fruitfully compared. This would include contradictory studies of "theoretically neutral" policy areas, as we attempted to do here, as well as policy areas that have long been dominated by a particular theory. The latter would be especially interesting, for they would be investigating whether a dominant theory in a policy area is dominant because it is the most effective or simply because it is the most established.

The contradictory analysis in this study was limited by the fundamental incommensurability of the theories being investigated, and any future contradictory analyses will have to grapple with this issue. The theories' incommensurability means that proving one theory does not disprove others and that multiple theories can be empirically supported simultaneously. We accommodated this by attempting to assess each theory on its own terms, but future contradictory studies may be able to push beyond this approach. While the theories will remain incommensurate for the foreseeable future, it may be possible to undertake contradictory analyses that focus on specific elements of theories that are commensurate and mutually exclusive, and attempt to adjudicate between them. For example, PET and the ACF have contrasting conceptions of what policy subsystems look like over the long term: PET conceives policy subsystems as successions of policy monopolies, while the ACF conceives policy subsystems as shifting configurations of competing and collaborating coalitions. These conceptions are somewhat at odds, and contradictory studies to adjudicate them, if possible, would be welcome contributions to theoretical development. There may be other opportunities for such contradictory studies, and public policy scholars should seek out these opportunities and seize them when they come along.

Lessons for Understanding Firearms Policy

Although we started out this book by observing that it is not really about firearms policy, it is fair to say that we have learned much about this policy area, so we close with some brief reflections in that regard. A finding that was reinforced in several approaches was the crucial role of high-profile events – whether termed "external shocks," "external events," "policy windows," or "punctuations" – often in the form of mass shootings like the Montreal Massacre that shocked the public and political elites alike. These events raised awareness, shaped public opinion, spurred the formation and/or mobilization of advocacy organizations, and helped set the government's agenda; moreover, these effects often interacted, for example, sparking political counter-mobilization by gun rights advocates. Our tests also underscored the important role played by the structural features of the state, such as majority governments, the electoral system, party system competition, bureaucratic organization, and the centralization of policy-making power around the prime minister. The centralization of power during periods of majority government looms particularly large and is consistently the factor that raises questions about the applicability to Canada of theories developed elsewhere. Following on that observation, there was strong evidence of the importance and agency of individuals and collective actors, including political leaders, policy entrepreneurs, political parties, and advocacy groups. A notable strength of both the ACF and the MSF was their capacity to trace the fine-grained influence of particular actors in the policy-making process, something that is less true of more structurally oriented accounts like PET, RCI, and the SCF. Finally, our tests confirmed the significant role of the media and issue framing, as the ACF, MSF, PET, and SCF all emphasized the importance of being able to articulate a policy idea as an attractive solution to a pressing problem. While some might see all of this as evidence that "everything matters," we would argue that, while certainly complex, firearms policy does encompass patterns that can be discerned though the rigorous application of public policy theories and frameworks, as we have undertaken here.

Since we began writing this volume, firearms and firearms-related crimes in Canada (and abroad) have regularly made headlines: a 2020 murder spree in rural Nova Scotia that killed twenty-two, now the worst mass shooting in Canadian history; the tragic 2017 mosque shootings in Quebec City; and a rash of handgun shootings in Canadian cities, especially Toronto. While there appears to be little political appetite to restore the long-gun registry, gun control advocates continue to pressure the government to further restrict handguns in cities, as well as semi-automatic weapons such as those used in Montreal and Nova Scotia and in the 2019 massacre in Christchurch, New Zealand. In 2019, Prime Minister Justin Trudeau proposed empowering cities to ban handguns, and shortly after the murders in Nova Scotia his government banned many "military-style" semi-automatic assault rifles, including (some would add "finally") the one used by the Montreal

Massacre shooter. That Order in Council granted a two-year amnesty for existing legal owners, however, and the government as of this writing has yet to implement a proposed buy-back scheme similar to those used in Australia and New Zealand. We make no effort to analyse such developments here, but close by observing that it is likely that any major changes in Canadian firearms policy will continue to draw a distinction between handguns and long guns and focus on weapons more commonly used in the military. As well, policy instruments will probably reflect the reality that there are a large number of firearms in Canada and that organized and strongly motivated pro-firearms groups will continue to wield influence. Finally, the firearms policy debate in Canada can be expected to retain its highly partisan and regionalized character. Whatever comes to pass, we believe that readers of this book will be well-equipped to undertake analysis of proposed and future changes in firearms policy and to appreciate the rich complexity of possible approaches and explanatory factors for understanding policy development.

Notes

Chapter 1

1 This study traces its origins to Heinmiller's Graduate Seminar in Public Policy in the fall of 2016 and was heavily influenced by his early work on this study. Curiously, this is not acknowledged in the paper.

Chapter 2

1 All Canadians were considered British citizens until 1947's *An Act Respecting Citizenship, Naturalization and the Status of Aliens* (S.C. 1946, c. 15).
2 Buyers of handguns and automatic weapons had to apply for a registration certificate from a firearms registrar, usually the local police force or a justice of the peace, which was then forwarded to the central RCMP registry in Ottawa.
3 Commission of an indictable (more serious) offence with a firearm would carry a mandatory minimum fourteen-year sentence. For the sake of comparison, the mandatory minimum sentence for second-degree murder was only ten years.
4 *An Act to amend the Criminal Code and the Customs Tariff in consequence thereof*, S.C. 1991, c.40.
5 Fifteen MPs or twenty senators could demand a parliamentary review of Orders in Council regarding firearms (Brown 2012, 211).
6 The Supreme Court of Canada ultimately ruled 5–4 in Ottawa's favour – with all three of Court's Quebec judges in dissent – citing the finding from the *Firearms Reference* (2000) that the registry fell under the federal government's criminal law power. The dissenting judges, while acknowledging that Quebec had no legal right to demand the registry's data, employed the controversial argument that the "unwritten principle" of federalism required inter-governmental cooperation and that the registry "in pith and

substance" also touched on provincial jurisdiction. As such, the dissenting judges argued that the destruction of the registry was a matter for federal and provincial political actors to negotiate.

Chapter 3

1 It is commonly said that constitutional law is "entrenched," that is, difficult to change, as it requires super-majority agreement. The 1982 *Constitution Act* actually contains several amending formulas (hence our use of the plural above) that relate to different parts of the constitution. The general or "default" formula (Section 38) is that a constitutional change requires the consent of parliament (House of Commons and Senate) and of the legislatures of at least two thirds of the provinces that contain at least 50 per cent of Canada's population according to the most recent census. However, a province may unilaterally amend provisions that affect only that province (Section 45); also, unanimous approval of parliament and all provincial legislatures is required for several changes, including to the amending formulas themselves, the monarchy's role in Canada, and the composition of the Supreme Court of Canada (Section 42).

2 The Northwest Territories, Nunavut, and Yukon are technically creatures of the federal government; cities and other municipalities elsewhere fall under provincial jurisdiction (*Constitution Act, 1867*, Section 92(8)).

3 The legal rights include, among others, the rights to counsel, the presumption of innocence, *habeas corpus*, a translator in court, and a trial within a reasonable time, and against cruel and unusual punishment and arbitrary detention.

4 The average length of a "parliament" is roughly thirty-nine months (calculated by authors from https://lop.parl.ca/About/Parliament/FederalRidingsHistory/hfer.asp?Language=E&Search=G).

5 These are distributed as follows: twenty-four each for Ontario and Quebec; ten each for New Brunswick and Nova Scotia; six each for Alberta, British Columbia, Manitoba, Saskatchewan, and Newfoundland and Labrador; four for Prince Edward Island; and one each for the Northwest Territories, Nunavut, and Yukon.

6 Senators must own $4,000 worth property – a significant sum in 1867 but considerably less so today, as the amount is not indexed to inflation – and may not be bankrupt or insolvent. Senators must also be at least thirty-nine years old and own some property in the province they ostensibly represent (as the Mike Duffy scandal in 2012–14 revealed, senators do not actually need to live primarily in the province they represent).

7 In 2014, while in opposition, Liberal leader Justin Trudeau initiated a major change in this regard, ejecting senators from his Liberal Party

caucus. Since becoming prime minister in 2015, he has appointed "independent" senators.

8 Information for this section is drawn from Parliament of Canada (House of Commons, n.d.).
9 Legislative committees are possible in the senate but have never been used (Senate of Canada 2015, 181).
10 For a satirical but striking (and often profane) depiction of the PMO in the British context, see the television series *The Thick of It* (Iannucci 2005–12) and spin-off movie *In the Loop* (Iannucci 2009).
11 Misleading, because there is no "post" one passes to win. A more accurate term would be "winner takes all" or "most popular wins it all."
12 In 2015, the average riding size in the most urbanized and populous provinces (Alberta, BC, Ontario, and Quebec) was 38 per cent larger than in the other six provinces (Elections Canada 2015). Moreover, riding sizes *within* each province can vary by +/–25 per cent around the average constituency population – a 50 per cent range, with even wider divergence permitted for small northern and Indigenous "communities of interest" (J. Smith 2002). Notably, this has the effect of underrepresenting visible minority voters and those who cannot vote (youths, new and longer-term non-citizen immigrants), who overwhelmingly live in Canada's largest cities (Pal and Choudhry 2007).
13 Data obtained from Official Voting Results, published by Elections Canada (http://www.elections.ca).
14 For example, in 2011, PC incumbent Kevin Sorenson won Crowfoot (Alberta) with 84 per cent of the popular vote, the largest share of any winning candidate. However, even with this landslide victory, he only won 49.7 per cent of the eligible voters, given the dismal turnout rate in his riding of 59.2 per cent (Elections Canada 2011).
15 See Lovink (1970) and Johnston and Ballantyne (1977) for critical replies to Cairns, and Cairns's (1970) rejoinder. None of the critics seriously challenge Cairns's main findings: SMP hurts small, national-focused parties, and it depresses regional diversity within the parliamentary caucuses of even large parties.
16 The Liberals won just two seats, both in Winnipeg.
17 Calculated from Elections Canada data (www.elections.ca). The Reform Party won four seats in Saskatchewan and one seat each in Manitoba and Ontario. The party benefited from concentrated support in the West; SMP penalized the party elsewhere. Conversely, SMP underrepresented Liberal support in the West: the party won more than one quarter of the popular vote in both Alberta and BC yet received only 19 and 15 per cent of the seats respectively. A mere 8 percentage point edge in the popular vote for Reform in BC was translated into *four times* as many seats as the Liberals

(24 to 6), while double the popular vote in Alberta (52% Reform to 25% Liberal) translated into five and a half times as many seats (22 to 4).

18 Again, SMP's distortions are on display here with a vengeance. The BQ won 23 per cent of the Quebec popular vote compared to the NDP's 43 per cent, but these were converted into four and fifty-nine seats respectively. Meanwhile, the Conservative and Liberals won five and seven Quebec seats with only 17 and 14 per cent of the vote respectively (Elections Canada 2011).

19 Flanagan (2008) observes that the Conservatives picked up several suburban ridings in Greater Vancouver, as well as seats in urban areas including Edmonton, Ottawa, Quebec City, and Winnipeg.

20 The convoluted referendum question was as follows: "Do you agree that Quebec should become sovereign after having made a formal offer to Canada for a new economic and political partnership within the scope of the bill respecting the future of Quebec and of the agreement signed on June 12, 1995?"

21 The rural population for 1981 to 2011 refers to persons living outside centres with a population of at least 1,000 and a population density of 400 persons per square kilometre (Statistics Canada 2011b). Since 2011, the census has distinguished between large (> 100,000 people), medium (30,000–99,000), and small (1,000–29,000) urban centres and rural areas (< 1,000 people or a population density of < 400 persons per square kilometre). Statistics Canada recalculated some earlier census periods according to this breakdown (Statistics Canada 2011a).

22 But see recent counter-evidence from McGrane, Berdahl, and Bell (2017), although they do not specifically explore attitudes toward leading "culture war" topics like gun control, abortion, and same-sex relations.

23 The "free market" dimension relates to views about market competition and private versus public ownership; "moral traditionalism" addresses beliefs about homosexuality, abortion, prostitution, divorce, euthanasia, and suicide; the "family values" dimension concerns views about the proper role of women in society, gender roles in families, single parents, and childrearing (Nevitte and Cochrane 2011, 258).

24 Space restrictions preclude a full list. Some of the most notorious shootings are commonly known simply by the name of where they occurred: Columbine (1999), Virginia Tech (2007), Fort Hood (2009), Sandy Hook (2012), Aurora (2012), Parkland (2016), Orlando Pulse (2016), and Las Vegas (2017).

25 Thirty-five people were killed and eighteen wounded by a gunman with semi-automatic rifles on 10 May 1996 in Port Arthur, spurring the Australian government's voluntary buy-back scheme, mentioned earlier. On 13 March 1996 in Dunblane, Scotland, a gunman killed sixteen primary school children

and their teacher with a handgun before committing suicide. A year later the UK passed legislation banning most handguns. An Australian white supremacist slaughtered fifty-one Muslim worshippers and injured forty-nine others at two mosques in Christchurch, New Zealand, on 15 March 2019, the deadliest mass shootings in modern New Zealand history. Less than one month later, the New Zealand parliament voted 119–1 to ban military-style semi-automatic and assault rifles and to introduce a buy-back regime.

Chapter 4

1   While the term "veto players" comes from Tsebelis (1995, 2002) and is explicitly associated with RCI, "veto points" is also used in other neo-institutionalist approaches, particularly historical institutionalism (HI). In some cases of HI research (for example, Immergut [2002]) they are offered as an alternative to preference- or interest-driven – that is, rational choice – explanations, by showing how institutions produced effects that key actors did not choose or prefer. But elsewhere – see, for example, Immergut (1990), Maioni (1997), Birchfield and Crepaz (1998), and Constantelos (2014) – veto "points" are used to explain how institutional configurations conditioned the ability of preference-driven political actors to influence policy outcomes. These latter usages are consistent with RCI. See also Peters (1999, 74–7) for some discussion of institutionalist usages of "veto points."

2   The last formal coalition government at the federal level was Sir Robert Borden's 1917 Union government during the First World War; however, they have been more common in the provinces. Formal coalition governments are distinguished from informal agreements by opposition parties to support a minority government's agenda.

3   This conclusion was confirmed by the Supreme Court of Canada's rulings in *R. v. Hasselwander*, [1993] 2 S.C.R. 398, and *R. v. Wiles*, 2005 SCC 84.

4   For instance, campaign platforms are not a reliable guide as they may not mention the policy issue at all, and governments may (and often do in Canada) reverse themselves on key policy promises made during the campaign.

5   In theory, the Senate could be a veto player, having most of the same legislative competencies as the House, and at times (such as during the first Chrétien and Harper governments) opposition parties are the majority in the Senate. Preliminary analysis reveals, however, that the Senate did not function as a veto point during any of the policy events discussed below – not even in 1995, when it was expected it might.

6   Moreover, Sayers found that population density was almost perfectly correlated with his more sophisticated index measure (personal correspondence with author, 8 February 2019).

7   Our deepest thanks to Brock University's data librarian Heather Whipple and to map librarian Sharon Janzen for providing this information.

8   https://lop.parl.ca/sites/ParlInfo/default/en_CA/Parliament/Parliaments.

9   The exception being C-391, which as a private member's bill did not technically signal the government's position by its introduction. Instead, we use the date of the final vote on C-391, 22 September 2010, to assess the various parties' positions.

10 Strict categories proved too difficult to construct for all dimensions. For example, if the measure concerned whether to allow or to restrict more types of weapons, which types would be "worth" more on the scale: handguns, or semi-automatics? As well, some measures work better in relative terms (such as punishments for gun crime), and it was preferable to use a consistent approach.

11 We excluded Bill C-2 (*Tackling Violent Crime Act*), passed by the Conservative minority government in 2008 with the support of the NDP and several Liberal MPs, because it was an omnibus bill that combined firearms provisions with several unrelated measures that opposition parties had supported previously, thus muddying the analysis. C-2's firearms-related amendments included these: two new firearms offences, increases to the mandatory minimum sentences for some firearms offences, the addition of firearm use as an aggravating factor in sentencing, and the creation of a reverse onus in bail hearings for those charged with violent firearms offences.

12 With the exception of C-80, which predates coverage in LEGISinfo and does not appear in HeinOnline as it only includes successfully enacted statutes. We rely on information from secondary sources for C-80.

13 Two Quebec Liberals also left for the BQ; another died in office in 1989 and was replaced by Gilles Duceppe, who joined the BQ (later to become its leader). Another Quebec PC MP resigned after being convicted of a criminal offence and was replaced in February 1990 by an NDP MP. An Alberta PC MP died shortly after the election and was replaced in 1989 by Deborah Grey, the first Reform MP. Also during the C-80 episode, an Alberta PC defected to the Liberals over the GST, and another from Nova Scotia left the PCs to sit as an independent. The calculations above and in Table 4.6 (see Appendix) reflect these developments.

14 The distinction between incrementalism and a sharp change in policy direction helps explain why C-17 is considered a major policy change here but not in the ACF chapter; only the latter type of change qualifies as "major" in the ACF. This is a good example of the incommensurability issue discussed in the introductory chapter: theories may define even the dependent variable (policy change) in somewhat different terms.

15 For example, in what would eventually become the greatest irony regarding the registry, Calgary West MP Stephen Harper voted in favour of C-68

at second reading based on the results of a mail-back survey of his riding (Bottomley 2004, 43). He reversed this on third reading, but three other Reform MPs ultimately voted for C-68 (Bottomley 2004, 49).

16 MPs Rex Crawford, Benoît Serré, and Paul Steckle.

17 The PC senators' amendments were rejected (53–46), and C-68 passed easily (64–28) (Bottomley 2004, 50).

18 Floor crossings (such David Emerson from the Liberals to Conservatives shortly after the election) and other changes to party standings between the election and when C-21 and -24 were introduced are accounted for in these figures.

19 The Conservatives gained an eleventh Quebec seat from the BQ in a by-election before the final vote on C-391.

20 The same bill was also introduced in the Senate by a Conservative deputy government leader, Gerald Comeau, as Bill S-5 (2009) but did not proceed further.

Chapter 5

1 There is some ambiguity surrounding the concept of degenerative politics. It is sometimes referred to as a pattern of policy-making and other times discussed as a structural or cultural factor shaping policy-making. Our usage of the term corresponds closely with the latter.

2 It should be noted that there is a normative element to the SCF given that degenerative politics is generally regarded pejoratively as inhibiting the development of "good" public policy that enhances equality, social justice, and full citizenship. SCF scholars acknowledge this normative element – often proudly – and it does not undermine the positivist aspects of the framework.

3 This emphasis on how the effects of policy at time "n" can constrain future policy change at time "n + 1"' (and beyond) gives the SCF something in common with policy feedback theory. Yet despite this commonality, the two are distinct theories with distinct origins as evidenced by the fact that they were covered in separate chapters and treated as separate theories in the second and third editions of the *Theories of the Policy Process* text.

4 In his study of Quebec immigration policy, Garon argues that immigrants are constructed as a deviant target group but are subjected to only superficial policy burdens, which is inconsistent with SCF expectations. However, a close reading of his study suggests that Garon underestimates the political power of immigrants. Given that immigrants constitute about 10 per cent of the Quebec population, are concentrated in ridings in the Montreal area, and have close ties to the Quebec Liberal Party, they have substantial political power and therefore should be categorized

as contenders rather than as deviants. The superficial policy burdens assigned to immigrants as contenders are entirely consistent with SCF expectations. Therefore, in this interpretation, Garon's study supports SCF as useful in explaining Canadian policy-making.

Chapter 6

1 In this section, the number of media mentions was calculated using the Canadian Major Dailies database.
2 As an illustration of the NFA's decline, its newspaper mentions bottom out in 2008 and 2009.

Chapter 7

1 Kingdon (1995) explicitly assumed that the three streams operate independently of one another. Zahariadis somewhat relaxed this assumption, stating that "although these streams are not completely independent of one another, they can be viewed as each having a life of its own" (Zahariadis 2003, 6). Treating the streams as heuristics accords well with Zahariadis's approach.
2 There is some debate about the theoretical interpretations and research methods used by Howlett in this study as evidenced by Soroka's (1999) critique and Howlett's (1999) rejoinder in the *Canadian Journal of Political Science*.
3 Because the data set was constructed to examine policy change and not agenda-setting, it only includes bills that made it onto the policy agenda and does not include efforts that tried and failed to get bills onto the policy agenda. To assess fully the MSF as a theory of agenda-setting, failed attempts to get on the policy agenda would also have to be included in the analysis. This is because the MSF makes probabilistic causal claims and these claims are symmetrical in the sense that both the presence and absence of issues on the policy agenda are explained by the theory: windows and entrepreneurs make agenda-setting more likely, and the absence of windows and entrepreneurs makes agenda-setting less likely. Our analysis only assesses the former, so, for examining agenda-setting, our data set is incomplete. For example, it is possible that many failed attempts at agenda-setting involved policy windows and entrepreneurs, which is contrary to MSF theory, but there is no way to evaluate this claim with our existing data set.

Chapter 8

1 Some have questioned whether the original PET formulation was intended as a theory of policy change, but this intention is stated clearly by Baumgartner and Jones in the opening line to Part One of *Agendas and*

Instability in American Politics: "We propose a punctuated equilibrium model of policy change in American politics, based on the emergence and recession of policy issues from the public agenda."

2 There is some debate about the theoretical interpretations and research methods used by Howlett in this study as evidenced by Soroka's (1999) critique and Howlett's (1999) rejoinder in the *Canadian Journal of Political Science.*

3 Prior to the 1995 *Firearms Act*, all firearms classified as prohibited and restricted were required to be registered and they were registered in the Restricted Weapons Registration System (RWRS). The *Firearms Act* introduced universal firearms registration and a new registration system, the Canadian Firearms Registration System (CFRS), was created to accommodate this in 1999. All firearms registered in the old RWRS had to be reregistered in the new CFRS by 1 January 2003. From 1999 to 2002, the RWRS and CFRS existed in concert, and the figures for these years are the total number of firearms registered in both systems.

4 This approach is different from the one used in Baumgartner and Jones's work. They typically rely on congressional committee activities as a proxy for venue shopping, an approach that is appropriate for the American political system, which is quite open and jurisdictionally fluid. In Canada, where federal jurisdiction over criminal law is clear and the government tends to dominate parliament, the political system is not as open and fluid and a different approach is needed. Our approach is appropriate, we argue, because it captures a wide range of Canadian policy venues, though it is certainly possible to conceive of other approaches that might also work.

5 The government actions for 1987 and 1988 reported in Figure 8.3 were actions by US governments reported in the *Globe and Mail*.

Works Cited

Alcantara, Christopher. 2013. "Preferences, Perceptions, and Veto Players: Explaining Devolution Negotiation Outcomes in the Canadian Territorial North." *Polar Record* 49(2): 167–79. https://doi.org/10.1017/S0032247412000125.

Alcantara, Christopher, and Jason Roy. 2014. "Reforming Election Dates in Canada: Towards an Explanatory Framework." *Canadian Public Administration* 57(2): 256–74. https://doi.org/10.1111/capa.12067.

Allison, Graham T. 1971. *Essence of Decision: Explaining the Cuban Missile Crisis.* Boston: Little, Brown.

Anderson, William F.A., and David A. MacLean. 2015. "Public Forest Policy Development in New Brunswick, Canada: Multiple Streams Approach, Advocacy Coalition Framework, and the Role of Science." *Ecology and Society* 20(4): 20. https://doi.org/10.5751/ES-07795-200420.

Angus Reid Institute. 2019. "Amid Concern over Spread of Gun Violence, Majorities Support Ban on Handguns, Assault Weapons." 23 May. http://angusreid.org/gun-control-handgun-ban.

Aucoin, Peter, Mark D. Jarvis, and Lori Turnbull. 2011. *Democratizing the Constitution: Reforming Responsible Government.* Toronto: Emond Montgomery.

Aucoin, Peter, Jennifer Smith, and Geoff Dinsdale. 2004. *Responsible Government: Clarifying Essentials, Dispelling Myths, and Exploring Change.* Ottawa: Centre for Management Development (now Canada School for Public Service). http://publications.gc.ca/collections/Collection/SC94-107-2004E.pdf.

Auditor General. 2002. "Chapter 10 – Department of Justice – Costs of Implementing the Canadian Firearms Program." *2002 December – Report of the Auditor General of Canada.* December. http://www.oag-bvg.gc.ca/internet/English/parl_oag_200212_10_e_12404.html.

Augustine, Philip W. 1986. "Protection of the Right to Property under the Canadian Charter of Rights and Freedoms." *Ottawa Law Review* 18(1): 55–81.

Australian National Audit Office. 1997. *The Gun Buy-Back Scheme* [Audit Report]. Canberra. https://www.anao.gov.au/sites/g/files/net4181/f/anao_report_1997-98_25.pdf.

Bakenova, Saule. 2008. "Making a Policy Problem of Water Export in Canada: 1960–2002." *Policy Studies Journal* 36(2): 279–300. http://doi.org/10.1111/j.1541-0072.2008.00266.x.

Bakvis, Herman. 2001. "Prime Minister and Cabinet in Canada: An Autocracy in Need of Reform?" *Journal of Canadian Studies* 35(4): 60–79. https://doi.org/10.3138/jcs.35.4.60.

Bandelow, Nils C., Colette S. Vogeler, Johanna Hornung, Johanna Kuhlmann, and Sebastian Heidrich. 2019. "Learning as a Necessary but Not Sufficient Condition for Major Health Policy Change: A Qualitative Comparative Analysis Combining ACF and MSF." *Journal of Comparative Policy Analysis* 21(2): 167–82. https://doi.org/10.1080/13876988.2017.1393920.

Barbehön, Marlon. 2020. "Reclaiming Constructivism: Towards an Interpretive Reading of the 'Social Construction Framework.'" *Policy Sciences* 53: 139–60. https:// doi.org/10.1007/s11077-020-09370-7.

Barnett, Laura, Tanya Dupuis, Cynthia Kirkby, Robin MacKay, Julia Nicol, and Julie Bechard. 2011. *Legislative Summary of Bill C-10*, 1–158. Ottawa: Library of Parliament.

Bartlett, William. 1995. *Legislative Summary. Bill C-68: An Act Respecting Firearms and Other Weapons*, 1–45. Ottawa: Library of Parliament.

Baumgartner, Frank R. 2006. "Punctuated Equilibrium Theory and Environmental Policy." In *Punctuated Equilibrium and the Dynamics of US Environmental Policy*, edited by Robert Repetto, 24–46. New Haven: Yale University Press.

Baumgartner, Frank R., and Bryan D. Jones. 2009. *Agendas and Instability in American Politics*, 2nd ed. Chicago: University of Chicago Press.

Baumgartner, Frank R., Bryan D. Jones, and Peter B. Mortensen. 2018. "Punctuated Equilibrium Theory: Explaining Stability and Change in Public Policymaking." In *Theories of the Policy Process*, 4th ed., edited by Christopher M. Weible and Paul A. Sabatier, 55–101. New York: Westview Press.

Beach, Derek, and Rasmus Brun Pedersen. 2016. *Causal Case Study Methods: Foundations and Guidelines for Comparing, Matching, and Tracing*. Ann Arbor: University of Michigan Press.

Bernardo, Tony. 2011. *Standing Committee on Public Safety and National Security – Evidence.* 17 November. https://www.ourcommons.ca/DocumentViewer/en/41-1/SECU/meeting-12/evidence#Int-4791776.

Berry, Frances Stokes, and William D. Berry. 2018. "Innovation and Diffusion Models in Policy Research." In *Theories of the Policy Process*, 4th ed., edited by Christopher M. Weible and Paul A. Sabatier, 253–97. New York: Westview Press.

Bickerton, James, Alain-G. Gagnon, and Patrick J. Smith. 1999. *Ties That Bind: Voters and Parties in Canada*. Toronto: Oxford University Press.

Birchfield, Vicki, and Markus M.L. Crepaz. 1998. "The Impact of Constitutional Structures and Collective and Competitive Veto Points on

Income Inequality in Industrialized Democracies." *European Journal of Political Research* 34: 175–200. https://doi.org/10.1111/1475-6765.00404.

Bird, Malcolm G. 2010. "Alberta's and Ontario's Liquor Boards: Why Such Divergent Outcomes?" *Canadian Public Administration* 53(4): 509–30. https://doi.org/10.1111/j.1754-7121.2010.00147.x.

Bittner, Amanda. 2007. "The Effects of Information and Social Cleavages: Explaining Issue Attitudes and Vote Choice in Canada." *Canadian Journal of Political Science* 40(4): 935–68. https://doi.org/10.1017/S000842390707117X.

Blais, André, Elisabeth Gidengil, Neil Nevitte, and Richard Nadeau. 2002. *Anatomy of a Liberal Victory*. Peterborough: Broadview Press.

Blankenau, Joe. 2001. "The Fate of National Health Insurance in Canada and the United States: A Multiple Streams Explanation." *Policy Studies Journal* 29(1): 38–55. https://doi.org/10.1111/j.1541-0072.2001.tb02073.x.

Block, Richard. 1998. *Firearms in Canada and Eight Other Western Countries: Selected Findings of the 1996 International Crime (Victim) Survey*. Working Document, Canadian Firearms Centre. Ottawa: Department of Justice. http://publications.gc.ca/collections/collection_2011/jus/J3-8-1997-3-eng.pdf.

Bottomley, Samuel A. 2004. "Locked and Loaded: Gun Control Policy in Canada." In *The Real Worlds of Canadian Politics: Cases in Process and Policy*, edited by Robert M. Campbell, Leslie A. Pal, and Michael Howlett, 19–79. Peterborough: Broadview Press.

Boucher, Ann. 2013. "Bureaucratic Control and Policy Change: A Comparative Venue Shopping Approach to Skilled Immigration Policies in Australia and Canada." *Journal of Comparative Policy Analysis*, 15(4): 349–67. https://doi.org/10.1080/13876988.2012.749099.

Boyce, Jillian, and Adam Cotter. 2013. *Homicide in Canada, 2012. Juristat*. Component of Statistics Canada Cat. no. 85-002-X, Canadian Centre for Justice Statistics, Ottawa: Statistics Canada.

Bratt, Duane. 2012. *Canada, the Provinces, and the Global Nuclear Revival*. Montreal and Kingston: McGill-Queen's University Press.

Brodie, Ian. 2018. *At the Centre of Government: The Prime Minister and the Limits on Political Power*. Montreal and Kingston: McGill-Queen's University Press.

Brown, R. Blake. 2012. *Arming and Disarming: A History of Gun Control in Canada*. Toronto: University of Toronto Press.

– 2017. "Firearm "Rights" in Canada: Law and History in the Debates over Gun Control." *Canadian Journal of Law and Society* 32(1): 97–116. https://doi.org/10.1017/cls.2017.5.

Cairney, Paul. 2007. "A Multiple Lenses Approach to Policy Change: The Case of Tobacco Policy in the UK." *British Politics* 2: 45–68. https://doi.org/10.1057/palgrave.bp.4200039.

– 2012. *Understanding Public Policy: Theories and Issues*. New York: Palgrave Macmillan.

– 2013. "Standing on the Shoulders of Giants: How Do We Combine the Insights of Multiple Theories in Public Policy Studies?" *Policy Studies Journal* 41(1): 1–21. http://doi.org/10.1111/psj.12000.

Cairns, Alan C. 1968. "The Electoral System and the Party System in Canada, 1921–1965." *Canadian Journal of Political Science* 1(1): 55–80. https://doi.org/10.1017/S0008423900035228.

– 1970. "A Reply to J.A.A. Lovink, 'On Analysing the Impact of the Electoral System on the Party System in Canada.'" *Canadian Journal of Political Science* 3(4): 517–21. https://doi.org/10.1017/S0008423900025944.

Campbell, Kim. 1996. *Time and Chance – the Political Memoirs of Canada's First Woman Prime Minister*. Toronto: Doubleday Canada.

Canadian Firearms Association. 2017. "Mission Statement." *Canadian Firearms Journal*, January–February.

Canadian Shooting Sports Association. 2018. *History of the Canadian Shooting Sports Association*. https://cssa-cila.org/shooting-sports/history.

Carty, R. Kenneth. 2013. "Has Brokerage Politics Ended? Canadian Parties in the New Century." In *Parties, Elections, and the Future of Canadian Politics*, edited by Amanda Bittner and Royce Koop, 10–23. Vancouver: UBC Press.

Carty, R. Kenneth, William Cross, and Lisa Young. 2000. *Rebuilding Canadian Party Politics*. Vancouver: UBC Press.

CBC News. 2006. *Tories Gut Liberals' Gun Registry*. 17 May. http://www.cbc.ca/news/canada/tories-gut-liberals-gun-registry-1.601544.

– 2009. "PM Shuts Down Parliament until March." *CBC News*. 30 December. http://www.cbc.ca/news/politics/pm-shuts-down-parliament-until-march-1.829800.

– 2015. *The Rise and Fall of Canada's Long-Gun Registry*. June. http://www.cbc.ca/news/multimedia/the-rise-and-fall-of-canada-s-long-gun-registry-1.2862001.

CBC News Online. 2006. *INDEPTH: Sponsorship Scandal*. 26 October. http://www.cbc.ca/news2/background/groupaction/index.html.

CBC Radio. 2018. *The Facts on Gun Ownership and Gun Crime in Canada*. 21 September. https://www.cbc.ca/radio/sunday/the-sunday-edition-september-23-2018-1.4831872/the-facts-on-gun-ownership-and-gun-crime-in-canada-1.4832326.

Cernetig, Miro. 1994. "B.C. Mayors Urge New Gun Laws; 18 Leaders Offer Support to Rock." *Globe and Mail*, 29 November, A1.

Choudhry, Sujit. 2006. "So What Is the Real Legacy of Oakes? Two Decades of Proportionality Analysis under the Canadian Charter's Section 1." *SCLR (2d)* 34: 501–35.

Christensen, Benjamin. 2020. "Ontario Pension Policy Making and the Politics of CPP Reform, 1963–2016." *Canadian Journal of Political Science* 53: 1–18. https://doi.org/10.1017/S0008423919000805.

Clarke, Harold D., Jane Jenson, Lawrence LeDuc, and Jon H. Pammett. 1996. *Absent Mandate: Canadian Electoral Politics in an Era of Restructuring*, 3rd ed. Vancouver: Gage.

Coalition for Gun Control. 2005. "The Gun Control Story." http://guncontrol .ca/about-the-coalition.

– 2014. "Discussion of Bill C-42." November. http://guncontrol.ca/wp-content /uploads/2015/03/CGC-brief-on-C-42.pdf.

Cohen, Michael D., James G. March, and Johan P. Olsen. 1972. "A Garbage Can Model of Organizational Choice." *Administrative Science Quarterly* 17: 1–25. http://doi.org/10.2307/2392088.

Conservative Party of Canada. 2006. "Stand Up For Canada – Conservative Party of Canada Election Platform 2006." http://www.poltext.org/sites /poltext.org/files/plateformes/can2006pc_plt_en._14112008_165519.pdf.

– 2008. "The True North Strong and Free – Stephen Harper's Plan for Canadians." http://www.poltext.org/sites/poltext.org/files/plateformes /can2008pc_plt_eng._13112008_193556.pdf.

– 2011. "Here for Canada – Stephen Harper's Low-Tax Plan for Jobs and Economic Growth." http://www.poltext.org/sites/poltext.org/files /plateformes/can2011pc_plt_en_12072011_114959.pdf.

Constantelos, John. 2010. "Playing the Field: Federalism and the Politics of Venue Shopping in the United States and Canada." *Publius: The Journal of Federalism* 40(3): 460–83. http://doi.org/10.1093/publius/pjq010.

– 2014. "Vetoes and Venues: Economic Crisis and the Roads to Recovery in Michigan and Ontario." *Canadian Journal of Political Science* 47(4): 827–53. http://doi.org/10.1017/S0008423914001073.

Cooper, Christopher A., and Patrik Marier. 2017. "Does it Matter Who Works at the Center? A Comparative Policy Analysis of Executive Styles." *Journal of Comparative Policy Analysis* 19(1): 1–16. https://doi.org/10.1080/13876988 .2015.1031543.

Cotter, Adam. 2014. *Firearms and Violent Crime in Canada, 2012. Juristat*. Statistics Canada Cat. no. 85-002-X, Canadian Centre for Justice Statistics, 1–39. Ottawa: Statistics Canada.

Courtney, John C. 2004. *Elections*. Vancouver: UBC Press.

Cukier, Wendy. 1995. *Justice and Legal Affairs Committee – Evidence*. 11 May. https://www.ourcommons.ca/Content/Archives/Committee/351/jula /evidence/134_95-05-16/jula134_blk-e.html.

– 2011. *Standing Committee on Public Safety and National Security – Evidence*. 17 November. https://www.ourcommons.ca/DocumentViewer/en/41-1 /SECU/meeting-12/evidence#Int-4792594.

Cukier, Wendy, and James Sheptycki. 2012. "Globalization of Gun Culture: Transnational Reflections on Pistolization and Masculinity, Flows and Resistance." *International Journal of Law, Crime, and Justice* 40: 3–19. http:// doi.org/10.1016/j.ijlcj.2011.09.001.

Cukier, Wendy, and Neil Thomlinson. 2004. "The Age of Missing Information: Canadian Media, Politics, and the Construction/Deconstruction of the 'Billion Dollar Registry.'" Paper presented at the Canadian Communications Association, Winnipeg, 5 June.

Cutler, Fred, and Richard W. Jenkins. 2002. "Where One Lives and What One Thinks: Implications of Rural–Urban Opinion Cleavages for Canadian Federalism." In *Canada: The State of the Federation 2001*, edited by Hamish Telford and Harvey Lazar, 367–90. Montreal and Kingston: McGill-Queen's University Press.

Dandurand, Yvon. 1998. *Firearms, Accidental Deaths, Suicides, and Violent Crime*. An Updated Review of the Literature with Special Reference to the Canadian Situation. International Centre for Criminal Law Reform and Criminal Justice Policy. Vancouver: Department of Justice.

Dauvergne, Mia. 2005. *Homicide in Canada, 2004. Juristat*. Statistics Canada – Catalogue no. 85-002, Vol. 25, no. 6, Centre for Criminal Justice Statistics, Ottawa: Statistics Canada.

Davis, James A. 1971. *Elementary Survey Analysis*. Englewood Cliffs: Prentice-Hall.

Delacourt, Susan. 2000. *Shaughnessy: The Passionate Politics of Shaughnessy Cohen*. Toronto: Macfarlane, Walter & Ross.

Department of Justice. 2015. "Public Perception of Crime and Justice in Canada: A Review of Opinion Polls." http://www.justice.gc.ca/eng/rp-pr/csj-sjc/crime/rr01_1/p5.html.

Dicey, Albert V. 1959. *Introduction to the Study of the Law of the Constitution*. 10th ed. London: Macmillan.

Docherty, David. 1997. *Mr. Smith Goes to Ottawa: Life in the House of Commons*. Vancouver: UBC Press.

– 2005. *Legislatures*. Vancouver: UBC Press.

Dowding, Keith. 2020. "Can a Case Study Test a Theory? Types and Tokens in Comparative Policy Analysis." In *Handbook of Methods and Applications in Comparative Policy Analysis*, edited by B. Guy Peters and Guillaume Fontaine, 49–65. Northampton: Edward Elgar.

Downs, Anthony. 1957. *An Economic Theory of Democracy*. New York: HarperCollins.

Dubois, Janique, and Kelly Saunders. 2017. "Explaining the Resurgence of Metis Rights: Making the Most of 'Windows of Opportunity.'" *Canadian Public Administration* 60(1). https://doi.org/10.1111/capa.12196.

Dupuis, Tanya, Cynthia Kirkby, and Robin MacKay. 2011. *Legislative Summary of Bill C-19*, 1–16. Ottawa: Library of Parliament.

Eckstein, Harry. 1975. Case Studies in Political Science. Vol. 7 in *Handbook of Political Science*, edited by Fred Greenstein and Nelson Polsby. Reading: Addison-Wesley.

Edmonton Journal. 2007. "Obituary – David A. Tomlinson." 25 September.

Eidelman, Gabriel. 2010. "Managing Urban Sprawl in Ontario: Good Policy or Good Politics." *Politics and Policy* 38(6): 1211–36. http://doi.org/10.1111/j.1747-1346.2010.00275.x.

EKOS Politics. 2017. *Here's a Simple Idea: Most Canadians Want a Strict Ban on Guns in Our Cities.* Ottawa, 4 December. http://www.ekospolitics.com/index.php/2017/12/heres-a-simple-idea-most-canadians-want-a-strict-ban-on-guns-in-our-cities.

Elections Canada. 1997. *Thirty-sixth General Election 1997: Official Voting Results Synopsis.* Ottawa: Elections Canada. Accessed May 23, 2018. http://www.elections.ca/content.aspx?section=res&document=index&dir=rep/off/dec3097&lang=e.

– 2011. *Forty-First General Election 2011: Official Voting Results.* Ottawa. http://www.elections.ca/scripts/ovr2011/default.html.

– 2015. *Canada's Electoral Districts.* March. http://www.elections.ca/content.aspx?section=res&dir=cir/list&document=index338&lang=e#list.

– 2017. *Voter Turnout at Federal Elections and Referendums.* 9 January. http://www.elections.ca/content.aspx?section=ele&dir=turn&document=index&lang=e.

Farrant, Greg. 2017. *Standing Committee on Public Safety and National Security - Evidence.* 15 November. https://www.ourcommons.ca/DocumentViewer/en/41-1/SECU/meeting-11/evidence#Int-4750887.

Flanagan, Thomas. 1997. "The Staying Power of the Legislative Status Quo: Collective Choice in Canada's Parliament after Morgentaler." *Canadian Journal of Political Science* 30(1): 31–53.

– 1998. *Game Theory and Canadian Politics.* Toronto: University of Toronto Press.

– 2008. "Urban–Rural Divide?: All Votes Are Created Equal in This Country." *Globe and Mail*, 28 March, A19.

– 2013. "Something Blue: The Harper Conservatives as Garrison Party." In *Conservatism in Canada*, edited by James Farney and David Rayside, 79–94. Toronto: University of Toronto Press.

Fleming, Anthony K. 2012. *Gun Policy in the United States and Canada: The Impact of Mass Murders and Assassinations on Gun Control.* New York: Bloomsbury.

Foot, Richard. 2000. "Gun Registry on Firing Line: In this Debate, You Either Like Firearms or You Don't." *National Post*, 19 February, B5.

Ford, Brian. 1995. *Justice and Legal Affairs Committee – Evidence.* 3 May. https://www.ourcommons.ca/Content/Archives/Committee/351/jula/evidence/119_95-05-03/jula119_blk-e.html.

Franks, C.E.S. 1987. *The Parliament of Canada.* Toronto: University of Toronto Press.

Friedland, Martin L. 1975–76. "Gun Control: The Options." *Criminal Law Quarterly* 18: 29–71.

– 1984. *A Century of Criminal Justice: Perspectives on the Development of Canadian Law.* Toronto: Carswell.

Friesen, Joe, and John Ibbitson. 2011. "Guns or Health Care: How Do You Win Over the Rural Voter?" *Globe and Mail*, 5 April, A1.

Ganghof, Steffan. 2003. "State of the Art Article: Promises and Pitfalls of Veto Player Analysis." *Swiss Political Science Review* 9(2): 1–25. https://doi.org /10.1017/S0261444800009836.

Garon, Francis. 2015. "Policy-Making for Immigration and Integration in Quebec: Degenerative Politics or Business as Usual?" *Policy Studies* 36(5): 487–506. http://doi.org/10.1111/j.1541-0072.2010.00380.x.

George, Alexander L., and Andrew Bennett. 2005. *Case Studies and Theory Development in the Social Sciences*. Cambridge, MA: MIT Press.

Gerring, John. 2007. *Case Study Research: Principles and Practices*. Cambridge: Cambridge University Press.

Giasson, Thierry, and David Dumouchel. 2012. "Of Wedge Issues and Conservative Politics in Canada: The Case of Gun Registry Elimination." Paper presented at the Midwest Political Science Association, Chicago, 12–15 April. https://www.researchgate.net/publication/266674806.

Gidengil, Elisabeth, Neil Nevitte, André Blais, Joanna Everitt, and Patrick Fournier. 2012. *Dominance and Decline: Making Sense of Recent Canadian Elections*. Toronto: University of Toronto Press.

Globe and Mail. 1992. "Mayors Call for Tougher Gun Control Laws." 30 November, A4.

– 1995. "Romanow Threatens Gun Control Challenge." 19 December, A6.

Goffman, Erving. 1974. *Frame Analysis: An Essay on the Organization of Experience*. London: Harper and Row.

Government of Canada. 1994. *The Government's Action Plan on Firearms Control*. Ottawa: Department of Justice.

Green-Pederson, Christofer, and Lars Thorup Larsen. 2012. *Morality Policies in Western Europe: Parties, Agendas, and Policy Choices*. New York: Palgrave Macmillan.

Griffith, John, and Michael Ryle. 1989. *Parliament: Functions, Practice and Procedures*. London: Sweet and Maxwell.

Grinshteyn, Erin, and David Hemenway. 2016. "Violent Death Rates: The US Compared with Other High-Income OECD Countries, 2010." *American Journal of Medicine* 129(3): 266–73. https://doi.org/10.1016/j. amjmed.2015.10.025.

Gwyn, Richard. 2012. *Nation Maker: Sir John A. Macdonald: His Life, Our Times*. Toronto: Vintage Canada.

Haglund, David G. 2017. "The Paradigm That Dare Not Speak Its Name: Canadian Foreign Policy's Uneasy Relationship with Realist IR Theory." *International Journal* 72(2): 230–42. http://doi.org/10.1177/0020702017709976.

Hall, Peter A. 1993. "Policy Paradigms, Social Learning, and the State." *Comparative Politics* 25(3): 275–96.

Hall, Peter, and Rosemary Taylor. 1996. "Political Science and the Three New Institutionalisms." *Political Studies* 44: 936–57. https://doi.org/10.1111 /j.1467-9248.1996.tb00343.x.

Harel, Mario. 2011. *Standing Committee on Public Safety and National Security – Evidence.* 17 November. https://www.ourcommons.ca/DocumentViewer /en/41-1/SECU/meeting-12/evidence#Int-4791384.

Harper, Tim. 1995. "3 MPs Pay Price for Gun Bill Revolt." *Toronto Star*, 7 April, A10.

Hausegger, Lori, Matthew Hennigar, and Troy Riddell. 2015. *Canadian Courts: Law, Politics, and Process*, 2nd ed. Toronto: Oxford University Press.

Hayle, Steven. 2015. "Comparing Drug Policy Windows Internationally: Drug Consumption Room Policy Making in Canada and England and Wales." *Contemporary Drug Problems* 42(1): 20–37.

Heard, Andrew. 2014. *Canadian Constitutional Conventions: The Marriage of Law and Politics*, 2nd ed. Toronto: Oxford University Press.

Heinmiller, B. Timothy. 2013. "Advocacy Coalitions and the Alberta Water Act." *Canadian Journal of Political Science* 46(3): 525–47. http://doi.org/10.1017 /S0008423913000541.

– 2016. *Water Policy Reform in Southern Alberta: An Advocacy Coalition Approach.* Toronto: University of Toronto Press.

Heinmiller, B. Timothy, Matthew A. Hennigar, and Sandra Kopec. 2017. "Degenerative Politics and Youth Criminal Justice Policy in Canada." *Politics and Policy* 45(3): 405–31. https://doi.org/10.1111/polp.12204.

Heinmiller, B. Timothy, and Kevin Pirak. 2017. "Advocacy Coalitions in Ontario Land Use Policy." *Review of Policy Research* 34(2): 168–85. https:// doi.org/10.1111/ropr.12210.

Hennigar, Matthew A. 2010. "Reference re Same-Sex Marriage: Making Sense of the Government's Litigation Strategy." In *Contested Constitutionalism: Reflections on the Charter of Rights and Freedoms*, edited by James B. Kelly and Christopher P. Manfredi, 209–30. Vancouver: UBC Press.

Henstra, Daniel. 2010. "Explaining Local Policy Choices: A Multiple Streams Analysis of Municipal Emergency Management." *Canadian Public Administration* 53(2): 241–58. https://doi.org/10.1111/j.1754-7121.2010 .00128.x.

Hepburn, Bob. 2010. "US Gun Lobby Brings Hardline Tactics to Canada." *Toronto Star*, 13 May.

Herweg, Nicole, Christian Huß, and Reimut Zohlnhöfer. 2015. "Straightening the Three Streams: Theorising Extensions of the Multiple Streams Framework." *European Journal of Political Research* 54: 435–49. https://doi.org/10.1111/1475 -6765.12089.

Herweg, Nicole, Nikolaos Zahariadis, and Reimut Zohlnhöfer. 2018. "The Multiple Streams Framework: Foundations, Refinements, and Empirical

Applications." In *Theories of the Policy Process*, 4th ed., edited by Christopher M. Weible and Paul A. Sabatier, 17–54. New York: Westview Press.

Hiebert, Janet L. 2002. *Charter Conflicts: What Is Parliament's Role?* Montreal and Kingston: McGill-Queen's University Press.

Hiebert, Janet L., and James B. Kelly. 2015. *Parliamentary Bills of Rights: The Experiences of New Zealand and the United Kingdom*. Cambridge: Cambridge University Press.

Hoberg, George, and Jeffrey Phillips. 2011. "Playing Defence: Early Responses to Conflict Expansion in the Oil Sands Policy Subsystem." *Canadian Journal of Political Science* 44(3): 507–27. https://doi.org/10.1017/S0008423911000473.

Howlett, Michael. 1997. "Issue-Attention and Punctuated Equilibrium Models Reconsidered: An Empirical Examination of the Dynamics of Agenda-Setting in Canada." *Canadian Journal of Political Science* 30(1): 3–29. http://doi.org/10.1017/S0008423900014918.

– 1998. "Predictable and Unpredictable Policy Windows: Institutional and Exogenous Correlates of Canadian Federal Agenda-Setting." *Canadian Journal of Political Science* 31(3): 495–524. http://doi.org/10.1017/S0008423900009100.

– 1999. "Rejoinder to Stuart Soroka: "Policy Agenda-Setting Theory Revisited: A Critique of Howlett on Downs, Baumgartner and Jones, and Kingdon.'" *Canadian Journal of Political Science* 32(4): 773–79. https://doi.org/10.1017/S0008423900016991.

– 2005–12. *The Thick of It*. Directed by Armando Iannucci.

Ibbitson, John. 2010. "Harper Exploits the Great Divide." *Globe and Mail*, 28 August, A6.

Igielnik, Ruth. 2017. *Rural and Urban Gun Owners Have Different Experiences, Views on Gun Policy*. Pew Research Center, 10 July. https://www.pewresearch.org/fact-tank/2017/07/10/rural-and-urban-gun-owners-have-different-experiences-views-on-gun-policy/.

Immergut, Ellen M. 1990. "Institutions, Veto Points, and Policy Results: A Comparative Analysis of Health Care." *Journal of Public Policy* 10(4): 391–416. https://doi.org/10.1017/S0143814X00006061.

– 2002. "The Swedish Constitution and Social Democratic Power: Measuring the Mechanical Effect of a Political Institution." *Scandanavian Political Studies* 25(3): 231–57. https://doi.org/10.1111/1467-9477.00070.

Ingold, Karin, and Frederic Varone. 2012. "Treating Policy Brokers Seriously: Evidence from Climate Policy." *Journal of Public Administration Research and Theory* 22(2): 319–46. http://doi.org/10.2307/23250884.

Jacobs, Alan M., and R. Kent Weaver. 2015. "When Policies Undo Themselves: Self-Undermining Feedback as a Source of Policy Change." *Governance* 28(4): 441–57. http://doi.org/10.1111/gove.12101.

Jegen, Maya, and Gabriel Audet. 2011. "Advocacy Coalitions and Wind Power Development: Insights from Quebec." *Energy Policy* 39: 7439–47. https://doi.org/10.1016/j.enpol.2011.09.012.

Jenkins-Smith, Hank C., Daniel Nohrstedt, Christopher M. Weible, and Karin Ingold. 2018. "The Advocacy Coalition Framework: An Overview of the Research Program." In *Theories of the Policy Process*, 4th ed., edited by Christopher M. Weible and Paul A. Sabatier, 135–72. New York: Westview Press.

Jenkins-Smith, Hank C., Daniel Nohrstedt, Christopher M. Weible, and Paul A. Sabatier. 2014. "The Advocacy Coalition Framework: Foundations, Evolution, and Ongoing Research." In *Theories of the Policy Process*, 3rd ed., edited by Paul A. Sabatier and Christopher M. Weible, 183–223. Boulder: Westview Press.

Johansen, David. 1991. "BP-268E: Property Rights and the Constitution." Library of Parliament Archives. https://lop.parl.ca/Content/LOP/Research PublicationsArchive/bp1000/bp268-e.asp.

Johnston, Richard. 2017. *The Canadian Party System: An Analytic History*. Vancouver: UBC Press.

Johnston, Richard, and Janet Ballantyne. 1977. "Geography and the Electoral System." *Canadian Journal of Political Science* 10(4): 857–66. https://doi.org/10.1017/S0008423900050927.

Jones, Bryan D., and Frank R. Baumgartner. 2005. *The Politics of Attention: How Government Prioritizes Problems*. Chicago: University of Chicago Press.

Jones, Bryan D., Frank R. Baumgartner, Christian Breunig, Christopher Wlezien, Stuart Soroka, Martial Foucault, Abel Francois, et al. 2009. "A General Empirical Law of Public Budgets: A Comparative Analysis." *American Journal of Political Science* 53(4): 855–73. https://doi.org/10.1111/j.1540-5907.2009.00405.x.

Kamal, Rifat Darina, and Charles Burton. 2018. "Policy Gridlock Versus Policy Shift in Gun Politics: A Comparative Veto Player Analysis of Gun Control Policies in the United States and Canada." World Affairs 181(4): 317–47. http://doi.org/10.1177/0043820018814356.

Karp, Aaron. 2007. "Chapter 2 – Completing the Count: Civilian Firearms." In *Small Arms Survey 2007: Guns and the City*, edited by Eric G. Berman, Keith Krause, Emile LeBrun, and Glenn McDonald, 39–71. Cambridge: Cambridge University Press. http://www.smallarmssurvey.org/publications/by-type/yearbook/small-arms-survey-2007.html.

Kelly, James B. 1999. "Bureaucratic Activism and the Charter of Rights and Freedoms: The Department of Justice and Its Entry into the Centre of Government." *Canadian Public Administration* 42: 476–511. http://doi.org/10.1111/j.1754-7121.1999.tb02037.x.

– 2005. *Governing with the Charter*. Vancouver: UBC Press.

Kingdon, John W. 1995. *Agendas, Alternatives, and Public Policies*, 2nd ed. New York: HarperCollins College.

König, Thomas, Marc Debus, and George Tsebelis. 2011. *Reform Processes and Policy Change: Veto Players and Decision-Making in Modern Democracies.* New York: Springer.

Kordan, Bohdan S. 2002. *Enemy Aliens, Prisoners of War: Internment in Canada during the Great War.* Montreal and Kingston: McGill-Queen's University Press.

Krippendorf, Klaus. 2013. *Content Analysis – an Introduction to Its Methodology,* 3rd ed. Los Angeles: SAGE.

Krouse, William J. 2012. *Gun Control Legislation.* CRS Report for Congress. Washington, D.C.: Congressional Research Service. https://fas.org/sgp/crs/misc/RL32842.pdf.

Kuypers, Jim A. 2009. "Framing Analysis." In *Rhetorical Criticism: Perspectives in Action,* edited by Jim A. Kuypers, 181–203. New York: Lexington Books.

Lakoff, George, and Mark Johnson. 1980. *Metaphors We Live By.* Chicago: University of Chicago Press.

LeDuc, Lawrence. 2011. "Realignment and Dealignment in Canadian Federal Politics." In *Canadian Parties in Transition,* edited by Alain-G. Gagnon and A. Brian Tanguay, 163–77. Toronto: University of Toronto Press.

Leesti, Tracey. 1997. *Weapons and Violent Crime. Juristat.* Statistics Canada Ca. no. 85-002-XPE, vol. 17, no. 7, Canadian Centre for Justice Statistics. Ottawa: Statistics Canada.

Lertzman, Ken, Jeremy Rayner, and Jeremy Wilson. 1996. "Learning and Change in the British Columbia Forest Policy Sector: A Consideration of Sabatier's Advocacy Coalition Framework." *Canadian Journal of Political Science* 29(1): 111–33. https://doi.org/10.1017/S0008423900007265.

Levitz, Stephanie. 2017. *69% of Canadians Support Outright Ban on Guns in Urban Areas: Poll.* 3 December. https://globalnews.ca/news/3894223/canadians-support-outright-ban-guns.

Lewis, J.P. 2013. "Elite Attitudes on the Centralization of Power in Canadian Political Executives: A Survey of Former Canadian Provincial and Federal Cabinet Ministers, 2000–2010." *Canadian Journal of Political Science* 46(4): 799–819. http://doi.org/10.1017/S0008423913000905.

– 2017. "A Wolf in Wolf's Clothing: The Stephen Harper Ministry." In *The Blueprint: Conservative Parties and Their Impact on Canadian Politics,* edited by J.P. Lewis and Joanna Everitt, 264–89. Toronto: University of Toronto Press.

Liberal Party of Canada. 1993. "Creating Opportunity: The Liberal Plan for Canada." https://web.archive.org/web/19961109135939/http://www.liberal.ca/english/policy/red_book/chapter5.html#safe.

– 1994. "1994 Liberal Policy Convention – Adopted Resolutions." https://web.archive.org/web/19961109132852fw_/http://www.liberal.ca:80/english/index.html.

Lindblom, Charles. 1959. "The Science of Muddling Through." *Public Administration Research* 19(2): 79–88. https://doi.org/10.1016/B978-0-08-017066-4.50015-1.

Lindgren, April, and Tim Naumetz. 2003. "Ontario Defies Gun Registry Law: 5 Provinces Now Refuse to 'Persecute' Gun Owners." *Ottawa Citizen*, 4 June, A1.

Litfin, Karen T. 2000. "Advocacy Coalitions along the Domestic–Foreign Frontier: Globalization and Canadian Climate Change Policy." *Policy Studies Journal* 28(1): 236–52. https://doi.org/10.1111/j.1541-0072.2000.tb02026.x.

Loat, Alison, and Michael MacMillan. 2014. *Tragedy in the Commons: Former Members of Parliament Speak Out about Canada's Failing Democracy.* Toronto: Random House Canada.

Lovink, J.A.A. 1970. "On Analysing the Impact of the Electoral System on the Party System in Canada." *Canadian Journal of Political Science* 3(4): 497–516. https://doi.org/10.1017/S0008423900025932.

Mackreal, Kim. 2013. "'Behave and Obey': How Party Discipline Hurts Politics." *Globe and Mail*, 5 February. https://www.theglobeandmail.com/news/politics/behave-and-obey-how-party-discipline-hurts-politics/article8235842.

Macnaughton, Eric, Geoffrey Nelson, and Paula Goering. 2013. "Bringing Politics and Evidence Together: Policy Entrepreneurship and the Conception of the At Home/Chez Soi Housing First Initiative for Addressing Homelessness and Mental Illness in Canada." *Social Sciences and Medicine* 82: 100–7. https://doi.org/10.1016/j.socscimed.2013.01.033.

Maioni, Antonia. 1997. "Parting at the Crossroads: The Development of Health Insurance in Canada and the United States, 1940–1965." *Comparative Politics* 29(4): 411–31. https://doi.org/10.2307/422012.

Malcolm, Joyce Lee. 1994. *To Keep and Bear Arms: The Origins of an Anglo-American Right.* Cambridge, MA: Harvard University Press.

Marier, Patrik, Stephanie Paterson, and Mariel Angus. 2014. "From Quacks to Professionals: The Importance of Changing Social Constructions in the Policy-Making Process." *Policy Studies* 35(4): 413–33. https://doi.org/10.1080/01442872.2013.877582.

Marland, Alex, Thierry Giasson, and Jennifer Lees-Marshment. 2012. *Political Marketing in Canada.* Vancouver: UBC Press.

Martin, Marie E., and Meg Streams. 2015. "Punctuated Equilibrium Theory: An Empirical Investigation of Its Relevance for Global Health Expenditure." *Public Budgeting and Financing* 35(1): 73–94. https://doi.org/10.1111/pbaf.12055.

Mauser, Gary A., and Michael Margolis. 1992. "The Politics of Gun Control: Comparing Canadian and American Patterns." *Environment and Planning C: Government and Policy* 10: 189–209. http://doi.org/10.1068/c100189.

Mawhinney, Hanne B. 1993. "An Advocacy Coalition Approach to Change in Canadian Education." In *Policy Change and Learning – an Advocacy Coalition Approach*, 59–82. Boulder: Westview Press.

McGlashen, Lindsay. 2014. *The Office of the Auditor General of Canada: Beyond Bean Counting.* Background paper no. 2011-71-E. Ottawa: Library of Parliament.

McGrane, David, and Loleen Berdahl. 2013. "'Small Worlds' No More: Reconsidering Provincial Political Cultures in Canada." *Regional and Federal Studies* 23(4): 479–93. https://doi.org/10.1080/13597566.2013.794415.

McGrane, David, Loleen Berdahl, and Scott Bell. 2017. "Moving Beyond the Urban/Rural Cleavage: Measuring Values and Policy Preferences across Residential Zones in Canada." *Journal of Urban Affairs* 39(1): 17–39. https://doi.org/10.1111/juaf.12294.

Millar, Heather, Matthew Lesch, and Linda A. White. 2019. "Connecting Models of the Individual and Policy Change Processes: A Research Agenda." *Policy Sciences* 52: 97–118. https://doi.org/10.1007/s11077-018-9327-3.

Milner, Henry, ed. 1999. *Making Every Vote Count: Reassessing Canada's Electoral System*. Toronto: Broadview Press.

Mitchell, Penni. 2010. "The Big Guns." *Herizons* 5.

Mondou, Mathieu, and Eric Montpetit. 2010. "Policy Styles and Degenerative Politics: Poverty Policy Designs in Newfoundland and Quebec." *Policy Studies Journal* 38(4): 703–22. https://doi.org/10.1111/j.1541-0072.2010.00380.x.

Montpetit, Eric. 2009. "Governance and Policy Learning in the European Union: A Comparison with North America." *Journal of European Public Policy* 16(8): 1185–203. https://doi.org/10.1080/13501760903332720.

– 2011. "Scientific Credibility, Disagreement, and Error Costs in 17 Biotechnology Policy Subsystems." *Policy Studies Journal* 39(3): 513–33. http://doi.org/10.1111/j.1541-0072.2011.00419.x.

Montpetit, Eric, Erick Lachapelle, and Alexandre Harvey. 2016. "Advocacy Coalitions, the Media, and Hydraulic Fracturing in the Canadian Provinces of British Columbia and Quebec." In *Policy Debates on Hydraulic Fracturing: Comparing Coalition Politics in North America and Europe*, edited by Christopher M. Weible, Tanya Heikkila, Karin Ingold, and Manuel Fischer, 53–79. New York: Palgrave Macmillan.

Montpetit, Eric, Christine Rothmayr, and Frederic Varone. 2005. "Institutional Vulnerability to Social Constructions: Federalism, Target Populations, and Policy Designs for Assisted Reproductive Technology in Six Democracies." *Comparative Political Studies* 38(2): 119–42. http://doi.org/10.1177/0010414004271080.

Morden, Michael. 2016. "Theorizing the Resilience of the Indian Act." *Canadian Public Administration* 59(1): 113–33. https://doi.org/10.1111/capa.12162.

Muttart, Daved. 2007. *The Empirical Gap in Jurisprudence: A Comprehensive Study of the Supreme Court of Canada*. Toronto: University of Toronto Press.

Nadeau, Richard, and Éric Bélanger. 2012. "Quebec versus the Rest of Canada, 1965–2006." In *The Canadian Election Studies: Assessing Four Decades of*

Influence, edited by Mebs Kanji, Antoine Bilodeau, and Thomas J. Scotto, 136–53. Vancouver: UBC Press.

National Firearms Association. 1999. "The Practical Firearms Control System." www.canfirearms.ca/Skeeter/NFA/PFCS.pdf.

– 2014. *Critique of Bill C-42: The Common Sense Firearms Licensing Act.* 7 November. https://nfa.ca/wp-content/uploads/2015/09/C-42-criticisms -revised-Nov-7-2014.pdf.

Nevitte, Neil, and Christopher Cochrane. 2011. "Value Change and the Dynamics of the Canadian Partisan Landscape." In *Canadian Parties in Transition*, edited by Alain-G. Gagnon and A. Brian Tanguay, 255–75. Toronto: University of Toronto Press.

Newman, Joshua, and Brian Head. 2017. "The National Context of Wicked Problems: Comparing Policies on Gun Violence in the US, Canada, and Australia." *Journal of Comparative Policy Analysis* 19(1): 40–53. https://doi .org/10.1080/13876988.2015.1029334.

Nohrstedt, Daniel. 2011. "Shifting Resources and Venues Producing Policy Change in Contested Subsystems: A Case Study of Swedish Signals Intelligence Policy." *Policy Studies Journal* 39(3): 461–84. https://doi.org /10.1111/j.1541-0072.2011.00417.x.

Oberlander, Jonathan, and R. Kent Weaver. 2015. "Unraveling from Within? The Affordable Care Act and Self-Undermining Policy Feedback." *The Forum* 13(1): 37–62. http://doi.org/10.1515/for-2015-0010.

OECD. 2011. *OECD Regional Typology*. Directorate for Public Governance and Territorial Development, OECD. http://www.oecd.org/cfe/regional-policy /OECD_regional_typology_Nov2012.pdf.

O'Malley, Eoin. 2007. "The Power of Prime Ministers: Results of an Expert Survey." *International Political Science Review* 28: 7–27. https://doi.org/10.1177 /0192512107070398.

Orsini, Michael, and Miriam Smith. 2007. "Critical Policy Studies." In *Critical Policy Studies*, edited by Michael Orsini and Miriam Smith, 1–18. Vancouver: UBC Press.

Ostrom, Elinor. 1990. *Governing the Commons: The Evolution of Institutions for Collective Action*. New York: Cambridge University Press.

– 2007. "Institutional Rational Choice: An Assessment of the Institutional Analysis and Development Framework." In *Theories of the Policy Process*, 2nd ed., edited by Paul A. Sabatier, 21–64. Boulder: Westview Press.

Ostrom, Elinor, Roy Gardner, and James Walker. 1994. *Rules, Games, and Common-Pool Resources*. Ann Arbor: University of Michigan Press.

Overton, Iain. 2016. "Canada Has a Gun Problem." *Globe and Mail*, 16 April, F9.

Page, Christopher. 2006. *The Roles of Public Opinion Research in Canadian Government*. Toronto: University of Toronto Press.

Pal, Leslie A. 2003. "Gun Control." In *The Government Taketh Away: The Politics of Pain in the United States and Canada*, edited by Leslie A. Pal and Kent Weaver, 233–62. Washington, D.C.: Georgetown University Press.

Pal, Michael, and Sujit Choudhry. 2007. "Is Every Ballot Equal?: Visible-Minority Vote Dilution in Canada." *IRPP Choices* 13(1): 1–32.

Parliament of Australia. 2017. *National Firearms Amnesty 2017.* 27 June. https://www.aph.gov.au/About_Parliament/Parliamentary_Departments/Parliamentary_Library/FlagPost/2017/June/National_Firearms_Amnesty.

Parliament of Canada. 1991. "Debates (Hansard), House of Commons." 6 June, http://parl.canadiana.ca/view/oop.debates_HOC3403_01/1155?r=0&s=1.

– 1995a. "Debates (Hansard), House of Commons." 13 March. http://www.ourcommons.ca/DocumentViewer/en/35-1/house/sitting-165/hansard.

– 1995b. "Debates (Hansard), House of Commons." 28 March. http://www.ourcommons.ca/DocumentViewer/en/35-1/house/sitting-178/hansard.

Parliament of Canada – House of Commons. n.d. *About Committees: What Is a Parliamentary Committee?* https://www.ourcommons.ca/Committees/en/About.

– n.d. *Compendium of Procedure – Legislative Process.* https://www.ourcommons.ca/About/Compendium/LegislativeProcess/c_g_legislativeprocess-e.htm.

Patten, Steve. 2016. "The Evolution of the Canadian Party System: From Brokerage to Marketing-Oriented Politics." In *Canadian Parties in Transition*, edited by Alain-G. Gagnon and A. Brian Tanguay, 3–28. Toronto: University of Toronto Press.

Perreault, Samuel. 2013. *Police-Reported Crime Statistics in Canada, 2012.* Juristat. Statistics Canada Cat. no. 85-002-X, Canadian Centre for Justice Statistics. Ottawa: Statistics Canada.

– 2017. *Canadians' Perceptions of Personal Safety and Crime, 2014.* Juristat. Cat. no. 85-002-X, Canadian Centre for Justice Statistics, Ottawa: Statistics Canada.

Peters, B. Guy. 1999. *Institutional Theory in Political Science: The 'New Institutionalism.'* London: Pinter.

– 2020. "The Comparative Method and Comparative Policy Analysis." In *Handbook of Research Methods and Applications in Comparative Policy Analysis*, edited by B. Guy Peters and Guilliame Fontaine, 20–32. Northampton: Edward Elgar.

Pierce, Jonathan J., Holly L. Petersen, and Katherine C. Hicks. 2017. "Policy Change: An Advocacy Coalition Framework Perspective." *Policy Studies Journal* 48(1): 64–86. https://doi.org/10.1111/psj.12223.

Pierce, Jonathan J., Saba Siddiki, Michael D. Jones, Kristin Schumacher, Andrew Pattison, and Holly Peterson. 2014. "Social Construction and Policy Design: A Review of Past Applications." *Policy Studies Journal* 42(1): 1–29. https://doi.org/10.1111/psj.12040.

Pilon, Dennis. 2007. *The Politics of Voting: Reforming Canada's Electoral System.* Toronto: Emond Montgomery.

Powell, Betsy, and Tracy Huffman. 2005. "City records 59th homicide of '05; 41 gun killings this year surpass number in any other year." *Toronto Star,* 20 September, B4.

Pralle, Sarah B. 2003. "Venue Shopping, Political Strategy, and Policy Change: The Internationalization of Canadian Forest Advocacy." *Journal of Public Policy* 23(3): 233–60. https://doi.org/10.1017/S0143814X03003118.

Pruysers, Scott. 2014. "Canadian Party Politics in the 2000s: A Re-examination of the Regionalization Thesis." *Canadian Political Science Review* 8(1): 27–42.

Pruysers, Scott, Anthony Sayers, and Lucas Czarnecki. 2020. "Nationalization and Regionalization in the Canadian Party System, 1867–2015." *Canadian Journal of Political Science* 53(1): 151–69. https://doi.org/10.1017/S0008423919000957.

Puddister, Kate. 2019. *Seeking the Court's Advice: The Politics of the Canadian Reference Power.* Vancouver: UBC Press.

Puddister, Kate, and James B. Kelly. 2017. "With or Without You: Quebec, the Conservative Movement, and the Pursuit of Majority Government." In *The Blueprint: Conservative Parties and Their Impact on Canadian Politics,* edited by J.P. Lewis and Joanna Everitt, 150–71. Toronto: University of Toronto Press.

Quebec (Attorney General) v. Canada (Attorney General). 2015. 2015 SCC 14 (Supreme Court of Canada, 27 March).

Rana, Abbas. 2017. "Rural Liberal MPs 'Awfully Nervous' about Upcoming Gun Legislation, Any Tinkering Could Be Trouble." *The Hill Times,* 3 April. https://www.hilltimes.com/2017/04/03/rural-liberal-mps-awfully-nervous-upcoming-gun-legislation-suspecting-gun-registry-backdoor/101657.

Rathjen, Heidi, and Charles Montpetit. 1999. *December 6, from the Montreal Massacre to Gun Control: The Inside Story.* Toronto: McClelland and Stewart.

RCMP (Royal Canadian Mounted Police). 2012. *Commission of Firearms 2011 Report.* Ottawa.

– 2016. *History of Firearms Control in Canada: Up to and Including the Firearms Act.* September. http://www.rcmp-grc.gc.ca/cfp-pcaf/pol-leg/hist/con-eng.htm.Retallack, Matthew. 2020. "Paradigmatic Policy Change or Unintended Subordination of Rural Autonomy: The Case of Source Water Protection in Ontario, Canada." *Policy Sciences* 53(3–4): 85–100. https://doi.org/10.1007/s11077-020-09369-0.

Rexe, Deanna. 2015. "Anatomy of a Tuition Freeze: The Case of Ontario." *Canadian Journal of Higher Education* 45(2): 41–59.

Ritchie, Ian, and Greg Jackson. 2014. "Politics and 'Shock': Reactionary Anti-Doping Policy Objectives in Canadian and International Sport." *International Journal of Sport Policy and Politics* 6(2): 195–212. https://doi.org/10.1080/19406940.2013.773358.

Rock, Allan, interview by B. Timothy Heinmiller. 30 January 2019.

Rowlands, Ian H. 2007. "The Development of Renewable Electricity Policy in the Province of Ontario: The Influence of Ideas and Timing." *Review of Policy Research* 24(3): 185–207. https://doi.org/10.1111/j.1541-1338.2007.00277.x.

Roy, Jason, Andrea M.L. Perrella, and Joshua Borden. 2015. "Rural, Suburban, and Urban Voters: Dissecting Residence-Based Voter Cleavages in Provincial Elections." *Canadian Political Science Review* 9(1): 112–27.

Russell, Peter H. 2004. *Constitutional Odyssey: Can Canadians Become a Sovereign People?*, 3rd ed. Toronto: University of Toronto Press.

– 2008. *Two Cheers for Minority Government: The Evolution of Canadian Parliamentary Democracy*. Toronto: Emond Montgomery.

– 2017. *Canada's Odyssey: A Country Based on Incomplete Conquests*. Toronto: University of Toronto Press.

Sabatier, Paul A. 1986. "Top-Down and Bottom-Up Approaches to Implementation Research: A Critical Analysis and Suggested Synthesis." *Journal of Public Policy* 6(1): 21–48. https://doi.org/10.1017/S0143814X00003846.

– 1988. "An Advocacy Coalition Framework of Policy Change and the Role of Policy-Oriented Learning Therein." *Policy Sciences* 21(2–3): 129–68. https://doi.org/10.1007/BF00136406.

– 1993. "Policy Change over a Decade or More." In *Policy Change and Learning – an Advocacy Coalition Approach*, by Paul A. Sabatier and Hank C. Jenkins-Smith, 13–39. Boulder: Westview Press.

– 1999. "The Need for Better Theories." In *Theories of the Policy Process*, 1st ed., edited by Paul A. Sabatier, 3–18. Boulder: Westview Press.

Sabatier, Paul A., and Hank C. Jenkins-Smith, eds. 1993. *Policy Change and Learning: An Advocacy Coalition Approach*. Boulder: Westview Press.

Sabatier, Paul A., and Hank C. Jenkins-Smith. 1999. "The Advocacy Coalition Framework: An Assessment." In *Theories of the Policy Process*, edited by Paul A. Sabatier, 117–66. Boulder: Westview Press.

Sabatier, Paul A., and Christopher M. Weible. 2007. "The Advocacy Coalition Framework – Innovations and Clarifications." In *Theories of the Policy Process*, 2nd ed., edited by Paul A. Sabatier, 189–220. Boulder: Westview Press.

Samara Centre for Democracy. 2011. *"It's My Party": Parliamentary Dysfunction Reconsidered*. http://www.samaracanada.com/downloads/ItsMyParty.pdf.

Savoie, Donald. 1999. *Governing from the Centre: The Concentration of Power in Canadian Politics*. Toronto: University of Toronto Press.

– 2008. *Court Government and the Collapse of Accountability in Canada and the United Kingdom*. Toronto: University of Toronto Press.

– 2010. *Power: Where Is It?* Montreal and Kingston: McGill-Queen's University Press.

Sayers, Anthony M. 2013. "City Ministers: The Local Politics of Cabinet Selection." In *Parties, Elections, and the Future of Canadian Politics*, edited by Amanda Bittner and Royce Koop, 94–118. Vancouver: UBC Press.

Scharpf, Fritz W. 1997. *Games Real Actors Play: Actor-Centered Institutionalism in Policy Research*. Boulder: Westview Press.

– 2000. "Institutions in Comparative Policy Research." *Comparative Political Studies* 33(6–7): 762–90. https://doi.org/10.1177/001041400003300604.

Schlager, Edella. 2007. "A Comparison of Frameworks, Theories, and Models of the Policy Process." In *Theories of the Policy Process*, 2nd ed., edited by Paul A. Sabatier, 293–319. Boulder: Westview Press.

Schneider, Anne, and Helen Ingram. 1988. "Systematically Pinching Ideas: A Comparative Approach to Policy Design." *Journal of Public Policy* 8(1): 61–80. https://doi.org/10.1017/S0143814X00006851.

– 1993. "The Social Construction of Target Populations." *American Political Science Review* 87(2): 334–46. https://doi.org/10.2307/2939044.

– 1997. *Policy Design for Democracy*. Lawrence: University Press of Kansas.

Schneider, Anne L., Helen Ingram, and Peter deLeon. 2014. "Democratic Policy Design: Social Construction of Target Populations." In *Theories of the Policy Process*, 3rd ed., edited by Paul A. Sabatier and Christopher M. Weible, 105–49. Boulder: Westview Press.

Schreier, Margaret. 2012. *Qualitative Content Analysis in Practice*. London: Sage.

Schwartz, Robert, and Teela Johnson. 2010. "Problems, Policies, and Politics: A Comparative Case Study of Contraband Tobacco from the 1990s to the Present in the Canadian Context." *Journal of Public Health Policy* 31(3): 342–54. https://doi.org/10.1057/jphp.2010.19.

Schwartz, Robert, and Allan McConnell. 2009. "Do Crises Help Remedy Regulatory Failure? A Comparative Study of the Walkerton Water and Jerusalem Banquet Hall Disasters." *Canadian Public Administration* 52(1): 91–112. https://doi.org/10.1111/j.1754-7121.2009.00061.x.

Schwoerer, Lois G. 2000. "To Hold and Bear Arms: The English Perspective." In *The Second Amendment in Law and History: Historians and Constitutional Scholars on the Right to Bear Arms*, edited by Carl T. Bogus, 207–27. New York: New Press.

Scodanibbio, Lucia. 2011. "Opening a Policy Window for Organisational Change and Full-Cost Accounting: The Creation of BC Hydro's Water Use Planning Program." *Ecological Economics* 70: 1006–15. https://doi.org/10.1016/j.ecolecon.2010.12.022.

Segaert, Aaron A. 2008. *"Urban/Rural Differences and the Culture War in the United States and Canada."* PhD diss., Department of Sociology, McMaster University, Hamilton.

Senate of Canada. 2015. "Senate Procedure in Practice." *Parliament of Canada – Senate of Canada*. June. https://sencanada.ca/media/93509/spip-psep-full-complet-e.pdf.

SES Research. 2006. "Scrapping the Federal Gun Registry." http://www
.nanosresearch.com/sites/default/files/POLONT-W06-T173.pdf.

Shepsle, Kenneth A. 2008. "Rational Choice Institutionalism." In *The Oxford Handbook of Political Institutions*, edited by Sarah A. Binder, R.A.W. Rhodes, and Bert A. Rockman, 23–39. Oxford: Oxford University Press.

Sheptycki, James. 2009. "Guns, Crime, and Social Order: A Canadian Perspective." *Criminology and Criminal Justice* 9(3): 307–36. https://doi.org/10.1177/1748895809336379.

Simon, Herbert A. 1956. "Rational Choice and the Structure of the Environment." *Psychological Review* 63(2): 129–38. https://doi.org/10.1037/H0042769.

– 1957. *Models of Man: Social and Rational–Mathematical Essays on Rational Human Behavior in a Social Setting*. New York: Wiley.

Simpson, Jeffrey. 2001. *The Friendly Dictatorship*. Toronto: McClelland and Stewart.

Skogstad, Grace. 2017. "Policy Feedback and Self-Reinforcing and Self-Undermining Processes in EU Biofuels Policy." *Journal of European Public Policy* 24(1): 21–41. https://doi.org/10.1080/13501763.2015.1132752.

– 2020. "Political Parties and Policy Change in Canadian Agricultural Marketing Institutions." *Journal of Comparative Policy Analysis*. https://doi.org/10.1080/13876988.2020.1749519.

Skogstad, Grace, and Tanya Whyte. 2015. "Authority Contests, Power, and Policy Paradigm Change: Explaining Developments in Grain Marketing Policy in Prairie Canada." *Canadian Journal of Political Science* 48(1): 79–100. https://doi.org/10.1017/S0008423914001115.

Smith, David E. 2003. *The Canadian Senate in Bicameral Perspective*. Toronto: University of Toronto Press.

Smith, Jennifer. 2002. "Community of Interest and Minority Representation: The Dilemma Facing Electoral Boundaries Commissions." *Electoral Insight* 4(2): 14–19.

Smith, Miriam. 2018. *A Civil Society? Collective Actors in Canadian Public Life*, 2nd ed. Toronto: University of Toronto Press.

Smith, Neale, Craig Mitton, Laura Dowling, Mary-Ann Hiltz, Matthew Campbell, and Shashi Ashok Gujar. 2016. "Introducing New Priority Setting and Resource Allocation Processes in a Canadian Healthcare Organization: A Case Study Analysis Informed by Multiple Streams Theory." *International Journal of Health Policy and Management* 5(1): 23–31. https://doi.org/10.15171/ijhpm.2015.169.

Snow, Dave. 2019. "The Social Construction of Naturopathic Medicine in Canadian Newspapers." *Policy Studies*. https://doi.org/10.1080/01442872.2019.1704234.

Somerset, A.J. 2016. "Triggered: Outrage over a Well-Meaning Billboard Reminds Us That Gun Control Fears Are Alive in Canada." *The Walrus*, 16 September.

Soroka, Stuart. 1999. "Policy Agenda-Setting Theory Revisited: A Critique of Howlett on Downs, Baumgartner and Jones, and Kingdon." *Canadian Journal of Political Science* 32(4): 763–72. https://doi.org/10.1017/S000842390001698X.

Soroka, Stuart N., and Christopher Wlezien. 2010. *Degrees of Democracy: Politics, Public Opinion, and Policy.* Cambridge: Cambridge University Press.

Sproule-Jones, Mark, Carolyn Johns, and B. Timothy Heinmiller,. 2008. *Canadian Water Politics: Conflicts and Institutions.* Montreal and Kingston: McGill-Queen's University Press.

Statistics Canada. 1977. *Estimates of Population for Canada and the Provinces, June 1, 1977.* Cat. No. 91-201) Ottawa: Statistics Canada. https://www.statcan.gc.ca/pub/11-516-x/pdf/5500092-eng.pdf.

– 2011a. *Archived – from Urban Areas to Population Centres.* 11 February. https://www.statcan.gc.ca/eng/subjects/standard/sgc/notice/sgc-06.

– 2011b. *Population, Urban and Rural, by Province and Territory.* 4 February. http://www.statcan.gc.ca/tables-tableaux/sum-som/l01/cst01/demo62b-eng.htm.

– 2013. *Deaths, by Cause, Chapter XX: External Causes of Morbidity and Mortality (V01 to Y89), Age Group and Sex, Canada, Annual (Number).* Table 102–0540, 2012, CANSIM. Ottawa: Statistics Canada. www5.statcan.gc.ca/cansim/a26?lang=eng&retrLang=eng&id=1020540&tabMode=dataTable&sr.

– 2016. *Population Counts, for Canada, Provinces and Territories, Census Divisions, Population Centre Size Groups and Rural Areas, 2016 Census – 100% data.* https://www12.statcan.gc.ca/census-recensement/2016/dp-pd/hlt-fst/pd-pl/Table.cfm?Lang=Eng&T=703&S=87&O=A.

– 2020. "Population Estimates, Quarterly." https://www150.statcan.gc.ca/t1/tbl1/en/tv.action?pid=1710000901.

Stein, Karin. 2001. *Public Perception of Crime and Justice in Canada: A Review of Public Opinion Polls RR2001-1e.* Research and Statistics Division. Ottawa: Department of Justice.

Stenning, Philip C. 2003. "Long Gun Registration: A Poorly Aimed Longshot." *Canadian Journal of Criminology and Criminal Justice* 45(4): 479–88.

Stewart, Hamish. 2012. *Fundamental Justice: Section 7 of the Canadian Charter of Rights and Freedoms.* Toronto: Irwin Law.

– 2015. "Bedford and the Structure of Section 7." *McGill Law Journal* 60(3): 575. http://doi.org/10.7202/1032679ar.

Stritch, Andrew. 2015. "The Advocacy Coalition Framework and Nascent Policy Subsystems: Trade Union Disclosure Policy in Canada." *Policy Studies Journal* 43(4): 437–55. http://doi.org/10.1111/psj.12112.

Sudbury Star. 2006. "Tories Look for Best Way to Kill Registry." 16 February, A9.

Supreme Court of Canada. 2000. "Reference re Firearms Act." 15 June. https://scc-csc.lexum.com/scc-csc/scc-csc/en/item/1794/index.do.

Swigger, Alexandra, and B. Timothy Heinmiller. 2014. "Advocacy Coalitions and Mental Health Policy: The Adoption of Community Treatment Orders in Ontario." *Politics and Policy* 42(4): 246–70. https://doi.org/10.1111/polp.12066.

Tasker, Paul. 2020. "Trudeau Announces Ban on 1,500 Types of 'Assault-style' Firearms – Effective Immediately." *CBC News*, 1 May. https://www.cbc.ca/news/politics/trudeau-gun-control-measures-ban-1.5552131.

Taylor-Vaisey, Nick. 2015. "Who Won Canada's Rural Vote? Tories Took the Majority of Rural Seats, but Liberals Found Their Spots." *Maclean's*, 11 November. https://www.macleans.ca/politics/ottawa/who-won-canadas-rural-vote/.

Thom, Linda. 1995. *Justice and Legal Affairs Committee – Evidence*. 24 April. https://www.ourcommons.ca/Content/Archives/Committee/351/jula/evidence/106_95-04-24/jula106_blk-e.html.

Thomas, Timothy. 2001. "An Emerging Party Cleavage: Metropolis vs. the Rest." In *Party Politics in Canada*, edited by Hugh Thorburn and Alan Whitehorn, 431–44. Toronto: Prentice Hall.

Thompson, Debra, and Jennifer Wallner. 2011. "A Focusing Tragedy: Public Policy and the Establishment of Afrocentric Education in Toronto." *Canadian Journal of Political Science* 44(4): 807–828. http://doi.org/10.1017/S000842391100076X.

Tomlinson, David A. 1995. *Justice and Legal Affairs Committee – Evidence*. 24 April. https://www.ourcommons.ca/Content/Archives/Committee/351/jula/evidence/106_95-04-24/jula106_blk-e.html.

Toronto Star. 2005. "2005: Year of the Gun. Is This the End?" 31 December, A1.

Towns, William, and Daniel Henstra. 2018. "Federal Policy Ideas and Involvement in Canadian Urban Transit, 2002–17." *Canadian Public Administration* 61(1): 65–90. https://doi.org/10.1111/capa.12247.

Tsebelis, George. 1990. *Nested Games: Rational Choice in Comparative Politics*. Berkeley: University of California Press.

– 1995. "Decision Making in Political Systems: Veto Players in Presidentialism, Parliamentarism, Multicameralism and Multipartism." *British Journal of Political Science* 25(2): 289–325. http://doi.org/10.1017/S0007123400007225.

– 2002. *Veto Players: How Political Institutions Work*. Princeton: Princeton University Press.

– 2011. "Veto Player Theory and Policy Change: An Introduction." In *Reform Processes and Policy Change: Veto Players and Decision-Making in Modern Democracies*, edited by Thomas König, Marc Debus, and George Tsebelis, 3–18. New York: Springer.

van Dijk, Jan, John van Kesteren, and Paul Smit. 2007. "Ownership of Firearms and Handguns in Countries and Main Cities (percentages): 1989–2005 ICVS and 2005 EU ICS." In *Criminal Victimisation in International Perspective: Key findings from the 2004-2005 ICVS and EU ICS*. Vienna: UN Office on Drugs and Crime.

Vienneau, David. 1994. "Justice Minister Backs Stronger Gun Control." *Toronto Star*, 21 April, A1.

Wade, Terence, and Roger Tennuci. 1994. *Technical Report – Review of Firearms Registration*. Department of Justice.

Walchuk, Brad. 2012. "A Whole New Ballgame: The Rise of Canada's Fifth Party System." *American Review of Canadian Studies* 43(2): 418–34. http://doi .org/10.1080/02722011.2012.705867.

Walks, R. Alan. 2005. "The City–Suburban Cleavage in Canadian Federal Politics." *Canadian Journal of Political Science* 38(2): 383–413. https://doi.org /10.1017/S0008423905030842.

Wallace, Bruce. 1998. "For the Love of Power." *Maclean's*, 19 October, 16–21.

Wasko, Kevin, and Brenda O'Neill. 2007. "The Urban/Suburban/Rural Cleavage in Canadian Political Opinion." Paper presented at the annual meeting of the Canadian Political Science Association, Saskatoon.

Weaver, R. Kent. 2010. "Paths and Forks or Chutes and Ladders: Negative Feedbacks and Policy Regime Change." *Journal of Public Policy* 30(2): 137–62. https://doi.org/10.1017/S0143814X10000061.

Weaver, R. Kent, and Bert A. Rockman. 1993. *Do Institutions Matter? Government Capabilities in the United States and Abroad*. Washington, D.C.: Brookings Institution.

Weible, Christopher M. 2014. "Advancing Policy Process Research." In *Theories of the Policy Process*, 3rd ed., edited by Paul A. Sabatier and Christopher M. Weible, 391–407. Boulder: Westview Press.

– 2018. "Introduction: The Scope and Focus of Policy Process Research and Theory." In *Theories of the Policy Process*, 4th ed., edited by Christopher M. Weible and Paul A. Sabatier, 1–16. New York: Westview Press.

Weible, Christopher M., Paul A. Sabatier, and Kelly McQueen. 2009. "Themes and Variations: Taking Stock of the Advocacy Coalition Framework." *Policy Studies Journal* 37(1): 121–40. https://doi.org/10.1111/j.1541-0072.2008.00299.x.

Weston, Greg. 1989. "The Gun Lobby; Groups Target Politicians for their Right to Play with Guns." *Ottawa Citizen*, 16 December, B1.

White, Graham. 2010. "Cabinets and First Ministers." In *Auditing Canadian Democracy*, edited by William Cross, 40–64. Vancouver: UBC Press.

White, Linda A. 2012. "Must We All Be Paradigmatic? Social Investment Policies and Liberal Welfare States." *Canadian Journal of Political Science* 45(3): 657–83. https://doi.org/10.1017/S0008423912000753.

Wikipedia. 2018. *List of Massacres in Canada*. https://en.wikipedia.org/wiki /List_of_massacres_in_Canada.

Wills, Terrance. 1994a. "Justice Minister backs stronger gun control". *The Gazette* (Montreal). March 25: A1.

– 1994b. "Tougher Gun Control Promised: PM Seeks Bill by Fall." *The Gazette*, 16 May 16, A1.

Wilson, Shaun, and Nick Turnbull. 2001. "Wedge Politics and Welfare Reform in Australia." *Australian Journal of Politics and History* 47(3): 384–402. https://doi.org/10.1111/1467-8497.00235.

Wilson-Smith, Anthony. 1995. "Rock Fights for Gun Control." *Maclean's*, 5 June.

Worsham, Jeffrey. 2006. "Up in Smoke: Mapping Subsystem Dynamics in Tobacco Policy." *Policy Studies Journal* 34(3): 437–52. https://doi.org/10.1111/j.1541-0072.2006.00181.x.

Young, Lisa, and Joanna Everitt. 2004. *Advocacy Groups*. Vancouver: UBC Press.

Zahariadis, Nikolaos. 1998. "Comparing Three Lenses of Policy Choice." *Policy Studies Journal* 26(3): 434–44. https://doi.org/10.1111/j.1541-0072.1998.tb01911.x.

– 2003. *Ambiguity and Choice in Public Policy – Political Decision Making in Modern Democracies*. Washington, D.C.: Georgetown University Press.

– 2005. *Essence of Political Manipulation: Emotions, Institutions, and Greek Foreign Policy*. New York: Peter Lang.

– 2014. "Ambiguity and Multiple Streams." In *Theories of the Policy Process*, 3rd ed., edited by Paul A. Sabatier and Christopher M. Weible, 25–58. Boulder: Westview Press.

Zohlnhöfer, Reimut. 2009. "How Politics Matter When Policies Change: Understanding Policy Change as a Political Problem." *Journal of Comparative Policy Analysis* 11(1): 97–115. https://doi.org/10.1080/13876980802648300.

Zohlnhöfer, Reimut, Nicole Herweg, and Christian Huß. 2016. "Bringing Formal Political Institutions into the Multiple Streams Framework: An Analytical Proposal for Comparative Policy Analysis." *Journal of Comparative Policy Analysis* 18(3): 243–56. https://doi.org/10.1080/13876988.2015.1095428.

Index

abortion policy, 10, 65, 200, 208n23
advocacy coalition framework
(ACF), 6–7, 55, 166, 196–7;
actor beliefs, 112–16, 119, 128;
assumptions and focus of, 16,
112–18, 191–2; bodies of theory
from, 112–13; causal factors in,
15–16, 124–5, 134–5, 191–2, 198–9;
coalitions, advocacy (*see* advocacy
coalitions); hypotheses of, 112–14,
117–19, 124–6, 129–30, 133–5;
major policy change, analysis
of, 113–17, 124–6, 128–35, 191–2;
policy core beliefs, 112–14, 119,
121–6, 130–3; policy subsystem,
analysis of, 113–19, 123–4, 130,
202–3; scope conditions (*see*
scope conditions); umbrella
organizations, 119–22
advocacy coalitions, 188; dominance
of, 114, 116, 125–6, 128–9; effecting
policy change, 55–6, 114–16, 128–34;
gun control, 37, 113–14, 119–24,
126–34, 191, 199; legal authority,
114–15, 125, 130, 198; negotiations
among, 112–16, 128, 133; pro-gun,
26–7, 42–3, 119–26, 128–34, 191;
stability of, 114–15, 123. *See also*
lobbying; negotiated agreement

agenda coupling, 152–4, 192–3
agenda-setting, 13, 86; agents of, 55,
152, 212n3; analysis of, 7, 152–4,
192–3, 196; multiple streams
framework and, 138–41, 162,
187–8, 199–200; policy formation
and, 138, 140, 162, 192–3, 212n3;
punctuated equilibrium theory,
169–70, 201
Alberta, 35, 55, 131, 207n12; firearm
regulation, 35, 41, 60, 79, 119;
parties elected in, 33, 53–4, 207n17;
studies of policy-making in,
117–18, 170
Allison, Graham T. (*Essence of
Decision*), 5–6, 65
Allmand, Warren, 28, 32–3, 122,
148–9
ammunition, 28; licensing for, 23, 32,
37–8, 79, 101; restrictions on, 21–6,
41–2; storage of, 30, 98, 123
Anderson, William F.A., 6–7, 118
assault weapons: banning, 38, 101;
restrictions on, 29, 32, 77; unsafe
firearms users and, 95, 98, 103
Atlantic Canada, 47, 53–4, 58
auditor general, 39, 57, 157; mandate
of, 48–9; national firearms reports,
33–4, 131, 144, 171, 178, 191

55, 117, 124–6, 128–35, 187, 191–2; punctuations (*see* policy punctuations); robust, 68, 73, 75, 85; testing theories of (*see* theory testing); theory of major, 113–17, 124–35, 154–5, 165–74, 187–8

policy elites, 51, 108, 203; social constructions of, 88–91, 93, 97; target groups and, 90, 95, 103, 107

policy entrepreneurs, 48, 140–2, 146–53, 187, 192–3, 203

policy environment, firearms, 191–2; contextual factors of, 39–42, 44–9, 52, 56–63; status quo of, 26–8, 71, 75–6, 82, 134–5, 187; structures of, 39–40, 49, 52, 64–7, 186–8, 193–6; use of term, 39

policy equilibria, 170–3, 176, 179–80, 200–1

policy events, RCI analysis, 76–83, 87, 209n5

policy feedback theory, 14–15, 211n3

policy-makers, 7, 33; agency of, 39, 138; attention to issues, 10, 94, 96–7, 140, 145–6; constraints on, 43–5, 49; factors influencing, 39, 56, 62, 90–1, 99, 127 (*see also* policy environment, firearms); partisan, 60, 94, 96

policy-oriented learning, 117, 125–9, 132–3, 187, 191

policy outcomes, explaining, 197, 209n1; lack of, 6, 14, 93, 194; social constructions and, 88–9, 103–6, 190; theories' effectiveness at, 104–7, 124, 169, 176, 190, 194; variation in, 16–18, 124

policy processes, 117; impeding, 125, 136; multiple streams framework, 136–8, 141, 192–3, 200; social

construction framework, 88–9, 92, 113, 190, 198; theories of, 3–5, 8–14, 165, 195–7, 201–2

policy punctuations, 168–70, 179, 181, 194–5, 200; Canadian firearms policy, 171–3, 175–8, 180

policy windows, 140–6, 149–52, 187, 192–3, 203

political entrepreneurs, 153–61, 187, 190, 193, 197, 200

polling, public opinion, 124, 145; gun control, 60, 72, 156

population density, voting behaviour, 75, 208n21. *See also* rural ridings; suburban ridings; urban ridings

positivism, 89, 211n2

Possession and Acquisition Licence (PAL), 80; introduction of, 23, 32, 37–8, 79

power, political, 30, 197–8; advocacy coalitions, 55–6, 114–16, 125–6, 128–34, 191–2; concentration of, 49–55, 65–6, 74, 146, 200–3; judicial, 42, 44; ministerial, 30, 37, 45–6, 49–55, 186–9; safe versus unsafe firearms users, 62, 90–2, 94–100, 103–6, 190

prime minister, role of, 39, 45, 47, 69, 74, 85; concentration of power, 49–51, 62, 66, 203

Prime Minister's Office (PMO), 49–51, 56

Privy Council Office (PCO), 49–51

probabilistic claims. *See* causal claims

Progressive Conservatives: Conservative Party merger, 35–6, 53–4, 133; gun lobbyists and, 96, 99–100, 110, 122; firearm policies, 28–9, 38, 76–9, 82–7, 146; Liberals versus, 31, 127–30, 146, 149